Education, State a
Anatomy of Neolil

Dave
With revolutionary greetings
Ravi
22/3/14

Education, State and Market: Anatomy of Neoliberal Impact

Edited by
Ravi Kumar

AAKAR

Education, State and Market: Anatomy of Neoliberal Impact
Edited by *Ravi Kumar*

© Editor

First Published 2014

ISBN   978-93-5002-282-5 (PB)

All rights reserved. No part of this book may
be reproduced or transmitted, in any form or
by any means, without prior permission
of the Publisher.

Published by
AAKAR BOOKS
28 E Pocket IV, Mayur Vihar Phase I, Delhi 110 091
Phone : 011 2279 5505 Telefax : 011 2279 5641
info@aakarbooks.com; www.aakarbooks.com

Printed at
Saurabh Printers Pvt. Ltd., A 16, Sector IV, Noida

For My Parents
and
In Memory of Prof. G.K. Chadha

Contents

Acknowledgement	ix
1. Education, State, and Market: Anatomy of Neoliberal Impact: An Introduction *Ravi Kumar*	1
2. Changing Discourses on Inequality and Disparity: From Welfare State to Neoliberal Capitalism *Vikas Gupta*	19
3. The Story of Dismantling of Higher Education in India: The Unfolding Crisis *G. Haragopal*	58
4. Commoditizing Higher Education: The Assault of Neoliberal Barbarism *Madhu Prasad*	76
5. Caught between 'Neglect' and a Private 'Makeover': Government Schools in Delhi *Radhika Menon*	114
6. The Language Question: The Battle to Take Back the Imagination *Harjinder Singh 'Laltu'*	139
7. Constitution of Language: Neoliberal Practices in Multi-lingual India *Samir Karmakar*	161

8. A Relevant Economics for India: Dark Past, Bleak Future 186
Rajesh Bhattacharya

9. Mapping the Changes in Legal Education in India 212
Srinivas Burra

10. Countering Neoliberal Conception of Knowledge, Building Emancipatory Discourse: A Historical Overview of Phule-Ambedkar's Critique and Gandhian Nai Taleem 236
Anil Sadgopal

11. A Dialogue for Mass Movement for Democratic Education System 265
D. Ramesh Patnaik

12. *Afterword:* Narratives of Resistance: The Case of Struggle for a Common School System in Tamil Nadu 276
Prince Gajendra Babu

Notes on Contributors 283
Index 287

Acknowledgement

Indian educational discourse is yet to respond to the onslaught of neoliberal capital in a concerted manner. This volume emerges out of a workshop organized to understand the crisis that the Indian education system is confronted with. A vacuum has been felt on the library shelves, in the university syllabi and for individual readers for a volume which would try to understand the impact of an unbridled market on different aspects of education. This volume is an initiative in the direction filling that vacuum which is also a contested field in the politics of knowledge production.

The workshop, and therefore the volume, could become possible because of the interest shown by Carsten Krinn, Resident Representative, South Asia at the Rosa Luxemburg Stiftung. At a time when the rule of private capital seeks to destroy all that is public he felt the need to undertake an analysis of how mechanisms of capital work in the arena of education. Vinod, Pragya, and Rajiv at Rosa Luxemburg Stiftung, South Asia Office, also facilitated the whole process of organizing the workshop. The workshop was organized by the Department of Sociology, South Asian University, which could not have been possible without the encouragement of Sasanka Perera, Dean of Faculty of Social Sciences. G.K. Chadha, President, South Asian University and Rajiv Saxena, Vice-President, South Asian University and A.K. Mallik, Registrar, South Asian University ensured that the organization of the workshop was smooth. My colleagues at the Department of Sociology were supportive of the whole exercise. Atul Chandra, Researcher associated with the project, not only took care of the nitty-gritty of organizing the workshop, but also came up with suggestions regarding the speakers for panel discussion.

My students have always been a great source of inspiration. They remain the source of intellectual stimulation. I would specially thank Umesh, Parveen, Mondip, Nafis, Anayika and Ragini. Uzma helped me with copyediting at the last moment. I am further grateful to Padmalini G. Rao for taking a final look at the manuscript.

Samson George in the Faculty of Social Sciences was his usual exuberant self to help out in every possible way. Finally, this volume could not be possible for the revision of texts by the respective authors. Given the time constraints, K.K. Saxena from Aakar Books ensured that processes of reviewing, copyediting and designing were done without any delay.

1

Education, State, and Market: Anatomy of Neoliberal Impact

An Introduction

Ravi Kumar

The Context

The physical landscape has altered—in not only cities but also the countryside. In the vast open fields on two sides of the highways stand ugly looking buildings thrusting down our imagination the delicate story of a resurgent India. Malls, plush apartments, education institutions, and everything that could be put to sale surround us as consumers to buy the product. This is the new landscape—the cities, towns, once nondescript district headquarters—everywhere, the narrative of a homogenous world, a universalized idea of 'market is the regulator and provider of everything' can be seen. Those who argued for local/mini narratives and denounced the category of 'universal' are confronted with this new world order. A new narrative has become dominant—one that breeds unprecedented and starker inequality, thwarts the idea of social justice, and converts social concerns into marketable commodities.[1]

The neoliberal world, nonetheless, sells the same dream to everyone by saying *you can also buy it*, that *you only need to work hard* to let the economy/company grow at a faster pace. In other words, the distant world of happiness embodied in the ability to buy everything may be drawn closer, it says, by ensuring that capital accumulation must happen unhindered, without revealing that the accumulated capital is not likely to be shared in a manner wherein the dreams can be bought by everyone. Like the uncivil neo-rich driving with their blinding headlights on and loud music to escape the realities of the world, the new economy seeks to blind you with the size of its buildings, flyovers, plush offices, residences, and markets all around: highways replete with shops selling degrees in medicine, engineering, and everything possible under the sky without much of quality control; the city with mall and hotel-like schools and inaccessible cinema halls that make entertainment class specific; the arrogance of money that spits at the face of anything you considered 'civil' and 'decent' few decades back; and a battery of research institutions that would constantly pump you with information through their pink newspapers and magazines about how good life has become, measuring quality through everything that market does and provides for. The new economy hides poverty from naked eyes, it makes your city look as if the poor do not exist. The motto seems to be, *hide them in every possible way, by throwing them out to the peripheries of the city or outside of it.*

This is the new world—the neoliberal world, where everything has been commoditized and quantified. It tells you that there is *possibility* everywhere, but when it comes to providing concessions and subsidies, it harps on the tune of *resource crunch*. We have seen the brazenness and ugliness of money power in the past decade or so in India. Every now and then, money that is littered around through scams, et cetera, shows how much resource actually we have to fund education and health for all.[2] However, the official documents reiterate how important it is to bring in the private sector if the whole of India is to be educated. It argues that there is a dearth of resources and that the State on its own cannot manage to provide education and healthcare to its citizens. This is the dominant discourse coming from the State as well as non-State actors in neoliberal times. As recent as the 12th Five Year Plan document says that 'Private providers (including NGOs and non-profits) can play an important role in elementary education. Their legitimate role in expanding elementary education needs to be recognized and a flexible approach needs to be adopted to encourage them to invest in the sector' (GoI 2013: p. 64).

Commodification of everything that surrounds us is happening. We have been told recently by the Nestle Chairman Peter Brabeck that water should be treated as a commodity: '"Water is a commodity with a market value like any other foodstuff," says Brabeck. "Personally I believe it's better to give a foodstuff a value so that we're all aware that it has a price," he concluded, in remarks that could be construed as supportive of the idea of privatizing the world's water supply.' (*Politix* 2013)

In practice, water has been privatized much before with rivers and their water being handed over to private enterprises to generate electricity and sell them for profiteering. People are upset and angry over how rivers being handed over in this manner become invisible and inaccessible to common people (Mazoomdar 2013). There is an overt centralization of decision-making that has happened under the new economic regime. Riding on the rhetoric of participatory democracy and decision-making it actually alienates masses from the process. And this not only becomes clearer from the way natural resources are being handed out to the corporate houses across the country, but also from the way the participatory institutions are subverted by the existing class, caste, and gendered inequalities in societies. The way school level committees function across the country are a proof of this myopic conception of 'participative institutions'.

In the bigger picture, participation in democratic process is becoming a costly affair as the number of millionaires increase in the Parliament. So, those making policies would obviously be working in the interests of those whose class interests they represent. Some of the estimates point out that there has been a quantum jump in the number of millionaires in the Indian Parliament.

Hence, the context within which one would have to analyse the neoliberal impact on education is a complex one—wherein each and every aspect of social, political, and cultural life is determined by the new economic regime. This is accompanied by declining organized and sustained resistance against it as well. There are sporadic protests but they are politically unclear and misplaced against the new regime, which provides it a smooth sail in pursuit of its goals. In order to better understand the above context, it is relevant to look at what neoliberalism actually does to our lives in general and education in particular.

Characterizing Neoliberalism

Neoliberalism arrived when the prosperity and stability of 'controlled capitalism' was shaken by the 'oil shocks' of 1970s as the price of oil uncontrollably increased overnight. The 'new' liberals or the neoliberals heralded the inefficacy of the Keynesian model and laid down the principle of minimal or no-State intervention and more powers to the market to work according to its 'will' (Steger and Roy 2010). It needs to be recalled that economists like John Maynard Keynes, in the aftermath of the Great Depression, 'advocated massive government spending in a time of economic crisis to create new jobs and lift consumer spending'. By advocating this, he was challenging 'classical liberal beliefs that the market mechanism would naturally correct itself in the event of an economic crisis and return to an equilibrium at full employment' (Steger and Roy 2010: p. 6). Hence, Keynes or the British Prime Minister Clement Attlee and American President Franklin D. Roosevelt were not critiquing market but they were only opposed to its unlimited and unbridled freedom to operate. They were emphasizing a certain kind of regulation and control by the State. It was in this context that one could see nationalization of industries and certain sectors happening in the post-World War II phase.

When neoliberalism arrived, it was arguing for a self-regulated market and its expansion in all possible arenas with a minimal role for the State. It hardly leaves any sphere of our life untouched—such is its desire to colonize our existence. 'Neoliberalism straddles a wide range of social, political and economic phenomena at different levels of complexity' (Saad-Filho and Johnston 2005: p. 1). Scholars argue that one may look at neoliberalism as (1) an ideology, (2) a mode of governance, and (3) a policy package (Steger and Roy 2010).

As an ideology, its chief advocates are 'global power elites that include managers and executives of large transnational corporations, corporate lobbyists, influential journalists and public-relations specialists, intellectuals writing for a large public audience, celebrities and top entertainers, state bureaucrats, and politicians' (Steger and Roy 2010: p. 11). In fact, Harvey argues that 'One substantial core of rising class power under neoliberalism lies... with the CEOs, the key operators on corporate boards, and the leaders in the financial, legal, and technical apparatuses that surround this inner sanctum of capitalist activity' (Harvey 2007: p. 33). The task of this class is also to create a public discourse that portrays the idealized images of a consumerist and free market world. In other words, they are responsible as ideological apparatuses to weave a world of false dreams, web of illusions, and a range of aspirations that can never be achieved. Consequently, one gets what McLaren and Farahmandpur (2005: p. 193) write:

> Capitalism has become so intensified that it represses our ability to acknowledge the process of repression itself. It naturalises repression so completely that the current economic horror has come to be seen as part of the everyday woof and warp of things that we have blithely come to name 'the daily grind'. Consequently, even progressive educators who are vigorously engaged in the debate fail to address the fateful implications of capitalism's confiscation of freedom and kidnapping of hope.

Neoliberalism is indubitably the hegemonic discourse today, as it pervades the 'ways of thought to the point where it has become incorporated into the common-sense way many of us interpret, live in, and understand the world' (Harvey 2007: p. 3).

As a mode of governance, neoliberalism bases itself on principles that are 'rooted in entrepreneurial values such as competitiveness, self-interest, and decentralization. It celebrates individual empowerment and the devolution of central state power to smaller localized units. Such a neoliberal mode of governance adopts the self-regulating free market as the model for proper government' (Steger and Roy 2010: p. 12). Brown argues that neoliberalism needs to be seen 'as a political rationality', which 'also involves a specific and consequential organization of the social, the subject, and the state' (p. 693). He cautions that this political rationality is not constituted as a 'spillover' from economic neoliberalism but as an 'imposition of the market rationality'. He argues:

> A political rationality is not equivalent to an ideology stemming from or masking an economic reality, nor is it merely a spillover effect of the economic on the political or the social... a political rationality is a specific form of normative political reason organizing the political sphere, governance practices, and citizenship. A political rationality governs the say-able, the intelligible, and the truth criteria of these domains. Thus, while neoliberal political rationality is based on a certain conception of the market, its organization of governance and the social is not merely the result of leak age from the economic to other spheres but rather of the explicit imposition of a particular form of market rationality on these spheres. Neoliberalism as a form of political reasoning that articulates the nature and meaning of the political, the social, and the subject must be underscored because it is through this form and articulation that its usurpation of other more democratic rationalities occurs. (Brown 2006: pp. 693–4).

The idea of public good becomes an alien concept for neoliberal order as it strives to reduce everything to the private sphere. Giroux says that

> Not only does neoliberalism bankrupt public funds, hollow out public services, limit the vocabulary and imagery available to recognize anti-democratic forms of power, and produce narrow models of individual agency, it also undermines the critical functions of any viable democracy by undercutting the ability of individuals to engage in the continuous translation between public considerations and private interests by collapsing the public into the realm of the private. (Giroux 2004: p. 494)

There are no longer 'public servants' or 'public offices'; there are only enterprises, entrepreneurs and workers, who would very often be told that they are part of a family—that is, the enterprise. Hence, it was no surprise when, 'in the early 1980s, a novel model of public administration known as "new public management" took the world's state bureaucracies by storm. Operationalizing the neoliberal mode of governance for public servants, it redefined citizens as "customers" or "clients" and encouraged administrators to cultivate an "entrepreneurial spirit"' (Steger and Roy 2010: p. 13).

The State becomes a facilitator of corporate interests and works towards ensuring profit maximization for them. It manipulates legislature, executive, and judiciary to the advantage of corporations. There are instances when it 'assumes much of the risk while the private sector takes most of the profits. If necessary, furthermore, the neoliberal state will resort to coercive legislation and policing tactics (anti-picketing rules, for example) to disperse or repress collective forms of opposition to corporate power' (Harvey 2007: p. 77). What can explain this better than the fact that the Indian State gives land to corporate business houses at subsidized rates and even acquires and buys land for them? The Delhi Government, after privatizing electricity supply, keeps paying the corporate house huge amounts of subsidy, whereas the corporation keeps making profit through exorbitant electricity prices. The Indian State has written off Rs four lakh crores as tax waivers to corporate houses just between 2004–05 and 2011–12 (Sainath 2012).

On the policy front, the neoliberal mantra is '(1) deregulation (of the economy); (2) liberalization (of trade and industry); and (3) privatization (of state-owned enterprises)'. In the process of implementing this, one experiences: massive tax cuts (especially for businesses and high-income earners); reduction of social services and welfare programmes; replacing welfare with 'workfare'; use of interest rates by independent central banks to keep inflation in check (even at the risk of increasing unemployment); the downsizing of government; tax havens for domestic and foreign corporations willing to invest in designated economic zones; new commercial urban spaces shaped by market imperatives; anti-unionization drives in the name of enhancing productivity and 'labour flexibility'; removal of controls on global financial and trade flows; regional and global integration of national economies; and the creation of new political institutions, think tanks, and practices designed to reproduce the neoliberal paradigm. (Steger and Roy 2010: p. 14).

Neoliberalism is, undoubtedly, a system of governance, an effort to dictate and determine how we live our lives, and a doctrine that believes in taking away the rights of those who cannot pay or afford to live in this world where you would pay money even to pee, where everything gets into private hands—from your individual security to the collective good, obviously aimed at feeding the insatiable appetite of the private capital. Capitalism, as usual, does its best to ensure that the system runs in best possible way so as to minimize acts of resistance and optimize the possibility of accumulation. It is for this that 'neoliberal capitalism performs the dual task of using education to train workers for service sector jobs and produce lifelong consumers' (Giroux and Giroux 2006: p. 21).

Education becomes one of prime instruments to generate what can be termed a segmented labour force for capital and, simultaneously, to facilitate the rule of capital. This new avatar has hardly added anything worth saying that it can be deemed as even marginally better than the other avatars. And that is so because of what it does:

1. The market becomes the organizing principle of all aspects of our life—political, economic, social, and cultural—as commodification pervades all of them.
2. The distinction between public and private diminishes/vanishes as private takes over everything that is public, including the sanctified so-called security systems.
3. Politics increasingly and overtly becomes a domain of the ruling elite, as number of millionaires and billionaires rise in formal democratic structures.
4. While 'resource crunch' becomes an excuse for the State's inability to manage health, education, pension, et cetera, the State, simultaneously, doles out huge monetary benefits to corporate houses as tax waivers and subsidies.
5. Poverty increases in real terms (if not in definitional terms of the State, which manipulates its definitions and figures) and so does the gap between those who can afford to be buyers in the new commodified economy and those who

cannot.
6. The market expands and creates monopolies in such a way as to give impression that it can cater to everyone (according to their capacity and, thus, not ignoring any segment of population) trying to generate illusions about its predatory nature.
7. Through an unprecedented control over ideological apparatuses, the market creates a chimera of 'hope' and 'aspirations' that keep telling the masses about unlimited 'possibilities' under neoliberal capitalism. This temporal intoxication is broken by crises that the economy faces repeatedly.
8. By pumping into individual imagination illusory impressions of the world, it tries to push its darker side into oblivion (such as farmer suicides, hunger deaths, malnourishment, environmental catastrophes, et cetera) though they resurface time and again.
9. The idea of 'social justice' is destroyed as the State reduces its role and hands everything to the market, which believes in its criteria of 'competition' and mutilated notion of 'merit'. Social concerns and historical constructs are no longer factored in the idea of 'justice'.
10. There is growing intolerance towards *dissent* and *dialogue*. It is seen as hampering the smooth functioning of the institution and is taken as an 'attack' on its endeavour to attain the goals that it has set for itself.
11. It is more aggressive in terms of governance. Hence, it not only manipulates the existing bourgeois democratic structures such as the Parliament or regulatory bodies such as University Grants Commission but also resorts to physical violence against those who resist.
12. There is increasing surveillance of public as well as private lives. This emanates from the fear that private capital has come from masses engaging in acts of resistance and subversion. In the words of Giroux: 'Situated within an expanding culture of fear, market freedoms seem securely grounded in a defense of national security, capital, and property rights. When coupled with

a media-driven culture of panic and hyped-up levels of insecurity, surviving public spaces are increasingly monitored and militarized' (2004: p. 496).
13. Because it believes in manipulating the rules of governance, it sets into motion a vicious cycle wherein the same gets replicated at the level of each and every institution. Instead of following a process of framing rules and regulations, the institutions make, modify, and change them everyday as per their convenience. This allows them to facilitate better surveillance and control, and to provide them the opportunity to factor in the interests of market.

Within the field of education, this phenomenon is the dominant discourse today, irrespective of public or private institutions. The spread of this demon that eats away public money and neglects the interests of the masses has generated great amount of work globally specifically looking at how it impacts education. These works have ranged from how corporatization and simultaneous militarization of the educational institutions have happened to the mutation of education policies as the State takes upon the role of the 'agent of capital' much more aggressively (Saltman 2003; Robertson 2005; Hill and Kumar 2008). Spread of the neoliberal virus across different physical locations has been explored at a more fundamental level (Hill 2009; Hill and Rosskom 2008). However, Most of these works have emerged from the Western context and relatively lesser number from the South Asian context, which is no different when it comes to the neoliberal arguments becoming dominant or getting translated into State policies. A need was always there which would look at the case of India and how the impact of neoliberalism is changing the education system.

Neoliberalism and Education in India

The education system in India never ever experienced such a huge transformation in such a short span of time. It is not only the quantum of change that needs to be analysed and understood but also the violent form that it takes—a violence that is not only momentarily physical but also intellectually coercive, compelling one to get claustrophobic within the confines of a university ideally considered a dialogic space. Visit one of the largest state universities in India—Delhi University—and you would get that feeling or do an ethnography of how mechanisms of university governance work in close collabouration with a group of teachers, it would reveal to you the pain and agony that most teachers and students undergo without having any say in what to teach and how to teach.

This transformation is located within a situation that has entrenched the rule of capital, as its owners march fearlessly and shamelessly on a campaign to expand the accumulation of capital in a situation where the anti-systemic forces in politics are also weakened. This transformation tried closing debates on a Common School System, put a closure to even the possibility of equality within elementary education or higher education, mobilized the liberal voices in its favour through different committees and commissions, formulated and implemented everything that would suit the rule of capital through synchronizing the imaginations of judiciary, executive, and legislature, and sent a clear message that the 'popular will' would not necessarily be factored in policies and politics. The distance between what people need and what is 'provided' by the State is dissonant. This must not appear surprising for anybody when the role of the State is determined by the needs and, therefore, designs of private capital. Inequality would continue to be there in all spheres of service delivery—from the education system to the health system—till the State is controlled by and works at the behest of owners of capital.

While there are evident changes at the policy level—from opening up the economy to commodifying education as any other to be bought in the marketplace—there are different, and often complex, ways of effecting these changes. The direct, coercive, undemocratic policymaking practice of the State is one while using the so-called progressive voices to create an illusion of 'democracy' and 'welfarism' is another. So, the State opens up education to the private sector in an unprecedented manner (Kumar 2012) but it also mustered support for its plan to corporatize and homogenize education system through committees such as the Yashpal Committee (Chandra 2012: pp. 160–1; Kumar 2012: p. 145). At a micro level, this could also be seen in some of the committees appointed at the provincial level (GoB 2007). In the process of doing this, the State, for private capital to prosper, has done away with the history of welfarism and negated all its commitments made during the phase of its welfarist avatar (Sadgopal 2006). Analysts argue that the State has gradually put an end to possibilities of a long standing commitment such as the Common School System (Sadgopal 2010) and the arguments of 'something is better than nothing' has become a justification for any move towards withdrawal of the State from its basic responsibilities.

One of the thrust areas of the neoliberal assault can be seen in the changes in the content of what is being taught. The decline of social sciences and predominance of technology institutes are only one dimension of it. The other dimension is the nature of teaching-learning that happens in these institutions. Opened not as part of a long-standing vision to enhance the disciplines and their knowledge stock, these institutions have been mushrooming everywhere. South India is no longer the only hub of private institutions; one can now find them all over the country. Over 250 technical and management institutes had shut down as of 2012 (Basu 2012). Even social sciences have been trying to join the rat-race of being a job-oriented (read market-oriented) discipline by offering as many diplomas as they can. The idea of knowledge as critical and as an instrument that teaches the idea of liberation has been skillfully and deftly set aside. As McLaren and Farahmandpur write '...even progressive educators who are vigorously engaged in the debate over global capitalism and theories that oppose one another within it frequently fail to address the fateful implications of capitalism's confiscation of freedom and kidnapping of hope' (2005: p. 193).

The idea of education has changed. It is no longer something which generates hope and dares one to dream for a world free of inequality and exploitation. The 'good education' equips one with the necessary skills to serve the factories of different types —from automobile units to the universities. It is developed in tandem with the changing notion of what is a 'good society'.

'The logic of privatization and free trade—where social labour is the means and measure of value and surplus social labour lies at the heart of profit—now odiously shapes archetypes of citizenship, manages our perceptions of what should constitute the 'good society', and produce necessary functions for capital in relation to labour' (McLaren 2005: p. 23). The dominant idea of education reproduced through the school and university system is about reproducing the system in which one lives. And the changes that one experiences in the system are in that direction. It is this new idea, which quantifies everything, standardizes everything and looks for ever-new ways of measuring how well students and teachers are serving (or going to serve) the demands of the economy and the thought processes necessary for sustaining the system. The principles and concepts of autonomy, innovation, and social good have changed and they are now interpreted in a way that would cater to the needs of the market.

In the same way as everything undergoes a change, the teaching labour force has become more and more a part of the trends in the labour market. Contractualization and informalization of this labour force is quite common and on the anvil, whether it is school education or the university system. One of the functions of job insecurity is to instill a sense of fidelity through the fear of losing the job. This function makes one a much better carrier of dominant ideas across the disciplinary spectrum. In some of them it may appear subdued, while in others, it is overt. In order to have an education system that contextualizes itself in the social order and teaches and learns its dynamics to get over its scorn and repression, it becomes essential that the issues of the teaching labour force are understood well.

These transformations happened—though not without opposition, which has been fragmented and politically not united—while the anti-systemic political formations became increasingly social democratic and, hence, weakened all across the country. The politics on the streets diminished as the politics of legislative revolution overtook a section of the left imagination. The synchrony between the two and the significance of the street fights took a backseat. Vanaik puts this more succinctly when he says that 'the balance between parliamentary-electoral pursuits and extra-parliamentary mobilizational activity must always be titled strongly towards the latter' (2013: p. 13). The imagination of Left politics, which could have been one of the forces confronting the neoliberalization of education, has turned out to be myopic.

This myopia emerges as a greater result of the failure to ground education within working class politics and the class question, rather than a result of the arguments of mere accessibility (which is no doubt also important). A critique that could transcend into a sphere that establishes the linkages between capitalism and the consequent educational policies and the politics of knowledge production has been very weak. Hence, there have been non-party pressure groups and individuals that emerged as an opposition to this whole educational crisis in the country. How far their programmatic understanding and analysis becomes politically significant can be analysed separately. There have been, no doubt, powerful analyses emerging out of this context, which laid threadbare the nuanced ways in which political rationality guised as 'governance' has consistently manipulated and destroyed the State managed education (see Sadgopal 2006; 2010).

The changes that have taken place can be mapped at different layers and that kind of work is yet to be done at a more elabourate level in India. These different layers would include: (1) how changes have occurred at the policy level; (2) how do they impact at the layers of pedagogy within classrooms/disciplinary orientations or at the larger levels of language; and (3) how one would imagine the possibilities of resistance in this context.

The chapters in this volume are an effort to understand precisely these three aspects. As already stated, there is an increasing need to bring together more work to understand the nuances of how everyday structures of our life, which would include the sites of learning, are affected by neoliberal capitalism and its unceasing desire to devour everything that comes its way. This book offers only a miniscule part of that exercise.

While the chapters by Hargopal and Madhu Prasad deal with the issues of how policies work in the sphere of higher education, Vikas Gupta has tried to historically locate the shift that has happened from welfarism to neoliberalism in the educational sphere. Radhika Menon brings insights from the field to understand how these processes work, wherein the commodification of education affects the worst those who cannot afford to buy it. Srinivas Burra and Rajesh Bhattacharya show how disciplines get shaped in conjunction with the dominant economic logic of the times. Bhattacharya argues that the 'contemporary practices of teaching and research in economics in India don't prepare students, teachers and researchers to engage with the Indian political economy in a sophisticated and socially relevant way' and he explains why it happens. Similarly, Burra's paper narrates the historical trajectory that led to the shaping of the discipline of legal studies and how global factors have shaped the discipline. These factors may not become apparent when one looks at them as a participant, but taking a macro and longitudinal view always allows one to look at the aspects that influence them. Harjinder Singh 'Laltu' and Samir Karmakar have tried to look at the language question and how it is confronted with a crisis in contemporary times. Ramesh Pattnaik argues for a mass movement to ensure that education remains fully managed by the State. He writes, 'It is time for activists and academics alike to go to the masses to integrate their subjective theories with the objective experience of the people in order to advance the campaign for a democratic education system'. On the other hand, Anil Sadgopal argues for building an emancipatory discourse using the works and discourses of Jyotiba Phule, B.R. Ambedkar, and Gandhi. Prince Gajendra Babu, in his short reflective piece, shows how resistance is happening within the limits of given legal-juridical boundaries.

The volume establishes beyond doubt how perilous is neoliberalism for education. However, there is a need to not only further explore the theme but also move beyond by looking into possibilities and alternatives.

REFERENCES

Basu, Mihika (20 November 2012) '58 tech institutes apply for closure to AICTE', *Indian Express*, available at http://www.indianexpress.com/news/58-tech-institutes-apply-for-closure-to-aicte/1033484/ (Accessed on 23 January 2013)

Brown, Wendy (December, 2006) 'American Nightmare: Neoliberalism, Neoconservatism, and De-Democratisation', *Political Theory*, Vol. 34, No. 6, pp. 690–714

Chandra, Paresh (2012) 'The Struggle and its Generalization: The Case of the University', in Kumar, Ravi (ed.) *Education and the Reproduction of Capital: Neoliberal Knowledge and Counterstrategies*, Palgrave Macmillan: New York, pp. 153–70

Giroux, Henry A. (2004) 'Public Pedagogy and the Politics of Neoliberalism: Making the Political more Pedagogical', *Policy Futures in Education*, Vol. 2, Nos. 3 & 4, pp. 494–503

Giroux, Henry A. and Giroux, Susan Searls (2006) 'Challenging Neoliberalism's New World Order: The Promise of Critical Pedagogy', *Cultural Studies! Critical Methodologies*, Vol. 6, No. 1, pp. 21–32

Government of Bihar (2007) *Report of the Common School System Commission*, 8 June. Patna: Government of Bihar

GoI (2013) *Twelfth Five Year Plan (2012–2017) Social Sectors*, Vol. III, Sage Publications: New Delhi

Harvey, David (2007) *A Brief History of Neoliberalism*, Oxford University Press: Oxford.

Hill, Dave and Kumar, Ravi (eds. 2008) *Global Neoliberalism and Education and its Consequences*, Routledge: New York and London

Hill, Dave and Rosskam, Ellen (eds. 2008) *The Developing World and State Education: Neoliberal Depredation and Egalitarian Alternatives*, Routledge: New York and London

Hill, Dave (2009) *The Rich World and the Impoverishment of Education: Diminishing Democracy, Equity and Workers' Rights*, Routledge: New York and London

Kumar, Ravi (September-December 2010) 'Education and the Politics of Capital: Perspective and Agenda for Resistance against Neoliberalism', *Social Scientist*, Vol. 38, No. 9/12, pp. 51–60

Kumar, Ravi (October, 2012) 'The Charge of Neoliberal Capital and Higher Education in India,' *Journal of Critical Education Policy Studies*, Vol. 10, No. 2, available at <http://www.jceps.com/?pageID=article&articleID=267> (Accessed on 10 November 2012)

An Introduction 17

Mazoomdar, Jay (2013) 'Another Disaster in the Making', *Tehelka*, available at http://www.tehelka.com/another-disaster-in-the-making/ (Accessed on 26 September, 2013)

McLaren, Peter and Farahmandpur, Ramin (2005), *Teaching Against Global Capitalism and New Imperialism: A Critical Pedagogy*, Rowman and Littlefield: Lanham

McLaren, Peter (2005) *Capitalists and Conquerors: A Critical Pedagogy Against Empire*, Rowman and Littlefield: Lanham

Politix (2013) 'Nestle Chairman: Water should not be a Human Right' available at http://politix.topix.com/homepage/5677-nestle-chairman-water-should-not-be-a-human-right (Accessed on September 25, 2013)

Robertson, Terry (2005) 'Class Issues: A Critical Ethnography of Corporate Domination within the Classroom', *Journal for Critical Education Policy Studies*, Vol. 3, No. 2, available at http://www.jceps.com/index.php?pageID=article&articleID =52, accessed on 10 March 2007

Sadgopal, Anil (2006) 'Dilution, Distortion and Diversion: A Post-Jomtien Reflection on the Education Policy', in Ravi Kumar (ed.) *The Crisis of Elementary Education in India*, New Delhi: Sage

Sadgopal, Anil (September-December 2010) 'Right to Education vs. Right to Education Act', *Social Scientist*, Vol. 38, Nos. 9-12, pp. 17–50

Sainath, P. (March 26, 2012) 'To fix BPL, nix CPL', *The Hindu*, available at http://www.thehindu.com/opinion/columns/sainath/article3223573.ece (Accessed 20 November 2012)

Saltman, Kenneth J. and Gabbard, David A. (2003) *Education As Enforcement: The Militarization and Corporatization of Schools*, Routledge: New York

Steger, Manfred B. and Roy, Ravi K. (2010) *Neoliberalism: A Short Introduction*, Oxford University Press: Oxford

Vanaik, Achin (13 October 2012) 'Future Perspectives for the Mainstream Indian Left', *Economic & Political Weekly*, Vol. XLVII, No. 41, pp. 12–4

NOTES

1. The increasing violence against women in cities like Delhi has led to new mobile applications and new commodities to flourish themselves as if they would end the violence against women. Hence, rather than questioning the patriarchies which inevitably culminate into violence against women the consumers are being

effectively told that market can also provide solutions to the problem.
2. A quick calculation of amount of money eaten up by the corporate houses, political elite and bureaucracy through scams such as Fodder Scam, Coal Scam, 2G Scam, Commonwealth Games Scam, Allottment of Gas Reserves Scam, Madhu Koda Scam, etc., reveal that there is no dearth of resources and if this money could be used for providing education and health services through state managed institutions to everybody then the situation would have been different in this country.

2

Changing Discourses on Inequality and Disparity: From Welfare State to Neoliberal Capitalism

Vikas Gupta

Introduction

How do we ensure that every child receives equitable quality inclusive education as a fundamental right in accordance with his/her specific needs and requirements? Can the provision for education be left to someone's compassion, philanthropy, market fundamentalism, or corporate social responsibility? Or, should we bring the principles of equality and social justice to the centrestage of the discourse and politics of education?

Modern secular 'Right to equality' would recognize that in terms of physical traits, prowess, mental attitude and aptitude, cultural inheritance/historical legacy, skills and abilities, economic capacity, and social position, each individual is differently endowed and unique, but deserves equal treatment as a complete 'ethical' human being.[1]Difference is a universal reality, but it is not a frozen and ahistorical phenomenon: socioeconomic, political, and technological changes may 'reproduce', mitigate, or augment it. Whether differences amongst people exist originally or have historically evolved, we cannot use these as a justification for denying someone human dignity and entitlement to rights on an equal basis with others, because whilst the enjoyment of rights and human dignity may diminish these differences, their denial would aggravate disparities. In fact, we all need the guarantee of entitlements and protection on equal basis with others, precisely because there are differences in the world. Of course, we need to engage with difference as a secular phenomenon.[2]

However, since the normative ideal adhering to which the system or the world has been constructed, continues to exclude various kinds of groups simultaneously, and since 'exclusion' is a multi-layered and multi-causal phenomenon (involving in different contexts various sets of historical, sociological, economic, political, sexual, biological, or racial and similar other factors), therefore, there must be a larger politics of this exclusion; and by implication, it should be better to fight it from a broader front that includes and at the same time transcends all particularities. Otherwise, howsoever important, patchwork measures enabling only fractions of population to become part of 'mainstream' may not necessarily succeed in overthrowing discriminatory structure in order to establish a fair one. Mostly, however, this is what we see happening in education in the name of 'inclusionism'. The discourse on equality has perhaps left some scope for segregation of people and groups from the 'mainstream'. For instance, until quite recently, it was not perceived as problematic to seclude certain groups of people for their education in separate schools, though it clearly implied seeking to integrate left-out groups of people within the 'mainstream' of social life at a later stage, without reorienting and restructuring its foundation—the system of education. Therefore, inclusion ideology appears to be an important corrective.

Nonetheless, it appears that the neoliberal idea of inclusion has become more attractive these days, because, as distinct from the ideologies that laid core emphasis on the doctrine of equality, it does not pose the same degree of challenge of equitable redistributive justice in such explicit terms. It is far less marked by the tension of redistribution on equal basis between 'haves' and 'have nots', between privileged and disprivileged, and between included and excluded. Inclusion of some marginalized or hitherto excluded groups and people may be allowed without equitable redistribution of means, fruits and opportunities, without substantially redrawing the balance of class formation and power relations in favour of actual majority. Howsoever important, inclusion of hitherto excluded people without targeting the larger hegemonic normativity may not be sufficient for progressing towards a more equalitarian and less-prejudiced socially equitable order. At best, such efforts of inclusion and 'gradual expansionism' would result in seemingly legitimizing the existing discriminatory order and in the labeling of the targeted communities and people as 'special', 'specially appeased', specially protected', and therefore by implication, naturally weak and inferior. It may be one thing to promise to some specific opportunities to any particular section with the stated purpose of including it in the mainstream. However, that may not necessarily imply the affirmation of the equality principle, unless it is constantly reaffirmed and practiced in unequivocal terms, by emphasizing on equitable redistribution and enjoyment of not merely educational, but other related rights as well.

The role of the State is extremely crucial in this process, because notwithstanding the actual reality of it becoming a class instrument, it is the only institution that may transcend particular class or community interests in favour of the interests of entire citizenry. However, in the last section of this paper, where we will present an overview of the main trends of neoliberal policies in education culled from various recent examples/events, we will see that the contemporary political economy of education is moving in a different direction. At the same time, it is also true that notwithstanding occasional moments, when the principle of equality acquired a somewhat stronger position in the discourse as reviewed in the first part of this essay, the State in India has never truly championed this principle. It has been earlier concerned with integrationism, pluralism, and modernization, and now with inclusionism. Yet, until quite recently, the State had never formally distanced itself from the constitutional responsibility of promoting equality through State initiatives and from the vision of providing transformative, socially-oriented, and humanitarian education.

Perhaps, the reason of not disowning this responsibility and maintaining bleak presence of this liberal socialist view might be related with the requirement of sustaining the State's legitimacy and its inability to sideline effectively the assertion of equality, made by the historically discriminated people. However, in recent decades, the State's avowal of this responsibility seems to have become bleaker, and a new ideology of inclusionism is coming into vogue. This change is coinciding with, and in fact caused by the ascendancy of the neoliberal ideology of global capitalism. What therefore, we observe is that whilst seemingly adopting welfarist measures more vehemently than ever before, the State is relinquishing its traditional responsibilities, retaining for itself, only the role of a financial reimbursor and the possessor of monopoly over every legitimate form of violence. In collision with various non-Governmental agencies, and at times in order to appease elite interests within the Government itself, the State is immensely augmenting structural stratification in the system of education, and siphoning financial resources to corporate and religious houses for the inclusion of a certain number of marginalized people at different levels of this increasingly hierarchized order, depending upon their individual or socioeconomic capacities. Would this scenario lead to equitable quality inclusive education? Can market-oriented ideologies and practices achieve this objective? This paper suggests that presently these should be some of the crucial questions for investigation. Though fully aware of the inequities already present historically, as also documented in the first part of this paper, in the ultimate analysis, we hope, this essay would enable us to see how the contemporary political economy of education is marking significant departures in our ways of conceiving the role of the State, the place of rights in relation to the State and other agencies, and the meaning of fundamental rights themselves.

Discourse on Education Under Post-Independence Welfare State and Its Paradoxes

In this section of the present essay, we argue that although there were some new dimensions in the discourse on education in the early post-Independence period, the system of education continued to bear the burden of its colonial legacy. The overarching concerns were integrationalism, pluralism, and modernization, but seldom equality, in the sense of equitable redistributive social justice; and therefore, there continued to exist various trends of exclusion and inequalities. Nonetheless, at least during this period, we find that the State did not formally abandon into the hands of other agencies its responsibility of providing education and demonstrated faith in public system. Further, the official discourse envisaged the role of education, not merely with reference to the developmental agenda of modernizing nation state, but also in terms of the objectives of social transformation through child-centred pedagogies, and community-oriented transformative learning processes of school. True, such a vision did not correspond with the ground realities. However, it was not simply a catastrophe of implementation, because, as we shall see below, the official policies had very often their own significant limitations and contradictions, owing to which, the State could not go beyond gradual expansionism to adopt some truly radical measures, though at times these were suggested. Yet, this gradual expansionism was different from the minimalist approach adopted by the State in recent decades.

Though Ambedkar proposed to make elementary education a fundamental right (Teltumbde 2013), the Indian Constitution finally provided—howsoever important—a directive principle on elementary education in Article 45 in Part IV with the expectation of its realization by the Indian State within 10 years. Of course, this provision was very important in its own right as it was the only directive principle where the Constitution provided a timeline suggesting urgency in this regard (Sadgopal 2010B: p. 296). Nonetheless, we find that following this constitutional provision, and despite the existence of a set of fundamentally newer concerns in the discourse on education, post-Independence Indian Nation-State could not free education from the yoke of its colonial inheritance. We know that a powerful discourse on national education had emerged during anti-colonial freedom struggle, which had some common concerns and resolutions; but of course, it did not have harmony on each and every issue as it was 'contested terrain' (Bhattacharya1998 and 2003). During the freedom struggle, whilst one group laid emphasis on the expansion of modern education without too much worrying about the question of its Western and colonial character, another group exhibited profound disillusionment with the existing system of education. The latter group too wanted to expand education; however, it simultaneously also advocated the need for reconstructing education on principles different from those that were the main characteristic features of colonial system (AIFRTE[3] 2011; Bhattacharya 2003). Of course, these groups did not represent watertight categories, completely homogenous, internally unified and in agreement on an alternative; they nonetheless symbolized two trends. However, the post-Independence Nation-State chose to follow the expansionist trend, and not the one that stressed on alternative models and favoured complete reconstruction.

Further, notwithstanding some exceptional and occasional voices raising questions of poverty and class-inequalities, or the powerful efforts of people like Gandhi to bring this issue to the centrestage of educational planning, or nationalist attacks on the colonial State for divesting India from its riches, the problem of poverty and class-inequalities did not become a central feature of the discourse on national education; and the post-Independence Nation-State also did not break away from this pattern. It has been suggested, that,

> a significant lack in the nationalist discourse on education was that it did not seriously consider the economic aspect of mass education as it was dominated by certain Anglo-Saxon notions of child-centred education as distinct from the Gandhian scheme of basic education, which had various aspects such as self-sufficiency, vision of the Sarvodaya Society, and the liberation of the child from the tyranny of textbooks, rote memory and examinations, and his enrichment by reality and action (Shukla 1998).

Nonetheless, it may be said that though class inequality was a relatively marginal aspect of this discourse, it was owing to the perception of a socially-oriented role of education, that the visionaries of the freedom struggle and their counterparts in the early post-Independence phase, did not conceive of education as a commodity or service, that can be sold and bought in the market by its individual possessors. As a public good, or more correctly as an instrument of liberation (AIFRTE 2011; Velaskar 2012), education was conceived to play a larger goal in society, than the commercial motives of the colonial State and its allies. Therefore, the post-Independence Nation-State. hoped to address the challenges posed by the iniquitous class relations and resultant poverty, by keeping the fee for education considerably nominal, by distribution of some scholarships, and by maintaining a system of education comprised of directly State run and Government aided institutions, alongside with some unaided private institutes. The State, however, kept the system very restricted in size and openness, and made no concerted efforts to reconstruct it, in order to truly transcend its class character as suggested for instance, by Lala Lajpat Rai, Mahatma Gandhi, Sri Aurobindo (Aurobindo 1924; Gandhi 1938; Rai 1966) and others, during the freedom struggle, by creating a truly national system of education.Therefore, the benefit of seemingly welfarist provisions did not reach the majority of those people traditionally, excluded from the sphere of formal education.

Further, it can be said that in the discourse of education during the welfarist regime of the post-Independence Nation-State, we did not find the hard questions of community-based material discrimination being addressed. It focused on the emotional integration of communities, instead of paying attention to social justice, in concrete material terms of larger socioeconomic and material life. Therefore, it took almost sixty years for the independent Nation-State to constitute a committee for probing the socioeconomic and educational status of the Muslim community in India (Government of India 2006). Before it, the sole focus remained, at least in the initial decades, on emotional integration, as is evident from a Government of India report on this theme at the beginning of the second decade. As the opening statement, this report quoted Jawaharlal Nehru from a Speechat Bangalore, October, 1955, which illustrates the basic objective.

We should not become parochial, narrow-minded, provincial, communal and caste-minded, because we have a great mission to perform. Let us, the citizens of the Republic of India, stand up straight, with straight backs and look up at the skies, keeping our feet firmly planted on the ground, and bring about this synthesis, this integration of the Indian people. Political integration has already taken place to some extent, but what I am after is something much deeper than that—an emotional integration of the Indian people so that we might be welded into one, and made into one strong national unit, maintaining at the same time all our wonderful diversity' (Government of India 1962).

Thus, unity and diversity became the overarching motto of newly established Nation-State. This steamroller of integration within a hegemonic nationalism also continued to dominate the contents of prescribed textbooks; and a rigid system of written examination further sanctified this dominant nationalist narrative and the resultant exclusion of other concerns from 'official knowledge' (Kumar 2001).

Although, the agenda of integrationalism has been the overarching influence on educational discourse and 'official knowledge' throughout the period since Independence, by the 1970s, we find that a lot of emphasis was laid on the values of pluralism, as we will see in the following paragraphs. Further, as we have illustrated below, the inculcation of the values of pluralism, the task of building national character, and the objective of social transformation, were thought to have been achieved through school community interactions. But these expectations were not fulfilled, owing partly to the absence of instituting concrete measures for realizing this interface and partly because, subsequently this concept was diluted and utilized by agencies of education, for very different objectives breeding thereby, another set of inequalities. However, before we explain this point, it may be noted here that without a doubt, the philosophy of pluralism is very important; and it is not adversarial otherwise to other discourses either. Yet, what we find is that psychological dimensions of integrationalism and pluralism of communities, have been the main focal points of the discourse of the post-Independence welfare State; and the discourse of social justice and equality of classes and individuals have been shrouded under these overarching concerns. In other words, notwithstanding its advantages, merits and necessity, the focus on integrationalism and pluralism in the discourse on education, during the welfarist regime of the early-Independence Nation-State in India, had a corresponding absence of the actual adherence and constant emphasis, on the right to equality and redistributive justice in material terms, as part of a broader vision of education, which sees it as part of the larger socioeconomic realm, and which perceives interconnection between different sets of rights. Therefore, the system of education in post-Independence India, could not effectively address the questions of equality and redistributive justice.

It continued to remain embedded in the colonial pattern of literary education, which was marked by socially biased official knowledge, 'majoritarian' culture, and a particular kind of discordance between school and the community—all heavily tilting it in favour of 'reproduction' and status quo (Gupta 2012). The apparatus of educational institutions and the grip of 'official knowledge' continued to marginalize in the classroom learning process, the social field of lived experiences (Gupta Forthcoming; Krishna 2007; Kumar 2008). The normative student in educational theory and practice in India, continued to be the Hindu upper caste, middle class male urban child. Therefore, the curriculum designed for the schools was shaped in such a way, that it catered to the needs and aspirations of the Hindu upper caste students, whilst orienting others towards the oppressive Hindu cultural world. The educational theory, teachers' training programmes, school curriculum and the teachers demonstrated apathy to the pathetic life conditions of marginalized people (Ilaiah 1996: pp. 71–101; Krishna 2007; Kumar 1983).

Nonetheless, there was one very important occasion when the objectives of equality, quality and quantity came at the centrestage of the educational discourse of post-colonial Nation-State in India. This moment was provided by the report of Indian Education Commission (1964–6) chaired by Prof. D.S. Kothari. Of course, guided by the developmental agenda of modernizing

Nation-State, which is also evident from the title of its report, and the much-abused model of integrationism in education, it, however, recommended for establishing the 'Common School System Based on the Concept of Neighborhood Schools' (CSS-NS). It also recommended for annual allocation of six percent of the GDP for education (Government of India 1966). Thus, as distinct from the contemporary neoliberal discourses to be discussed shortly, Kothari Commission offered two very concrete solutions, both in the form of State initiatives, which perhaps possessed potentials of transcending socioeconomic and cultural barriers, for achieving equality, quality, and quantity objectives in education.

However, the National Policy of Education (Government of India 1968) and other subsequent pronouncements did not truly uphold any of the two potential measures suggested by the Kothari Commission. The National Education Policy (Government of India 1968) nonetheless, kept the developmental agenda of Nation-State at the core, even whilst envisioning the school community relationship in education. It suggested, that the school and the community should be brought closer for work-experience, community service, national reconstruction, self-help, character formation, and developing a sense of social commitment (Government of India 1968: p. 41).

Similarly, the National Curriculum Framework (NCF) (NCERT 1975) discussed the need to promote school community interaction in a number of ways. It underlined pluralism as an important aspect of Indian society; and it acknowledged the distinction between prescribed curriculum and hidden curriculum, but at the same time, it also realized the need to protect constitutional objectives. Therefore, it suggested that, 'while the 'hidden' curriculum of a school cannot be totally done away with, the discrepancy between the 'hidden' and the 'prescribed' can be reduced by allowing some freedom to teachers and other curriculum workers, to adapt the curriculum to the needs of the individuals and the community, provided the basic values and the national goals are not sacrificed.' (NCERT 1975: p. 2). Here, both aspects, a meeting point as well as the tension between integrationism and pluralism are perceptible.

The NCF (NCERT 1975) further recommended in the context of teaching Civics and Environment, taking out students from the classroom and involving them in real life situations. They also recommended planning activities and programmes for children that recognized the pedagogic and transformative significance of school community interface (NCERT 1975: p. 22 and p. 55). It suggested that work experience, play, and games should form an important means of organizing meaningful learning experiences, cutting across language, mathematics, sciences and social sciences. There should be a continuous assessment of progress, through frequent evaluation of learning outcomes, and the community and the school should come closer through the use of the resources of the community in learning and by the school's helping in the improvement of the life and environment of the community (NCERT 1975: p. 36). Students and teachers on their part should participate in community life, whether it is cleanliness, health, sanitation, literacy, beautification, road construction, irrigation, childcare, or work in the farm, the factory, and the hospital (NCERT 1975: p. 53). Therefore, it recommended that there should be a minimum of 240 working days in a year, out of which 220 days would be for instruction and 20 days for school camps and community services, et cetera (NCERT 1975: p. 29).

The suggestions outlined above from the NCF (1975) would appear radical if seen in terms of the existing Indian education system, which is a continuation of the colonial model. It did not, and still does not, welcome the role of community in the management of schools, but this NCF was precisely demanding for the same. Its recommendations implied reciprocal interaction between the school and the community, an active learning process even transcending physical confines of the school, and in this course of action, also transforming the outside society. This proposed live pedagogic interaction between school and the outside communities would have been essential for eliminating prejudices, which are one of the root causes of discrimination and disparities. However, notwithstanding these objectives, the NCF (1975), or any subsequent official policy document thereafter, did not provide any systematic, concrete, and obligatory programme to use community as a pedagogic resource on a regular basis in the learning process of students. Even these recommendations, as laid down in the NCF (1975), were ultimately extremely limited, as these envisaged only some occasional moments when students would be taken out from school's physical space so that they get a temporary opportunity for learning by doing, and learning by observation of living reality and would attain transformative objectives. Similarly, it highlighted the need to bring closer the school, and the community in the task of evaluation of students, but in its recommendations on the subject of evaluation, it is not explained how community can be involved objectively in this process.

Of course, NCFs from 1985 onwards continue to occasionally discuss the idea of school community interaction, and they refer to objectives like active learning process and social development as well. However, these NCFs mostly placed this issue within their discussion of work experience, which was already reduced to a minor and extremely sidelined activity in the actual curricular practices of the school. For instance, the NCF (1985) suggested that all teachers should work as SUPW (socially useful productive work) teachers; and SUPW should be linked with outside community, as it would be good for social development (NCERT 1985: p. 18). Further, in the NCF (NCERT 1985), the conception of the reciprocal interaction between the school and the community was sadly confined to the rural schools alone. This conception was limited in another sense; NCF (NCERT 1985) merely discussed about the need to use natural or material resources, but it did not take up the issue how the outside community or society, with all its attractive features as well as with its evils could become a pedagogic resource in the learning process of students.

In the same manner, the NCF (NCERT 1988: p. 26) expected, that Social Science should aim at developing in the student, an understanding of his/her physical and social environment, both immediate and remote, in terms of time and space, and an appreciation of the cultural heritage of India and various cultures of the world. All of this social science was expected to achieve as if it is a living and active agent in itself akin to the

Changing Discourses on Inequality and Disparity 31

State, the teacher, the student, or the parent! How would it obtain these objectives when no concrete transformative pedagogic programme involving students, teachers, outside community and parents was outlined in the NCF, or any other policy document for the implementation of this vision? One may suppose that like other curricular frameworks, the NCF (NCERT 1988) also left this objective to be achieved by the textbook writers and the teachers, believing that the latter's mediation between the text and the student, would be able to devise precise ways of its realization. However, neither the National Commission for teachers (Government of India 1984) nor the National Policy of Education (Government of India 1986) or any other policy pronouncement thereafter, contained anything that would have brought this change enabling teachers, students and other community members to attain these objectives.

In fact, one should not fail to see the way in which the approach of National Commission for teachers attempted to distort the hitherto followed meaning of transformative education, implying the utilization of living phenomenon of outside society in the learning process of students: instead of seeing that larger meaning, the Commission merely focused on the need to mobilize community resources (Government of India 1984: p. 22). As we shall illustrate below, it was a true precursor to the contemporary or neoliberal dilution, in the vision regarding the role of community in education, which has further weakened the agency of teachers and has augmented inequalities in the system of elementary education.

Similarly, the National Education Policy (Government of India 1986) had announced that the resource persons in the community, irrespective of their formal educational qualifications, would be invited to contribute to the cultural enrichment of education, employing both the literate and oral traditions of communication. It further prescribed that in order to sustain and carry forward the cultural tradition, the role of old masters, who train pupils through traditional modes will be supported and recognized (Government of India 1986). Here, except one element of the discourse of transformative education, as outlined above, namely the cultural interaction between students and the outside professional practitioners, the larger vision was lost. In fact, the terms 'resource persons in the community, irrespective of their formal educational qualifications' have been exploited in the subsequent decades by local, provincial, national and international agencies as a green signal for the appointment of a large number of untrained/insufficiently trained, unqualified, under-paid, contractual teachers for majority of schools except for that minority of institutions, which cater to the children of elites. Is it not another form of inequality? In fact, it was under this framework that this policy adopted formally for the first time the 'erroneous principle' of multiple layers in education. It established upper layer in the form of Navodaya Vidyalayas for one set of students and lower layer in the form of non-formal education for another much wider group of children.

Thus, the discourse on the values of pluralism and pedagogic interaction between school and the community became feebler, thinner and narrower by 1980s; and from then onwards, it began to be utilized for the policies of 'structural adjustment', breeding newer forms of educational inequalities. We also find that from this time onwards, some other objectives began to be more emphasized in this discourse, such as the need to develop a national identity, spread of education to the marginalized sections of society, and adjusting education with modern technological developments like the computer technology (NCERT 1985). The expansion of education amongst the hitherto excluded sections should be of course the most important objective; and there does not seem to be a necessary contradiction between the philosophy of pluralism and the policy of expansionism; on the contrary, they should be complimentary to each other. However, it appears that this discourse of expansionism was grounded in the model of integrationise, to be replaced shortly by inclusivism, which pushed the philosophy of pluralism, and the question of equality and redistributive social justice in the rear. And more importantly, as we shall elaborate in the next section, it was based on a minimalist approach, which is related to the extrinsic pressures this time, because this is also the period, when as scholars have underlined, the influence of international agencies and ideologies of neoliberal global capitalism had started exerting decisive influence on Indian education (Sadgopal 2010a and 2010b). Therefore, in an effort to ideologically deconstruct policy framework and identify terminological/discursive shifts within it, specifically with regard to the question of the equality-quality conundrum in elementary education, one eminent scholar has aptly underlined that 'neither the concern for equality of educational opportunity nor for socialjusticeever found expression in educational terms' (Velaskar 2010). She suggests that for most part of the seventies and for the better half of the eighties, a policy of piecemeal and gradual expansionism governed the development of elementary education, where equality goals of education were blatantly short changed for elitist, modernization goals.

By the NCF (NCERT 2000), the emphasis has considerably shifted from the philosophy of pluralism to the idea of a supposedly 'inclusive education' capable of developing a 'national identity' and ensuring some recognition to 'indigenous knowledge'. One cloak for its religious agenda of Right wing Hinduism was, its emphasis on the need to introduce value education in the schools. While giving examples of the kind of values it would include, it was underlined that the objective of such a programme is to inculcate in the students the ancient Indian values (*prachinbhartiyamulyon*); and mostly such references were directed to religious texts and figures; and less to secular symbols of values as enshrined in the texts authored during the 'medieval' period of Indian history.[4] The NCF (NCERT 2000) preferred to use the term 'social cohesion' instead of pluralism and it recommended education about religions, the other cloak for its right wing agenda, in order to achieve this objective (NCERT 2000: Sections 1.1, 1.4.1, 1.4.4, 1.4.7, 2.2, 2.6, 2.8.8, and 2.8.9). It is interesting to note here that the NCF (NCERT 2000) quoted from a UNESCO document in order to justify its recommendation for religious education.

> It is from early childhood that children should be introduced to the discovery of 'otherness', and to the values of tolerance, respect,

and confidence in the 'other' that will bring about a change of behavior and attitudes towards others' (NCERT 2000: section 1.4.7).

The introduction of specific teaching of intercultural and inter-religious dialogue, through the adequate pedagogical tools, was conceived as a means to foster reciprocal knowledge of shared values, contained in the message issued by religious and spiritual traditions, which can be considered as a common spiritual and cultural heritage.

Thus, we find some crucial shifts occurring in the discourse on education in India. It first moved away from a modern, secular and political understanding of the concept of rights, at the core of which, was the philosophy of difference and equality as we had discussed in the introductory section of this essay with the emphasis on integrationalism, pluralism, inclusionism and modernization. Subsequently, it began advocating the need for cohesion and appreciation of common religious values, instead of identifying with the differences that exist amongst them. In other words, the NCF (NCERT 2000) at one hand discussed about the feeling of 'otherness', instead of concrete material differences and discriminations; and it on the other hand also emphasized the point of 'common spiritual and cultural heritage', whilst pluralism is about recognizing and appreciating multiple identities and allegiances. Both of these elements perfectly fit in the right wing theory of Hindu *rashtra*, where recognizing 'others' is essential in order to distinguish who is a Hindu so that these others may be compelled to get assimilated within the Hindu fold. The 'Hindu' is the one whose *pitribhu* (fatherland) and *matribhu* (motherland) is the same as that of his ancestors. 'Hinduism' in this conception, is a way of living, a cultural code of the original inhabitants of the country, where the 'others' will have to assimilate themselves' (Savarkar 1923/1962).

The philosophy of pluralism, and the vision of involving outside community in the pedagogic practices of school have been revived in the NCF (2005), alongside with the presence of inclusion ideology. In fact, it may be said without inviting perhaps too much of a risk that the NCF (2005) revived the discourse of 1975 on child, community and pluralism. The NCF (NCERT 2005) underlines the necessity of connecting learning process with the life outside the school, so that the learner can actually construct knowledge. This Curricular Framework lays emphasis on the need to recognize and respect the plurality and diversity of Indian society, and to use it as a pedagogic resource. This is proposed to reform the currently prevailing situation, where the information is being imparted to the students through the textbook culture. The classroom culture does not allow students to critically raise questions on everything they study or observe. The classroom teaching is generally either based on no frame or alternatively, the frame is too strong to facilitate opportunity for the accommodation of students' aspirations.

However, the emphasis on child, identity and local in the NCF (NCERT 2005) has been perceived by an eminent scholar as dangerous, because it may give encouragement to obscurantist trends of outside society to pollute school education. Further, he quite correctly suggested that one way, however defective in actual practice, that may still be employed to keep a check on actual content of teaching in schools, is the system of examinations. The critic believes, that the NCF (2005) is, however, intent on reducing these to mere farcical exercises (in the name of reducing burden on the students).

Nonetheless, we need to recognize the fact that even prior to this kind of renewed emphasis on child, identity, and local, the obscurantist trends were affecting schools in considerable degree, as have been underscored by various reviewers of curricular knowledge and the accounts of classroom transactions and experiences. Hence, surely, there is some need to rethink discordance of school and the outside community, a condition where, while the former gets influenced by the latter, but no conscious pedagogic interaction takes place in the reverse direction (Gupta forthcoming). Moreover, in his analysis, this critic treated the distinction between knowledge and information—as suggested in the NCF (2005)—and the emphasis on child and local as postmodern delusion. Though in general terms, this statement may well be true about the turn in academic discourse, yet, we cannot negate entire history of educational thought, both in India and outside, where Gandhi, Dewey and many others have already taken analogous positions.

The other problem is that in such discussions, 'community' is generally understood to imply only one meaning: primordial entity of obscurantist people possessing 'primitive beliefs', which seems quite in line with colonial and orientalist depictions of Indian society, while we have already seen at the beginning of this paper that it may be used and is used in very different ways. It is not that one is summarily denying the existence of obscurantism in the world outside the school—though it is not the only phenomenon of the cultural milieu outside the school—but it should not be treated, in such a manner to give impression of its essentiality and non-reformability as a racial pathology. Moreover, ignoring it cannot provide a solution, rather we need to interact with it very seriously. However, regardless of its recommendation for 'continuous comprehensive evaluation' of students, which has been accepted by the Government, the vision of NCF (NCERT 2005) ultimately remains unfulfilled, like the vision of earlier NCFs to concretely initiate a programme of transformative pedagogic interaction between school and community, to establish equality principle as the essential yardstick of educational policy and practice, and to enable the agency of teacher as an important link of this process. Moreover, as we shall see in our analysis of neoliberal ideology of education, in the last section of this paper, whatever progressive vision this NCF upholds, the extrinsic limits to its materialization are now too evident to be dismissed lightly.

We find that the term community is still being readily used these days in the discourse on decentralization of education. However, its meaning seems to have been considerably reduced and changed under the neoliberal discourse and practice of education. In such discussions, the term community implies local population and administration. Its role in education is conceived largely in terms of the need to transfer the ownership of school property to the local bodies, to claim locally available resources, to locally appoint para teachers, and to enlist the participation of local community in certain managerial aspects associated with schools, primarily with the view to improve access to education, as well as, with the stated objective of the 'empowerment' of community. In so doing, scholars (Leclercq 2008; Chatterjee 2004: 129–202, 229–38) have not examined the implications of this move for the principle of equality in education, for the transformative role that school community interaction should facilitate; and for the political economy of education. For instance, this approach not merely falls short of adequately focusing on the transformative pedagogic interaction between school and community, or community as a source of knowledge production. But, under various flagship programmes, such as District Primary Education Project (DPEP) and Sarva Shiksha Abhiyan (SSA) and various euphemisms, such as Venture Schools, Education Guarantee Scheme (EGS), alternative education, and *ekal* schools (single teacher schools), neoliberal State, in collusion with international agencies of global capital and religious organizations, has created newer layers of substandard schools for the education of the masses of this country. Thus, it is another form of inequality and disparity legitimized under the pretext of community based arrangements of education.

Neoliberal Vision of Education and its Implications for the Rights of Citizens: Contours of the Debates on RTE Act

In this section of the present essay, we will explain how in the recent years, the discourse has further moved away from the socially-oriented vision of transformative, democratizing, equalizing and humanitarian education? We have already seen that it had a bleak presence, of course with its own problems and limitations, under a welfare State up to at least the 1970s as it was more concerned with emotional integration and the philosophy of plural values. By the 1980s, the State started further distancing itself from this vision. In this section, we will explain how in the garb of economic liberalization, structural readjustment, public private partnership and open competition, education and knowledge are being transformed as marketable commodities? We shall see how not merely the capitalist class interests, but also neo-conservative forces in collaboration with neoliberal State comprise the vanguard of this historic transition. This exercise would also reveal how the State is increasingly relinquishing its social commitment in the hands of these private service providers and neo-conservative forces, which are left almost free to enjoy maximum fruits produced by oppressed classes. Therefore, it needs to be seen whether the neoliberal political economy of education would mark another drift away from the principle of equality, or does it possess potentials to create conditions conducive for the realization of equitable quality universal education?

We will first analyse the contours of the key scholarly positions on 86th Constitutional Amendment Act (Government of India 2001) and particularly the Right of Children for Free and Compulsory Education Act (Government of India 2009) (hereinafter RTE Act) with the purpose of underscoring the place of equality principle in this discourse as a parameter of evaluating these enactments. It would set the context for our subsequent discussion within this section of our paper, where we will present a brief outline of some exemplary events that have occurred following these legislations. We hope that these examples would compel us to raise some critical questions about the direction in which political economy of education is moving in our times and its implications for the conception of rights, including the right to equality as outlined in the introductory section of this essay.

In the period beginning since 1990s until now, we notice four sets of important events happening in the sphere of elementary mass education in India. First, elementary education was recognized as a fundamental right by Supreme Court in 1993 in the famous Unni Krishnan Judgment subsequently leading to 86th Amendment Act in the Constitution in 2001 by the Parliament and the legislation of RTE Act in 2009. Second, it was the time when Indian Governments began accepting international aid for elementary education. Third, it is also the time when we find Governments busy in launching one after the other different schemes of educational expansion and exalting their achievements through statistical data about enrollment and literacy, both in terms of general aggregates as well as its smaller break-ups with regard to different social categories and regional distribution. Fourth, if we look at the recent data for elementary education (DISE 2008–09 and 2009–10)[5], particularly the figures pertaining to facilities, infrastructure, enrollment, retention, drop out and completion; and the studies on attendance (Government of India 2007–08); although the space constraints do not permit extensive discussion of these statistical records, it is clear that the picture continues to remain appalling and pathetic.

Therefore, there are scholars who are very critical of Indian educational policies being framed under the influence of international capital and neoliberal ideology. For instance, it has been argued that neoliberalism has spawned a new expansionism wherein State provision is undercut by new globally inspired strategies of equity and quality, which masquerade as measures of equality and social justice next. Neo-educational strategies aim at new equity goals and dislodge earlier efforts of gradual State sponsored expansionism. At the same time, the new sovereign principles of equity and compensation are sought to be given a new life through highest forms of State action, such as the 86th amendment to Constitution (and the RTE Act) marking further deflection towards 'neoliberal reform' underscored by human capital theory, a new philosophy of instrumentalist, skill based knowledge and market-oriented values of efficiency, accountability and performance (Velaskar 2010).

It has also been suggested that instead of giving a right, the 86th Amendment Act tried to dilute the possibilities created by Unni Krishnan Judgment and other policy frameworks. Further, though the Indian ruling class has been historically unwilling to provide equitable quality universal elementary education, however, added to this was now the international pressure of structural adjustment imposed by World Bank and International Monetary Fund (IMF) following which the State has been trying to abdicate its constitutional responsibility (Sadgopal 2001a and 2001b). Many examples are given to substantiate this point, however, we will return to them in context of our following discussion of RTE Act.

There exist two starkly opposed camps of the general opinion about RTE Act (Government of India 2009). First, there are aficionados in somewhat celebratory mood on the enactment of this long awaited legislation, considering it as a creditable achievement of a poor nation after decades of delay—a milestone on which they expect more progress to ensue in the near future![6] Of course, even with the passing of this legislation, serious concerns of quality in education continue to cloud. However, there is also this alternative suggestion that the Government and international agencies are adhering to a 'minimalist approach' for the universalization of elementary education, which has posed one significant quality constraint in Indian education; and therefore, by implication, it is not the RTE Act as such, which we should hold accountable for this dilution.[7] After all, apart from some enabling acts of colonial era, judicial verdict of Supreme Court and 86th Amendment Act in the Indian Constitution (2001), no legislation in India before the RTE Act provided education as a fundamental right of all citizens. Further, it may be argued that whatever may be the nature and the flaws of this legislation, since it has made education a fundamental right, it may generate a new kind of discourse liberating education from the confines of inertia and welfarism. Another possibility could be that the passing of the RTE Act may have important consequences, owing to the potentials of litigation a fundamental right contains.

Yet, we need to understand a few crucial questions here. One area of bewilderment or enigma is that does the shift from the discourse of equitable quality education to the adoption of a 'minimalist approach' not amount to be a significant dilution in the notion of right itself?[8] Further, how significant are the possible judicial potentials of RTE Act? If fundamental inequalities are integral and therefore legitimized within the framework of this legislation, how much liberal interpretation and provisioning is possible? Moreover, how much judicial intervention has achieved since 2001, when elementary education was recognized by the Parliament as a fundamental right? Further, is it not some kind of a piecemeal approach, a continuation of earlier pattern and therefore, insufficient to

Changing Discourses on Inequality and Disparity 41

liberate masses of this country from the overall paradigm of educational inequalities? Has it not once again, postponed resolution of all three pertinent questions of education, namely equality, quality and quantity? This is what we wish to investigate through a brief sketch of the position of second camp on RTE Act, and an analysis of the events taking place within this framework in the sphere of Indian education.

Second camp consists of those detractors who find nothing creditable in the RTE framework and in fact bemoan RTE legislation, as a tactic of legitimizing already existing discriminatory system, a neoliberal instrument of privatization, and a lost opportunity to strike at the root cause of inequitous educational system and inegalitarian social order. This camp identifies many problems, some fundamental and others additional in the RTE Act, and also point examples from the subsequent events as proofs of their stand being vindicated. They argue, that this legislation denies Right to early childhood care and pre-primary education to children below 6 years of age; right to secondary education to children in the 14 to 18-year age group; and elementary education of equitable quality even to children in the 6 to 14-year age group. It does not include even the required student support measures to ensure retention, and regular participation of children in the 6 to 14-year age group; and neither develops government schools nor regulates private schools. It has provisions to allow private managements to hike fees as they like and to intensify the pace of commercialization; it provides for siphoning off public funds to private operators through reimbursement; and it opens flood gates to thorough commercialization of school education under reimbursement scheme. This camp believes that the RTE Act (2009) not only institutionalizes the present multi-layered and unequal school system, but also further widens inequalities and discrimination in all dimensions. It ends up in closure of government schools and takes the school system precisely in opposite direction to the long-cherished vision of Common School System (AIFRTE 2012–13). For almost last 200 years, both colonial and post-colonial State in India and the social elites have been taking shelter under baseless pretensions, to obfuscate the attention of people from the real issue, namely the need to establish a fully and directly public (State) funded common school system guarantying equitable quality education to all. Therefore, the second camp, insists for complete revamping of the present RTE act and replacing it with a new one, designed on the pattern of 'common school system based on the principle of neighborhood schools' (Sadgopal 2010a and 2011; Niranjanaradhya 2011; Gupta 2012).[9]

Of course, these camps exist alongside with some other very significant trends. First, there are scholars and activists who document lacunas in the RTE Act instead of completely rejecting it. They underline those issues that the rules framed (or yet to be framed) by Union or State Governments, for the implementation of this legislation needs to resolve. They also call attention to the non-compliance, non-implementation, or apathy to this act prevalent in most of the states and Union Territories (Mehendale 2010; Jha and Parvati 2010).[10] However, in doing so, unlike the second camp, they leave the larger ideological framework of RTE Act, somewhat unproblematized.

Second trend is discernible in the tirades on the ways of resource mobilization, or neoliberal ideology of educational management as evident for instance, in the debates generated by the advocacy, maneuvering and application for public private partnership (PPP) for the implementation of RTE Act. Of course, not without its contestation, however, the neoliberal ideological position—repellent to the direct State funding of education and champion of its greater privatization and PPP—had acquired a very powerful position in the discourse on education, by the time of the drafting and subsequent legislation of RTE Act. This debate commenced with a particularly provocative statement, which has become the constant revolving point of reference, namely the supposedly extraordinarily high salaries of teachers appointed by the government bodies on permanent basis. It was suggested that even an allocation of six per cent of the gross domestic product (GDP) to the education budget, as originally recommended by Kothari Commission, would not be sufficient to fund universal school education until the very distant future if the government school system is used as the only instrument.

Therefore, it was argued that universal elementary education could be provided by employing teachers on considerably low salaries under PPP in low budget schools.[11] (Jain and Dholakia 2009 and 2010; Sarangapani 2009; Ramachandran 2009; Jain and Saxena 2010; Kumar 2010; Tooley 2007).

However, numeracy through three hours of daily engagement adjusted around child labour schedules—allegedly provided in such low budget schools—does not amount to being a school. Schools need to provide for holistic allround development of children; this requires adequate space and facilities, time to be spent at school, a sound curriculum, and qualified teachers who can ensure that children have worth-while learning and development experiences and opportunities (Sarangapani 2009). On the other hand, to argue that alternative schools or private schooling can take care of the needs of primary schoolgoing children, is to effectively condemn the poor and the marginalized to a second rate education since they can never afford private and expensive schooling (Ramachandran 2009). Since the formulation and implementation of the Right to Education Act should be essentially in consonance with Right to Equality, we therefore need to examine various forms and meanings of PPP in this context: how is it going to impact different sections of population and what would be its implications for our idea of equitable quality inclusive education for all?

Let us suppose that this calculation is right, that we may not be able to achieve universal elementary education through State funded system of education even when six per cent budget of GDP is allocated for this purpose. It is very likely because, there has accumulated a deficit of allocation over last five decades since the recommendation of Kothari Commission, as the Government never implemented the implementation of this proposal. However, for this reason, what do we need to resolve is that whether finance is purely a matter of economics, or it is predominantly a question of the priorities of our political economy? For instance, even if we accept, for the sake of argument, this neoliberal row about high salaries of teachers, we need to resolve a variety of other questions too. Salary is a relative concept. After all, teachers are not the only sort of State employees getting these supposedly high salaries. What about the salaries of other Government employees? What about the too-high salaries of some select few employees in the private sector, and its interrelated corollary opposite in the form of too-low salaries of others? Can we isolate the question of salary of employees of one sector and cadre from the other sector and cadre? Should we continue with untrained or less trained and under-qualified contractual teachers for the masses of our country and trained, qualified permanent teachers for the elites? What about huge tax exemptions of various kinds to various corporate houses? All these have their claims on GDP and ultimately all of this goes from the pocket of each citizen. But, this we would perceive only when we allow fullness to our vision. The point is that salaries are part of a larger political economy. Why do these advocates of PPP not press for restructuring this political economy itself so that, a lot of money that is lost in tax exemptions or illegally amassed by both the Government and the private sector and their employees is saved and accumulated through proper taxation to be utilized for public good, such as food, health, and education?

Similarly, another core tenet of neoliberalism, which it seeks to implant in the minds of people is the belief in the essential or natural superiority of private or capitalist ventures over public funded-managed systems and institutions. It does not tell the real causes of the failure of certain public systems; through a highly generalized of an otherwise variegated situation, it seeks to essentialize their failure as inevitable. The celebratory responses of scholars on the verdict of Supreme Court upholding the constitutional validity of RTE Act on the question of 25 percent reservation for disadvantaged children in private schools, and even the language of this judgment itself ultimately played only the role of affirming to the view of the superiority of private schools. These reflections (Mander 2012), underlined the need for compassion and shrouded the negative implications of this provision for the Right to Equality. Knowingly or unknowingly, this kind of focus served the State to shun its obligation to protect and promote social and educational equality. By implications, this ultimately valorized the superiority of private schools as an oxymoron, giving a further push to the competition to admit children in these institutions under an enterprise, seemingly designed for social justice, but actually shifting attention away from the real issue, namely to strengthen public system of education (Teltumbde 2012; Patnaik 2012–13).

The favour of privatization and PPP is related with another significant shift engendered by neoliberal discourse. It is its clear and public avowal of profit motives in education. Though the RTE Act has the non-profit motive of the institution as one of the conditions of recognition, on this ground, no school has been derecognized till date. Moreover, there is no provision in the RTE Act to put a check on fee hike. On the contrary, under the mid-term appraisal of the 11th plan, the Government strongly favoured profit-making institutions in the sphere of education (Tilak 2011). The Government has already recognized before World Trade Organization (WTO) higher education as a tradable service by offering it in the General Agreement on Trade and Services (GATS); and it has also been suggested that the five bills on higher education presently lying before the Parliament intend to operationalize this agenda of WTO in Indian education (Patnaik 2012). Here we need to recognize two more points.

First, both higher education and school education are essentially and organically linked with each other: teachers for schools are prepared in higher education; and students are prepared in schools for undertaking advance courses in higher education for both professional and academic pursuits. Therefore, privatization of one is bound to impact the other.

Second, even with regard to school education, this agenda of PPP was already clearly visible in the document on 'Public Private Partnership in School Education: a Concept Note' released by the Ministry of Human Resource Development, Government of India for public feedback in the year 2007 (Government of India 2007). Although a Government document, it is full of admiration of private enterprises and contempt of public sector. It does not realize the need to mention even in passing the vital contribution, which the Government schools have so far made in our country despite insufficient funding, poor infrastructure, lack of proper supervision, and unscientific policies. Yet this document highlights the alleged 'essentiality' of the inefficiency of Government to impart quality education to all in such a manner as if it is something inbuilt within the public system of education and therefore beyond reforms. In arguing so, even the examples of those elite institutions which are run and financed by the Government and still have been doing well, such as Indian Institutes of Management, Indian Institutes of Technology, NavodayaVidyalayas, Central Schools, PratibhaVikasVidyalayas, Model Schools etcetera, are completely ignored. It sidelines the fact that until quite recently, both the official discourse and popular perception regarded public or Government institutions as the benchmark of quality. It undermines the fact that by mainly focusing on certain elite institutions, and also by its denial to appropriately fund universal elementary education, the Government has forced other institutions to suffer with chronic inequity, inevitable in a multi-layered system of education. Even though there is no consensus that the private schools perform better, it is obvious that the performance of Government schools would depend ultimately upon the State provisioning of these institutions. However, ignoring these crucial counter-arguments, the MHRD Concept Note on PPP blamed Government schools for all evils and praised private initiatives for their managerial skills.

This idea of superiority of private schools is being propagated and assimilated in various ways. Even within an episode of a television programme Satyamev Jayate on Star Plus channel (dated 10 June 2012) along with its follow-up programme Asar broadcasted on ABP News (dated 15 June 2012), a public celebrity apparently campaigned for the rights of disabled persons but simultaneously pleaded for donation to a trust/aided school for inclusive education. Irrespective of how we resolve the question of his personal intention, did he not thereby inadvertently but inevitably club together the essential contradiction between the focus on rights on the one hand and benevolence and philanthropy on the other?

Alternatively, would it no more be seen as a contradiction in the new ideological dispensation where equality is not the norm and the State is not therefore its fundamental guarantor? It is additionally important to ask this question for the reason that he did not feel the need to highlight the indispensability of improving the pitiable condition of ordinary Government funded schools in order to ensure admission and progression of disabled children within a system of equitable quality education for all.

What is desired by neoliberal pressure groups is not merely privatization, but in collusion with the State, they are setting up the scenario of increasingly unregulated autonomy of private schools unhindered by any pressure or intervention from the civil society or the judiciary. It is also corroborated by various provisions instituted under the RTE Act, which merely provided a procedure to be followed and the norms to be adhered to in the process of giving/seeking recognition of private schools. But it does not lay down any mechanism for fee regulation in private schools; and it does not take any clear position about the training of teachers and their emoluments and service conditions, leaving it open for the private sectors, the international agencies, and the State , which is also acting as a market firm these days.

Further, neoliberalism is not merely satisfied with creating a separate, autonomous, and unregulated space for itself, it aims to permeate at every level of State apparatus through advisory bodies and non-Governmental organizations (NGOs). Therefore, both practice and policies have now explicitly taken up this objective of encouraging the active involvement of NGOs in various kinds of tasks traditionally performed by the State (Sadgopal 2006; Teltumbde 2013; Tilak 2011). Evidently, these NGOs are different from the conception of community, as earlier reviewed in this paper in the section on the discourse of education under welfare State. Further, their role is not merely envisaged in terms of the distribution of goods alone, but also as the providers of services including the task of teaching. Since the teachers are constantly burdened with non-teaching tasks, the teaching-learning process is being taken over by the less-educated, untrained 'volunteers' of NGOs compelled to work on extremely low salaries. Yet, many private organizations are now working very hard to prove that the teachers of government schools remain absent from the classrooms and are not interested in teaching without at all discussing the larger politics that deliberately keeps them involved in various kinds of non-educational activities and also burdens them with too much of paperwork (Lok Shikshak Manch 2012).

Furthermore, these NGOs also claim that the result of the work done by their initiatives in schools is substantial. Many NGOs claim that the retention and enrolment of children in schools has improved during the period of their work in school. It may be asked that if untrained, less salaried teachers can work with 'weak' children with such great results, then how well would they do with 'talented' children? Then, why is the work of these 'teachers' not being utilized for the children in central and prestigious private schools? Why are there educated, professionally trained teachers for the children from one group and less educated, untrained teachers for the children from another? (Lok Shikshak Manch 2012). Is it not another form of inequality?

Another aspect of neoliberalism is that instead of seeking to equally place everyone within a homogenous educational order, at best, it can include people at different levels of a multilayered system ranging from Government schools for elite categories to ordinary village schools; from high fee charging schools to low-budget schools run and managed by religious/corporate bodies; or within exclusivist institutions, home-based education, non-formal education, or alternative education. The prospects of someone's inclusion at one of these levels would depend on a variety of factors, such as his/her socio-political status, paying capacity, physical/mental abilities, reimbursement schemes siphoning huge public funds to corporate or religious houses, 'corporate social responsibility' (CSR), availability of scholarship, or donations/charity. Thus, at best, a few special measures may be taken so as to accommodate or appease a certain section of hitherto excluded groups at a relatively well-endowed level of this hierarchy without democratizing and equalizing 'mainstream system' itself so that rest of the people are relegated at various substandard levels of education. Hiding its failure to make the 'mainstream' receptive for such students, neoliberal State even plans to segregate certain students from others (including from their homes) in the name of inclusion through special schools for marginalized groups. In addition, such students are required to pay the cost of their education–their fundamental right (Yunus 2012).

In the same sequence of events, reproducing and augmenting inequalities was situated in the RTE Amendment Act (2010), which was approved by the Parliament in 2012. Through this amendment, the Government has enshrined a set of changes in the RTE Act, all marking further deflection away from the principle of equality, but we will note here only two of them. First, in complete violation of other disability law instruments, this amendment has legalized home-based education for 'severely disabled', a category for which there exists no universally accepted definition. I have discussed this issue at length elsewhere (Gupta 2012–13), however, it may be noted here that there is no reason to deny such children their equal right to full time formal education, when it is possible to take appropriate measures in order to protect their right to receive full time formal education. Second, the same amendment has also exempted minority institutions from the purview of section 21 and 22 of RTE Act pertaining to the role and constitution of SMCs (School Management Committees). Under the RTE Act, SMCs were otherwise made responsible for a variety of tasks such as for ensuring the adequate arrangements for education of disadvantaged students and for making the school development plan.[12] It was also a way of ensuring community participation in school management. Without any doubt, we need to respect and protect the fundamental right of communities to nourish their identity, but there is an urgent necessity of pondering over a new dimension created by commercialization of education and RTE Amendment Act (2010) passed by the Parliament in the year 2012. Our constitution makers, would not have ever imagined a situation, where neoliberal forces in collaboration with neo-conservative groups, would exploit the right of cultural communities to autonomously run and manage educational institutions for their profit motives and for spreading their communal ideology.[13] Therefore, it is a strong and justifiable apprehension that a large number of private schools may take shelter under this provision by making necessary manipulative accommodations in their management trusts/boards to acquire minority status and such institutions would thereby remain out of any kind of regulative framework. Would such a scenario not present an additional obstacle in the path of establishing a system that imparts equitable quality inclusive education for all and at the same time nourishes diversity of Indian society?

However, this vision seems to have been threatened not merely because of the above-mentioned exemption in the case of minority institutions, but in the overall context of contemporary education in India, which is witnessing greater hierarchization than ever before. For instance, rather than improving already existing public funded schools, the Government has decided to move in to two opposite but interrelated directions.

On the one hand, in the recent years, Government or local administration maintained schools have been or are being closed, merged, or sold to corporate houses in various states and Union Territories by the neoliberal State; (Sadgopal 2006; Teltumbde 2013) and on the other hand, the State has been endeavouring to further extend the nuisance of multi-layered system of schooling through its plan for opening 6,000 model schools in 'educationally backward blocks' of the country. Instead of leading to any uniform pattern of improvement and leveling of the system, for a variety of reasons, these are likely to form another layer of schools outside the ordinary Government schools. For instance, firstly, 2,500 of these model schools will be under PPP mode. Secondly, as per the proceedings of the meetings of Project Approval Board (PAB), for the model schools to be established fully under Government auspices, most of the states have chosen English as the medium of education instead of mother tongue of children. Thirdly, State

Governments have also decided to affiliate these schools with Central Board of Secondary Education (CBSE) rather than with their respective State boards, which also implies that they will borrow textbooks from NCERT, in preference to designing regionally appropriate curriculum and study material.

The neoliberal political economy of education has also devised ways of meeting this criticism that it compels students to join particular kinds of institutions depending upon their class-backgrounds and other abilities. Their solution is the 'School Choice model' supported by the 'voucher scheme' and 'public private partnership': a system wherein public funds would be siphoned to private firms. According to the protagonists of the 'school choice' model, it will expand the range of options available to people including those coming from economically weaker sections of society. The profitability of schools would motivate entrepreneurs to open more and more schools, enabling thereby larger number of children to get education. Nonetheless, the protagonists of this 'School Choice' model seem to have missed the fact that it would still reproduce, aggravate and legitimize inequalities, because in the context of different and unregulated fee structures of different schools, rich and poor students would ultimately go to separate schools despite being provided with school vouchers by the State. Besides other dangers, the 'School Choice' campaign also presents the threat of the coalition between communal and market interests, because the voucher scheme and PPP models would be at their disposal to extract public money for spreading their communal agenda and for segregating students on religious lines as well.

Thus, the discussion of these tenets and events as the examples of the newer principles of the political economy of neoliberalism compels us to ponder over certain questions concerning our understanding of rights, including the Right to Equality and the meaning and role of education and State. For instance, can we or should we leave fundamental rights of citizens of any particular group, community, or class under the protection of the benevolence/charity/philanthropy/ compassion/sacrifice/profit or corporate social responsibility

(CSR) of another individual, group, community, or class? Does such a focus bordering on various forms of benevolence not distort the modern notion of rights itself, which essentially centres on the principles of dignity and equality and according to which, rights are rooted in their recognition by the State and guaranteed protection under the laws of the land? Should we make personal or familial purchasing capacity of an individual or someone's donation and sacrifice a guarantee for enjoying a fundamental right? Further, is it sufficient to focus on the inclusive, or should any such discussion be essentially attended/accompanied by a focus on equality/equitable instead of plainly assuming that the former would involuntarily result in the latter? How helpful would it be to adopt specific measures adopted for the education of a particular category of students without simultaneously making serious efforts to restructure the fundamentally exclusionary character of an education system, which tends to exclude virtually a practical majority?

Investigating answers to these questions may enable us to better comprehend significant changes in the meanings of these two principles, right and equality in the recent times and the perceived/implied meaning and role of education. This paper has only tried to underscore certain shifts in educational discourse, policy, and practice. Do we need to rewrite these principles or redesign our policies? This should be a research agenda now.

REFERENCES

AIFRTE (2011) 'Editorial,' Reconstructing Education, Vol. 1 (1): p. 1.
AIFRTE (2012–13) 'Why Do We Oppose RTE Act? *Reconstructing Education*, Vol. 1 (4) & Vol. 2 (1): p. 55
Ansari, M.T. (ed.) (2001) *Secularism, Islam and Modernity: Selected Essays of Alam Khundmiri*, Sage Publications: New Delhi
Apple, Michael W. (1996) *Cultural Politics and Education*, Open University Press: Buckingham
Aurobindo, Sri (1924) *A System of National Education,* Arya Publishing House: Calcutta
Bhattacharya, Sabyasachi, Joseph Bara and Chinna Rao Yagati (eds.) (2003) *Educating the Nation: Documents on the Discourse of National*

Education in India (1880-1920), Kanishka: New Delhi
Bhattacharya, Sabyasachi (ed.) (1998) *The Contested Terrain: Perspectives on Education in India*, Orient Longman Limited: New Delhi
Chatterjee, Anne Vaugier (ed.) (2004) *Education and Democracy in India*, Manohar: New Delhi
Combat Law (2008) Nos. 7-8, (May-August)
Gandhi, Mahatma (1938) *Educational Reconstruction*, Hindustani Talimi Sangh: Wardha
Government of India (1962) *Report of the Committee on Emotional Integration*, Ministry of Education, Manager of Publications: New Delhi
Government of India (1966) *Education and National Development*, Ministry of Education
Government of India (1968) National Policy on Education
Government of India (1984) *National Commission for Teachers (1) Under the Chairmanship of Prof. Chattopadhyaya*
Government of India (1986) *National Policy on Education*
Government of India (2006) *Social, Economic and Educational Status of the Muslim Community of India: A Report of Prime Minister's High Level Committee under Cabinet Secretariat, Chairperson: Justice Rajindar Sachar.*
Government of India (2007) *Public Private Partnership in School Education: A Concept Note, Ministry of Human Resource Development*
Government of India (2007–08) *Study of Students' Attendance in Primary and Upper Primary Schools: Abridged Report*, Educational Consultants India Limited (EDUCIL)
Government of India (2009) *The Right of Children for Free and Compulsory Education Act*
Government of India (2012) *Right of Children for Free and Compulsory Education (Amendment) Act*
Gupta, Vikas (2012) 'Pluralism Versus Contest of Identities,' *Seminar*, 638: pp. 30–36
Gupta, Vikas, 'Learning Scientific History in Schools: An Insider's Account,' in Shrimali, K.M. et. al. *Teaching History*, Aakar Books: Delhi
Ilaiah, Kancha (1996) *Why I am not a Hindu: A Sudra Critique of Hindutva Philosophy, Culture and Political Economy*, Samya
Jain, Manish and Sadhana Saxena (2010) 'Politics of Low Cost Schooling and Low Teacher Salary,' *Economic & Political Weekly*, Vol. 45 (18)
Jain, Pankaj S. and Ravindra H. Dholakia (2009) 'Feasibility of Implementation of Right to Education Act,' *Economic & Political*

Weekly, Vol. xliv (25): pp. 38–43.

Jain, Pankaj S. and Ravindra H. Dholakia (2010) 'Right To Education Act and Public-Private Partnership,' *Economic & Political Weekly,* Vol. xlv (8): pp. 78–80

Jha, Praveen and Pooja Parvati (2010) 'Right To Education Act 2009: Critical Gaps and Challenges,' *Economic & Political Weekly,* Vol. 45: (13)

Krishna, M. Murali (2007) Marginalization of Dalits: Role of Oppressive Pedagogic Practices in Indian Schools: A Dalit Perspective. Paper presented in the International Conference on School Education, Pluralism and Marginality: Comparative Perspectives. Organized by Deshkal Society, 14 to 16 December at the India International Centre, New Delhi. Also published in Sleeter Christine et al. (eds.) (2012) *School Education, Pluralism and Marginality: Comparative Perspectives,* Orient Blackswan: Hyderabad

Kumar, Krishna (1983) 'Educational Experience of Scheduled Castes And Tribes,' *Economic & Political Weekly,* Vol. 18 (36): pp. 1566–72.

Kumar, Krishna (1989) *Social Character of Learning,* Sage Publications: New Delhi

Kumar, Krishna (2001) *Prejudice and Pride: School Histories of the Freedom Struggle in India and Pakistan,* Viking, Penguin Books: New Delhi

Kumar, Krishna (2008) 'Education and Culture: India's Quest for a Secular Policy,' in Krishna Kumar and Joachim Oesterheld (eds.) *Education and Social Change in South Asia,* Orient Longman: New Delhi, pp. 96–117

Kumar, Krishna (2012) 'Quality Constraints in Education,' Lecture delivered at Nehru Memorial Museum and Library (NMML), New Delhi, dated April 25

Kumar, Sunil Mitra (2010) 'Is There a Case for School Vouchers?' *Economic & Political Weekly,* Vol. xlv (7): pp. 41–6

Leclercq, Francois (2008) 'Decentralisation of School Management and Quality of Teaching,' in Kumar, Krishna and Joachim Oesterheld (eds.) *Education and Social Change in South Asia,* Orient Longman: New Delhi, pp. 475–505

Lok Shikshak Manch (2012) 'Beware! Danger Ahead,' *Reconstructing Education,* Vol. 1 (3): 26

Mander, Harsh (2012) 'Barefoot: Still Under Siege,' *The Hindu,* 5 May

Mehendale, Archana (2010) 'Model Rules for the Right to Education Act,' *Economic & Political Weekly,* Vol. xlv (4): pp. 9–12

NCERT (1975) *The Curriculum for the Ten-Year School: A Framework,*

National Council for Educational Trainning and Research (NCERT): New Delhi
NCERT (1985) *National Curriculum for Primary and Secondary Education*, New Delhi: NCERT.
NCERT (1988) *National Curriculum for Elementary and Secondary Education: A Framework* (Revised Version), NCERT: New Delhi
NCERT (2000) *National Curriculum Framework*, NCERT: New Delhi
NCERT (2005) *National Curriculum Framework*, NCERT: New Delhi
Niranjanaradhya, V.P. (2011) 'A Regressive Legislation for School Education in Progressive Child (Human) Rights Age,' in Pankaj Sinha (ed.) *Indian Laws Protecting Children: An Information Booklet*, Human Rights Law Network (HRLN): New Delhi
Nussbaum, Martha C. (2006) *Frontiers of Justice: Disability, Nationality, Species Membership*, The Belknap Press of Harvard University Press: Cambridge
Patnaik, Ramesh (2012) 'WTO-GATS-Education and India,' *Reconstructing Education*, Vol. 1 (2): pp. 4–9
Patnaik, Ramesh (2012–13) 'The Supreme Court Verdict in favour of 25% Reservation in Private Unaided Schools,' *Reconstructing Education*, Vol. 1 (4) and Vol. 2 (1): pp. 5–11
Rai, Lajpat (1966) *The Problem of National Education in India*, Publications Division: New Delhi
Rajya Sabha Synopsis of Debate, 20/07/2009. http://righttoeducation.in/sites/default/files/legislation/rajya_sabha_discussion_synopsis_20July09.pdf (Last visited on 15/06/2013)
Ramachandran, Vimala (2009) 'Right To Education Act: A Comment,' *Economic & Political Weekly*, Vol. xliv (28): pp. 155–7
Richardson, Henry S. (2006) 'Rawlsian Social-Contract Theory and the Severely Disabled,' *The Journal of Ethics*, Vol. 10 (4): pp. 419–62
Sadgopal, Anil (2001a) 'Between the Lines: Rights and Wrongs in Education Bill,' *The Times of India*, 28 November 2001
Sadgopal, Anil (2001b) 'Political Economy of Ninety Third Amendment Bill,' *Mainstream*, December
Sadgopal, Anil (2006) 'Dilution, Distortion and Diversion: A Post-Jomtien Reflection on Education Policy' in Ravi Kumar (ed.) *The Crisis of Elementary Education in India*, Sage Publications: New Delhi, pp. 92–136
Sadgopal, Anil (2010a) 'Right To Education Act vs Right To Education', *Social Scientist*, Vol. 38, pp. 9–12, 17–50
Sadgopal, Anil (2010b) 'The Neo-Liberal Assault on India's Education System,' in Michele Kelley and Deepika D'Souza (eds.) *The World*

Bank in India : Undermining Sovereignty, Distorting Development, Independent People's Tribunal on the World Bank in India, Orient BlackSwan: Hyderabad, pp. 296–324

Sadgopal, Anil (2011) 'Neoliberal Act,' *Frontline*, Vol. 28 (14): pp. 3–24

Sarangapani, Padma M. (2009) 'Quality, Feasibility and Desirability of Low Cost Private Schooling', *Economic & Political Weekly*, Vol. xliv (43): pp. 67–9

Savarkar, V.D. (1923/1962) *Hindutva: Who is a Hindu?* Bombay

Shukla, Suresh Chandra (1998) 'Nationalist Educational Thought: Continuity and Change,' in Sabyasachi Bhattacharya (ed.) *The Contested Terrain: Perspectives on Education in India*, Orient Longman Limited: New Delhi, pp. 29–53

Teltumbde, Anand (2012) 'RTE: A Symbolic Gesture,' *Economic & Political Weekly*, Vol. xlvii (19): pp. 10–11

Teltumbde, Anand (2013) 'Keep Off Education,' *Economic & Political Weekly*, Vol. xlvi (10): pp. 10–11

Tilak, Jandhyala B.G. (2011) 'Education for Profit,' *Economic & Political Weekly*, Vol. xlvi: (9), pp. 18–19

Tooley, J., P. Dixon and S.V. Gomathi (2007) 'Private Schools and the Millennium Development Goal of Universal Primary Education: A Census and Comparative Survey in Hyderabad, India,' *Oxford Review of Education*, Vol. 33 (5): pp. 539–60

Velaskar, Padma (2010) 'Quality and Inequality in Indian Education: Some Critical Policy Concerns,' *Contemporary Education Dialogue*, Vol. 7 (1): pp. 58–93

Velaskar, Padma (2012) 'Education for Liberation: Ambedkar's Thought and Dalit Women's Perspective,' *Contemporary Education Dialogue*, Vol. 9 (2): pp. 245–71

Yunus, Reva (2012) 'Converting 'Liabilities' into 'Assets'?,' *Reconstructing Education*, Vol. 1 (3): pp. 12–15

NOTES

1. This point about difference can be made though there have been different interpretations of liberalism, as whilst one scholar emphasizes uncomfortable implications of Rawlsian theory of social justice for women, disabled, non-human animals and transnational justice, another scholar defends this framework for severely disabled. See for this debate–Richardson 2006; Nussbaum 2006.
2. Here we have relied on Alam Khundmiri's definition of secularism. See Ansari 2001: Esp. Ch. 15, pp. 225–36.

3. AIFRTE Stands for All-India Forum for Right to Education.
4. NCERT 2000: CF. section 1.4.7 and 'Salient Features' and in-pasim. This point was also emphasized in the media reports.
5. For these figures, see–District Education Service for Education (DISE) indicators of facilities for the year 2008–9 and DISE indicators of enrollment for the year 2009–10 available at www.dise.in.
6. It was noticeable in the popular media, both print and electronic. Even the Rajya Sabha Debate, dated Monday, 20 July 20 2009, on RTE Bill confirms this impression, because despite some very important critical observations/criticisms, all the members approved it considering it as a momentous event. See–Rajya Sabha 2009.
7. Kumar 2012. He attributed this situation to the absence of a popular and strong social movement in India striving to accomplish (equitable) quality education as a fundamental right of every child, and also cautioned that if we will not devise our own criteria's for measuring quality, international agencies would increasingly impose their standardized tests.
8. Prof. Mahesh Rangarajan (renowned historian, political analyst and presently the Director, NMML asked this extremely pertinent question in the seminar referred in the preceding footnote.
9. For some critical reflections of this kind, also see the special issue on RTE Act, *Combat Law*, 2008. Scholars/activists associated with AIFRTE also champion this perspective. For details, visit http://www.aifrte.in.
10. The discussion on non-implementation began in the relevant circles particularly after the issuance of the MHRD Report Card on one year of RTE Act and subsequently renewed after the completion of three years' deadline for meeting the norms prescribed in the Schedule.
11. Following the lead provided by James Tooley and others, Pankaj Jain and Ravindra Dholakia made this point, which drew various responses to it in *Economic & Political Weekly*.
12. However, this amendment leaves a gray area about admission in such institutions by its silence about Section 13, which bans any kind of screening of children other than random selection.
13. Michael Apple has demonstrated the connection between Neoliberal And Neoconservative groups in–Apple 1996.

3

The Story of Dismantling of Higher Education in India: The Unfolding Crisis

G. Haragopal

That higher education in India, which has been labouriously built during the first four decades after Independence, is systematically being dismantled by both the neoliberal forces from the outside and educational business entrepreneurs from within, with the connivance of the political class in power and also in opposition. The convincing example is the recent assault on Delhi University—one of the largest educational establishments providing not only education to a very large number but also providing quality education at the undergraduate level. Some of the colleges of this university can not only compare with the finest colleges in the Western world but can also surpass several of their counterparts in most parts of the developing world. This university is not only known for jealously safeguarding its institutional autonomy but also for its militant struggles, for improving the freedoms and service conditions of the teaching community. The Indian State, for almost four decades, respected the academic community and positively responded not only to its demands, but also looked up to some of its world class faculty for advice and direction. The present Prime Minister Manmohan Singh and Nobel Laureate Amartya Sen, along with several other distinguished personalities, belong to this academic fraternity. Notwithstanding all its democratic traditions, academic

The Story of Dismantling of Higher Education in India

accomplishments, and illustrious history, the forces unleashed by the neoliberal model chose this university (precisely for its strengths), for invasion and believed that if they succeeded here, the rest of the educational system in the country would fall in line. This well-designed, well-orchestrated attack, engulfing the system, caught the entire university community by shock and surprise, and the forces of resistance were left with no time to organize themselves in encountering this academic affront. Given the internal academic structures, its well laid down procedures, and institutionalized norms of the university, nobody ever imagined that it could be overthrown so suddenly and so easily. But it is happening.

The neoliberal forces first ensured appointment of an authoritarian Vice-Chancellor who passionately, to the point of madness, represents global interests and was ruthless in dismantling all the internal structures at one go. The teachers and students inside and the democratic sections outside have been rendered almost helpless as the Vice-Chancellor's undemocratic, un-academic approach and indifference to the criticism, and unwillingness to open dialogue left no democratic space. He went ahead with a decision to subvert the National Education Policy of 10+2+3 and brought in 10+2+4 with unprecedented haste. He pushed through the decisions and bulldozed the formal decisions, making bodies like the Academic Council and ignoring the age-old, time-tested policy of formulating and changing the curriculum through the departmental faculty involvement and vetting through several academic boards that normally discuss and debate the pros and cons of the changes. In fact, it is this process that ensured accommodation of several viewpoints, worldviews, ideological standpoints, and enlarging frontiers of knowledge. Any new changes proposed earlier, involved prolonged debate and discussions. In the present regime, these processes have been thwarted and the curriculum prepared by a chosen few has been imposed from above. All the resistance was handled through the force of power, to the point of deploying the coercive arm of the Indian State against the intellectual power of the teaching community.

The introduction of the Four Year Undergraduate Programme (FYUP) was never in the active public debate. This was not demanded either by the students, teachers, or parents. The only reason, as stated by the Vice-Chancellor himself, is the international mobility of the students. Since American Universities have four year undergraduate programmes, Indian universities are forced to create conditions for smooth entry of foreign universities into the Indian educational market. The earlier Education Commission, popularly known as the Kothari Commission, took more than two years to formulate the National Policy on Education. This involved nationwide debate and also critical examination of global experience and experimentation. This policy began to be tampered with from the mid-1980s, after Indian rulers opted to borrow from international financial agencies like the IMF and the World Bank. Yet, the 1985 New Education policy was put to public debate for two years. Although, the final policy did not adequately reflect the concerns expressed in the public debate, at least the formality required by the democratic process was completed. This was perhaps the last democratic academic gesture of the Indian State towards higher education.

As the integration of India's so called development with global economy went further, by 1990s, educational system particularly higher education started experiencing severe jolts. A Knowledge Commission headed by Sam Pitroda, an NRI known for his open loyalties to the neoliberal model, was requested to provide direction to the Indian knowledge system. The working of this commission was a one-man show. He was the one who was commissioned to dismantle the democratically functioning of statutory bodies and subversion of the very essence of knowledge. While the Kothari Commission viewed education as the 'conscience of the nation' and 'critical assessor of way of life of a society', Pitroda took a totally utilitarian view of viewing knowledge as a catalyst of production and consumption. While the Kothari Commission envisaged education as a response to social needs and not wants, to Pitroda, every want was a need. Given this perverted view, the subordination of knowledge to market forces was taken by this

The Story of Dismantling of Higher Education in India

commission to higher levels. This was clear in the very functioning of the commission; Sam Pitroda did not care to consult his own members and ignored them so blatantly that the Vice-Chairman of the commission, Dr P.M. Bhargava a renowned scientist, had to resign from the commission in protest. Pitroda started sending dispatches (like Wood's dispatches during colonial period) to the Government of India that formed the basis for some of the policy choices. The policymaking process has been so trivialized that it touched its lowest ebb in independent India.

As the Knowledge Commission and its style of working created a new culture of public policymaking, the Vice-Chancellor of Delhi University, a prototype of Sam Pitroda, took the Pitrodian approach further. While Sam Pitroda, settled in America was chosen from outside to sub-serve the global capital, the DU experience shows that there are also academics within India, who are equally enthusiastic and vulnerable. It is a sharp pointer of the deepening logic that began in the mid-eighties. In this whole episode, the major casualty has been the constitutional commitments, transformative agenda, and upliftment of millions of Indian citizens who are struck in the stranglehold of poverty, illiteracy, and inequitous, in-egalitarian social structures. Education that has to facilitate mobility of people, particularly from the disadvantaged section, has been converted into a purchasable commodity for the propertied and privileged. The departure is so marked, that none of the social concerns figured in the official thinking on higher education at the present juncture.

The shift in Delhi University curriculum is also considered anti-poor, which is clearly visible in the anxieties expressed on behalf of marginalized sections. The Four Year Undergraduate Programme permits two stages of dropouts—one, at the end of two years and the degree they get is an Associate Baccalaureate, the other at the end of three years where the degree awarded is the Baccalaureate, and lastly, at the end of four years resulting in a Baccalaureate with Honours. Many may not be able to even pronounce these degrees. Opening these outlets in the midst of education, begs the question why and who drop out in the middle of an undergraduate program? It would certainly be the first generation of boys and girls who struggle hard to enter the system, with great difficulties and diffidence. It is they who would be the victims, for rural students do take time to cope up with the very culture of institutions of higher learning; the present policy provides an exit option without any concern about the future of these dropouts, as completion of a degree is the minimum prescribed qualification for entry into public employment or pursuit of a postgraduate education for mobility to higher levels of public spaces. It is certainly true that no boy or girl from upper castes, upper classes, and better income groups would ever drop out or opt out prematurely from higher education. It is obvious that the system contrives to eject disadvantaged boys and girls so that the job market at the higher levels does not get crowded for the privileged and the powerful.

The curriculum content is equally un-academic, substandard and devoid of imagination. A simple example is the introduction of a compulsory course on Gandhian thought. This does not include the Gandhian worldview, his critique of industrial civilization, or his radical views on power and the State... not even Gandhian secular outlook as against the fundamentalist forces, which could also be relevant to fight the growing communal climate. Instead of this broader Gandhian thought forming the substance of the course, Gandhism has been brought into the stream of moral education and included in lessons like the Satya Harishchandra story, pertaining to pre-feudal stage of development. It relates to the selling of his wife by Harishchandra to keep up his word: selling and buying of persons smacks of slave trade. Another episode is of Gandhi's promise to his mother that he will not take to non-vegetarian food and yet another instance is that of a theft that Gandhi commits as a child. One wonders what moral lessons could be drawn from such episodes and what moral values could be imparted? Given the growing feminist consciousness, the story of Harishchandra could be very repulsive. Apart from these issues, how can these stories, which should be restricted to storytelling for kindergarten children, be taught to undergraduate level students who ought to be asking far more

The Story of Dismantling of Higher Education in India 63

fundamental questions at that stage of pursuit of knowledge? A note circulated by the Physics Department of St Stephens College of Delhi University on this approach observed that these reforms are ham-handed and all the justification for introduction of the FYUP like flexibility, more inter-disciplinary, more in tune with worldwide practices are misleading. The note maintains none of these claims are built into the scheme at all. The Vice-Chancellor rejected all the experience of other institutions and designed an utterly rigid programme, which is in no way an improvement on the existing scheme. It is further observed that it is prepared with minimum interaction, and the Vice-Chancellor has no respect for his academic colleagues nor the best practices elsewhere in the world. They point out that the experiment is a disaster in the making.

II

The Delhi University episode fits very well into the story of higher education and the concerted attempt of the Indian ruling class to bring foreign capital into the service sector including education. Global capital, particularly the American, is in search of avenues for investment in the service sector since American political economy is services driven; two thirds of its economy is service economy. America, which emerged as a super power in the wake of the post-Second World War, is not a manufacturing economy and its agricultural share in the Country's total GDP is less than two per cent. Its vulnerable economy received a rude shock in 1973, when oil exporting nations decided to standardize the oil prices at a time, when American share in the international trade was very marginal. the US, not having many options to cope with the new situation, triggered wars in the entire oil belt and decided to export the services to the other countries using their international clout. It is this context, that shaped and determined the nature of (GATT), General Agreement on Trade and Tariff to start with and the (WTO) World Trade Organisation to end with. While GATT had a limited role in the world economy, the WTO, a transmuted form of the GATT, had a larger mandate of converting every conceivable human activity into a tradable commodity.

The WTO has three integrated multi-lateral agreements: one, General Agreement on Trade and Tariff (1994); two, Trade Related Intellectual Property Rights (TRIPS) and three; the General Agreement on Trade in Services (GATS). This incarnation of GATT 1994 is so different from GATT 1947. The earlier GATT was to help the world economy, particularly the developing economies. What was meant to protect larger global interests, has been hijacked by the Western economies, particularly the American. The GATS council recognized 161 services as tradable under twelve heads that include education, health, and culture. Now trade in education service is openly and officially recognized. All member countries are bound to GATS and India enthusiastically joined those multi-lateral agreements, entangling some of the most socially needed services to powerful world economies. The story does not end here.

The member countries will have to carry all the necessary measures as a part of structural adjustment by not only recasting their institutions, but create a whole set of new regulatory institutions conforming to WTO conditions and requirements. They have to carry the necessary legislations and repeal the municipal laws that are not hospitable to global demands and compulsions. It is in pursuance of this mandate that the Government of India prepared more than half a dozen legislations in higher education attempting to replace some of the existing institutions and setup new institutions which are not necessarily in the interest of the nation nor its people.

This corporate profit hunting approach has not only impacted the countries outside the US but deeply disturbed the health and educational services within the US. A telling note,

> How the American University Was Killed, in Five Easy Steps', circulated on the Internet presents a graphic account of the destruction of publicly funded universities in the US, the country which had a fairly enlightened education policy in the 1950s, based on affordability, easy access to universities which were the very heart of intense public discourse, passionate learning and vocal

The Story of Dismantling of Higher Education in India

citizen involvement in the issues of the times. Liberal arts stood at the centre of a college education and students were exposed to philosophy, anthropology, literature, history, sociology, world religions, foreign languages, and culture. 'This led' the note observes 'to the uprisings and growing numbers of citizens taking part in popular dissent—against the Vietnam war, against racism, against the destruction of the environment in a growing corporatized culture, against misogyny, against homophobia.' The American corporate sector did realize that these revolts were incubated in the university campuses and would have liked nothing more than to shut down the universities. 'Destroy them outright'.

The corporate world chose five easy steps: one, de-fund public higher education; two, de-professionalize and impoverish the professors and create unemployment and under employment of PhD qualified people; three, encourage the managerial class to take over university governance; four, move in corporate culture and corporate money; and five, destroy the students. The note adds 'Within one generation, in five easy steps, not only have the scholars and intellectuals of the country been silenced and nearly wiped out, but the entire institution has been hijacked, and recreated as a machine through which future generations will ALL be impoverished, indebted and silenced'. It adds, 'Now, low wage migrant professors teach repetitive courses they did not design to students who travel through on a kind of conveyor belt, only to be spit out, indebted and desperate into a jobless economy'. The note laments that 'The real winners, the only people truly benefitting from the big-picture meltdown of the American university are those people who, in the 1960s, saw those vibrant college campuses as a threat to their established power. They are the same people now working feverishly to dismantle other social structures, everything from Medicare and Social Security to the Post Office'. Looking at this wreckage of American academia, the note acknowledges: 'They have won.' They won in the sense that the vibrant dissent of the 60s is missing. The US could easily invade Iraq, Afghanistan, enact undemocratic laws, and strenthen surveillance mechanisms against its own citizens without any internal resistance.

This story is so meticulously reenacted by the Indian ruling elite, that this soon will be the story of Indian higher education. Indian case may prove more disastrous than the American. The rise of fascist forces in the recent past is a clear indicator and a large section of academicians have either reconciled or subjugated to these forces. In fact, the Tsunami is in the making.

III

The dismantling of Indian higher education began in the 1980s and picked up in the 90s all over India. The disinclination to promote publicly funded higher education to start with has manifested in the gradual collapse of the State Universities. There can be any number of examples, such as that of the experience of the State of Andhra Pradesh from South India, one of the worst, that is worth recounting. This state is one of the top six developed states of India, a rising hub for the IT sector and Hyderabad, one of the fastest growing capital cities of the country. This is also a state that has been facing radical left movements, particularly in the 70s and 80s, a period when globalization was spreading its tentacles. The World Bank chose this state as its labouratory and found in Chandra Babu Naidu, the then Chief Minister, an agent who can carry its agenda. The massive World Bank loan came with a number of conditionalities, one being de-funding of higher education. To start with, recruitment of the faculty to universities and colleges was stopped from the late-80s to a point of abolishing the college service commission that was in-charge of recruitment of college teachers. The outstanding universities of the state with a national standing like Osmania and Andhra University have been downgraded by cutting the block grants. This adversely affected the quality of libraries, labouratories, and infrastructure. The universities were asked to raise their own funds through self-financing programmes courses like management, professional, and vocational courses. Science faculty was incentivized to go for consultancy and patenting, which are all directly linked to the corporate economy. Disciplines like Arts, Humanities, Social Sciences and Basic Sciences were underfunded and the number of faculty in each discipline was reduced to the bare minimum. The Chief Minister announced that social science disciplines were no longer relevant, although he himself was supposed to be a social science student.

In the place of permanent faculty, the institution started employing part-time, purely temporary under-paid under-qualified faculty whose tenure was permanently temporary. This temporary and insecure faculty for decades together could neither commit to teaching nor to passionate research. The global forces succeeded in hitting at the image of the publicity funded universities by starving them of grants and saw to it that they are pushed to the verge of collapse. For the better-off sections and the newly emerging lumpen class, education in the private sector was opened. The number of private institutions, including medical and engineering colleges, went up phenomenally, sprouting like poultry farms in every nook and corner of the state. The rise of deemed or private Universities, particularly in professional education, was an unbelievable spectacle. Thus, professional education for the affordable and softer disciplines with poorer quality to the rural first generation students, completed the circle of class polarization.

The World Bank declared higher education as a non-merit good, meaning that investment in this sector yields more individual returns than social. This is considered justification enough to withdraw public funding and go for the individual himself spending his own money on education as he or she is supposed to be the sole beneficiary of higher education. This was a clever move to delink qualified manpower from the social good and transformative agenda. This fit in well with the capitalist economic postulate that the individual is driven by self-interest, and still worse, is the neoliberal assumption that human selfishness is a driving force of productive economy. This rupturing of the umbilical-cord between the individual and the larger society lets loose a set of vultures in all walks of life leading to the breakdown of cultural and civilizational values. This story is not specific to Andhra Pradesh; this is the scene all over India. Having successfully created the climate of privatization commercialization, and commoditization, the Government of India has been pressurized to bring in the necessary legislations and amend the existing national laws for the smooth entry of foreign capital in this critical service sector.

The Government of India prepared more than half a dozen bills, which were placed or to be placed before the Indian Parliament to legalize and legitimize privatization and globalization of education. These bills include: The Foreign Educational Institutions (Regulations of Entry and Operations) Bill, 2010; the Universities Research and Innovation Bill, 2012; the Higher Education and Research Bill, 2011; the Educational Tribunals Bill 2010; the National Accreditation Regulatory Authority for Higher Educational Institutions Bill, 2010; The Prohibition of Unfair Practices in Technical Educational Institutions, Medical Educational Institutions and Universities Bill, 2010; The National Commission for Minority Educational Institutions (Amendment) Bill, 2009. This list is demonstrative of the type of pressure on the system and willingness of men in power to undertake the task of recasting all the institutions with total obedience to corporate capital. None of these bills, nor their contents have ever been publicly debated in any part of India, nor were these demands ever raised by any section of people. This is enough evidence that, how the Indian State has come to circumvent the internal democratic process and sub-serve the needs and demands of global capital. Since analysis of all these bills is not possible, a few of them are taken up in this discussion to discuss the trends in higher education that are leading us to the doomsday of publicly funded higher education.

IV

Lets look at the Higher Education and Research Bill aimed at dismantling the University Grants Commission that was established on the recommendations of Radhakrishna Commission in the year 1956 through an Act of Parliament. This Act, and with slight modifications, continues to be in effect till the day. While the functioning of the UGC is not beyond controversy, the changes that are contemplated to replace the body under global pressure is the point to be pondered over. This replacement was the idea of Sam Pitroda which did not carry public support. As a damage control, the Government appointed a committee under the Chairmanship of Yashpal, who commanded respect and credibility among the Indian academia. This Committee which looked into the state of Higher Education felt that different agencies that have been set up from time to time to oversee technical, medical, and legal education need to be integrated to ensure a holistic approach to education, but that an Independent Regulatory Commission as proposed by the Ministry was certainly not the answer. On seeing the way the Ministry of Human Resource Development was proceeding in the name of his committee, Yashpal went on record the state that what was proposed by the Ministry was not the spirit of his Committee's recommendations.

The UGC Act of 1956 was a simple Act with enormous trust in the commission and its wisdom to guide the destiny of higher education, with least intervention from the Government. The mandate of the commission was 'to take all steps as may think fit for the promotion and co-ordination of University Education and for the determination and maintenance of standards of teaching, examination and research in Universities with full involvement and participation of the Universities and its faculty'. The UGC was required to assess the overall financial needs and provide those grants for development of universities. The commission was also to advise the Central and State Governments on the allocation of grants and establishment of new universities. The Act also states that, the commission was to perform such other functions as may be deemed necessary for advancing the cause of higher education in India.

The UGC, with all said and done, had earned an image and invoking its name always worked with the academic community. The community by and large respected its stand and direction. Such institutions nurtured over a period of time normally are protected and improvised, but the neoliberal agenda is out to dismantle them and bring in new structures without any legacy and historical traditions. Supplanting institutions is the major thrust of the neoliberal agenda.

An examination of the Higher Education and Research Bill, 2011 suggests a fundamental deviation from the established norms, values and structures. The preamble of the bill, of course, states that 'its aim is to promote autonomy of higher education institutions and universities for free pursuit of knowledge and innovations and to provide for comprehensive and integrated growth of higher education and research keeping in view of global standards of educational and research practices.' It is in pursuance of these objectives that the Ministry proposes the National Commission for Higher Education be established. Obviously, terms like 'creativity', 'socially relevant knowledge' are replaced by 'innovation' and 'global standards'. Instead of using 'frontiers of knowledge', now the buzz term is 'knowledge economy'. These terms and their full meaning are yet to be fully explored.

The provisions in the bill are in total contrast with the stated objectives of autonomy and free pursuit of knowledge. In the place of UGC, a cumbersome organizational structure with one chairman, three whole-time members, three part time members will be established. The selection committee of the chairman of the new Commission consists of the Prime Minister, the Speaker of Lok Sabha, the leader of opposition in the Lok Sabha and two ministers. Thus, the committee is completely political replacing the search committee consisting of three renowned academicians. Then, there is a collegium with complex membership which includes, the chairman and all members of the Commission, Chairpersons of State educational councils, head of each professional body, head of each research council, one Central University Vice-Chancellor, one director of Indian Institute of Management, one Vice-Chancellor of the National Law University, one person from medical education, a principal of an autonomous college, and so on. The membership also includes three persons to be nominated by the Central Government from amongst heads of Association of Industry, Trade and Commerce and two persons from non-governmental organizations (NGOs), and a few other ex-officio members. In addition, there are two other wings: a Board for Research Promotion and Innovation and Higher Educational Finance Service Corporation. The overall form of the organization in appearance, is broad based and looks democratic enough, if quantity is any indicator of democracy. However, the overall spirit is to create an independent Regulatory Commission as required by the WTO conditionality.

While the UGC Act is simple, the present Act states that the new commission will:

> one, 'promote accountability framework in regulatory system of higher education sector'; two, 'promote coordination between universities and industry'; three, 'relate higher education to the world of work and need of society'; four, 'regulate the entry and operation of foreign educational institutions'; five, 'specify norms to measure productivity in research programs'. These five functions cited are only a sample to indicate the direction of the educational policy. As far as autonomy is concerned, some of the provisions in the new Bill are totally a negation of freedom of educational institutions, including that of the apex body.

Look at some of the clauses: the commission shall prepare annually an evidence based statement on the status of higher education and report on the activities of the commission; the President of India will constitute a committee to evaluate and review the performance of the commission, which includes the extent of fulfillment of the objectives of the commission, future directions of the commission along with corrective measures and will them see whether it has been able to promote effective academic linkages, inter-institutional linkages and public-private partnership in higher education. The dreadful clause 67 says if, at any time the central government is of the opinion

(a) that, on account of circumstances beyond the control of the Commission, General Council, Board or Corporation, as the case may be, it is unable to discharge the functions or perform the duties imposed on it by or under the provisions of this Act; or

(b) This body as the case may be, has persistently defaulted in complying with any direction given by the Central Government under this Act, or in the discharge of the functions or performance of the duties imposed on it, by or under the provisions of this Act, and as a result of such default the financial position of the Commission, General Council, Board or Corporation, as the case may be, or the administration of the Commission, General Council, Board, the Corporation, as the case may be, has suffered; or

(c) that circumstances exist, which render it necessary in the public interest to so do, It may by notification, supersede the Commission, General Council, Board, the Board of Directors of the Corporation, as the case may be, appoint a person or persons as the Chairperson or the President, as the case may be, to exercise powers and discharge functions of the Commission, General Council, Board or Corporation, as the case may be, under this Act.

The Central Government has appropriated so much of power to itself that all the office bearers, statutory functionaries can be superseded. It includes a clause, 'public interest', which gives sweeping powers to remove any functionary. This is something the UGC Act could never remotely imagine. There are instances where chairpersons of the UGC, of high integrity and academic standing, questioned and challenged the Ministries, if they felt that Ministry's intervention was unwarranted. In the present Act, functionaries of courage of conviction would lose their job at the whims and fancies of the MHRD. This is the state of autonomy of the world of higher education. The rulers are ignorant of the fact that autonomy is always rooted in the philosophy of self-governance with internal checks and balances, without any external intervention. That all the wisdom lies with the Central Government is a negation of the culture of plurality of institutions and deconcentration of power. This growing authoritarian culture is the greatest enemy of democracy, which promotes despotism.

Another innovation of present reforms is the Universities for Research and Innovation Bill (2012). This is a misleading title. In fact, it is nothing but an attempt to set up private universities. This is amply clear from all the provisions of the bill. The objects and reasons for setting up these Universities are; 'if India has to achieve a leadership role in the future global knowledge economy, mere public expenditure on higher education is not going to be sufficient and a substantial part of funding must flow into the education sector through not-for-profit private participation.' The bill states that 'it aims to lay down an enabling legislative framework for setting up universities in both the private and public sectors.' It also adds, 'presently there is no central law which provides for this framework, hence the need for a central legislation.' The Bill contemplates different modes of establishment of universities: they can be either fully public funded or fully private funded or provide for public private partnership.

The other stated objectives are;

> these universities can establish campuses and study centres in foreign countries; two, they should search for solutions that are globally valid and establish such standards that match or surpass the needs of global competitiveness; three, the University is free to appoint persons involved in research of significance in any industry; four, to determine and receive payments of fees and other charges, as such university may deem fit, from students and any other persons; five; charge for its services including training, consultancy and advisory services.

It further spells out that the university is open to all persons of India provided one half of the students are Indian citizens.

The clause on admissions is so vague that while the bill says that 'Universities not publicly funded shall specify by statutes such criteria in the matters of admission as would account for diversities,' another clause says 'the percentage of reservation shall be determined taking into account the total number of seats available.' It incorporates provision of self-disclosure of affirmative action towards members of socially and economically disadvantaged groups. The question arises is, what happens to constitutionally guaranteed reservations? Why should they be left to the universities concerned? Does it mean that not being publicly funded, more frankly, the private universities need not follow nationally accepted reservation policy.

Yet another bill of 2010– 'The Foreign Educational Institutions (Regulation of Entry and Operation) Bill 2010 opens the high road for foreign capital into higher education. The bill provides for some regulations and restrictions for the entry of foreign universities. However, there is a clause which says, 'notwithstanding anything contained in the Act, the Central Government by notification, on the recommendation of the Advisory Board Constituted, having regard to the reputation and international standing of foreign educational institutions, can exempt them from operation of any of the foregoing provisions of the Act.' It also adds that all the matters including the penalties leviable shall be adjudicated by the National Educational Tribunal.

The idea of a National Educational Tribunal is mainly to remove some of the items including education from the jurisdiction of regular judiciary, which is bound by constitutional morality and may not have as much of manoeuvrability that tribunals will have. The proliferation of tribunals is a fallout of globalization. A group of High Court Judges, in one of their interactions at the Bhopal Judicial Academy, expressed their concern about tribunalization of justice. A look at the constitution of National Educational Tribunal indicates how such tribunals are bureaucratized. Out of the eight members, six of them are non-judicial members appointed by the Ministry and three of them are ex-officio members.

The other Bills are all aimed at fulfilling the conditions of the WTO or World Bank, or the compulsions of privatization of some of the services which were otherwise to be legitimately performed by the State agencies or public institutions. Since the nations and Nation States operate within their legal and constitutional boundaries, they are now required to go beyond their boundaries and recast their legal systems and institutions to suit the requirements of corporate and global interests.

The spate of legislation waiting for the ratification of Parliament are indicative of where education is headed. Never before in the history of India, have so many proposals in the form of bills been brought before the Parliament in one go. All these bills directly or indirectly negate the constitutional mandate and its egalitarian vision. This is a clear indicator that this will be the trend in societies where, the public interest is completely subordinated to the Nation State, which is itself subjugated to the global corporate interest. The force and power of global interests have acquired such momentum that the popular interests, democratic culture, and larger national interests are in no position to fight back. The silence of the academic community and democratic sections of civil society will deliver a deathblow, if they do not see and respond to the unfolding future. The sixty years of educational endeavours of Indian society will be devoured by the corporate and imperialist interests, leaving a big man-made tragedy behind for posterity to suffer.

REFERENCES

1. Universities for Research and Innovation Bill, 2012, *As Introduced in the Lok Sabha*, Bill No. 61 of 2012
2. The Higher Education and Research Bill, 2011, *To be Introduced in the Rajya Sabha*, Bill No. LX of 2011
3. Educational Tribunal Bill, 2010, *To Be Introduced in the Lok Sabha*, Bill No. 55 of 2010
4. Foreign Educational Institutions Regulation of Entry and Operations Bill, 2010, *As Introduced in the Lok Sabha*, Bill No. 57 of 2010
5. Academy of Scientific and Innovative Research Bill, 2010, *To Be Introduced in the Lok Sabha*, Bill No. 73 of 2010
6. The National Accreditation Regulatory Authority for Higher Educational Institutions Bill, 2010, *To Be Introduced in the Lok Sabha*, Bill No. 54 of 2010
7. 'How the American University was Killed, in Five Easy Steps', Mayraj Fahim fmayraj@yahoo.com, 17 June 2013 7:08:41 PM EDT http://junctrebellion.wordpress.com/2012/08/12/how-the-american-university-was-killed-in-five-easy-steps/ How The American University was Killed, in Five Easy Steps
8. 'How not to Modernize a University Dinesh Singh's Ham-Handed Efforts at Reform', St Stephen's College Physics Department
9. Education as a Tradable Service under GATS-WTO Regime by Ramesh Patnaik, A note circulated to AIFRTE, Hyderabad

Acknowledgments

Thanks are due to the Centre for the Study of Social Exclusion and Inclusive Policy and its faculty members, particularly S. Japhet, for providing a conducive climate for work, and Shashikala for negotiating my cumbersome handwritten drafts.

4

Commoditizing Higher Education: The Assault of Neoliberal Barbarism

Madhu Prasad

The term 'barbarism' has been used anthropologically to denote a 'prior' natural human condition: what was before the start of 'civilization' and its correlate 'progress'. A variant usage focuses on an untutored, pre-civil state of 'unreason'. The mutually reinforcing use of a complex set of elements—political and economic hierarchies, commerce and intercommunications, high densities of population, and historical dynamism— appears to sustain the coherence of the binary, and the idea that the threatened descent from a fragile 'civility' is constant seems to 'justify' authoritarian modes of disciplining or reining in such tendencies. Descriptively, this account does influence popular ideas of what 'barbarism' is, but analytically and as a guide to praxis, it falls far short of expectations. The above-mentioned elements fail to qualify either as components, or even as indices, of a distinct stage or form of human sociality and 'have no explanatory significance if treated as a checklist' (Feierman 1993: p. 178). Yet, the binary continues to be potently used in support of policies and acts of astounding cruelty in the name of defending 'civilization' and enforcing 'progress' and has been a particular favourite of neoconservatives in their free market crusades since the 1970s and in the war against terror since 9/11.

The socialist tradition has systematically linked

contemporary forms of barbarism with the very nature of capitalism as an exploitative mode of production. Marx had identified the logic of the incessant drive towards accumulation of capital—privileging dead labour over living producers, exchange value over intrinsic use value—as generating a dynamic before which any consideration for human values, and even for human survival, paled into insignificance. Referring to the role of force and brutality in capitalism, he asserted that 'the profound hypocrisy and inherent barbarism of bourgeois civilization lies unveiled before our eyes, turning from its home, where it assumes respectable forms, to the colonies, where it goes naked' (Marx 1853/1978: p. 86). Marx's analysis of the ecological destruction wrought by capitalism, which undermined the material conditions of existence itself, also points towards the possibility of regression. 'Even the need for fresh air ceases to be a need for the worker. Man returns to a cave dwelling, which is now, however, contaminated with the pestilential breath of civilization ... Light, air, etc.—the simplest *animal* cleanliness—ceases to be a need for man. *Filth*—this stagnation and putrefaction of man, the *sewage* of civilization ... —comes to be the *element of life* for him' (Marx 1844/1975: pp. 307–8). Marx's treatment of barbarism was complex and reflected the numerous contradictions embedded in capitalism, which raised the possibility of degeneration as surely as that of progress toward communism. In the *Communist Manifesto,* Marx and Engels noted that throughout the history of all hitherto existing civilization, 'oppressor and oppressed, stood in constant opposition to one another, carried on an uninterrupted, now hidden, now open fight, a fight that each time ended either in a revolutionary reconstitution of society at large, or in the common ruin of the contending classes' (Marx, Engels 1848/ 1976: p. 482). Fredrick Engels characterized the historic choice that bourgeois society places before human society as a 'crossroads, either transition to socialism or regression into barbarism.'

Lenin defined imperialism as the monopoly stage of capitalism in which 'the capitalists divide [and re-divide] the world not out of any particular malice, but because the degree of concentration which has been reached forces them to adopt this method in order to obtain profits. And they divide "in proportion to capital", "in proportion to strength", because there cannot be any other method of division under commodity production and capitalism' (Lenin 1917/1976: p. 689). Lenin's theory captured a world economic, financial and politico-military system where 'great powers' carved and re-carved up the globe in a macabre dance where 'peaceful alliances prepare the ground for wars and in their turn grow out of wars' (Lenin 1917/1976: p. 724). Only an internationalist socialist revolution could end the barbarism unleashed by the ferocity of monopoly capitalist competition.

Taking with 'fearsome seriousness' the meaning of Engels's phrase `regression into barbarism', Rosa Luxemburg saw the 1914–18 War as epitomizing this regression:

> Today we face the choice exactly as Fredrich Engels saw it a generation ago: either the triumph of imperialism and the collapse of all civilization... Or the victory of socialism, that means the conscious active struggle of the international proletariat against imperialism and its method of war. This is a dilemma of world history, an either/ or; the scales are wavering before the decision of the class conscious proletariat.

Recognizing that the 'modern working class's understanding of its historical vocation' had been 'dearly bought' because imperialism had won in this instance, she declared: 'But we are not lost, and will be victorious *if we have not unlearned to learn*. And if the present leaders of the proletariat ...do not understand how to learn, then they will go under "to make room for people capable of dealing with a new world" [emphasis added] (Luxemburg 1916: Chapter 1).

Michel Henry's recent philosophical rendering of the term opens up rich possibilities precisely because it deepens the focus on qualities and conditions that we regard as essential to human life. 'Everything has a value because everything is done by and for life.' Life, as that which experiences itself and expresses itself in a Cartesian pre-cognitive awareness of its unique subjectivity, 'arranges each thing in its own terms; from the outset, it gives rise to the kingdom of ends. This evaluation ... only has a value because life itself is the supreme value, ... (and) carries in its own flesh, the invincible desire to change oneself ... in growth and in the enjoyment of oneself—this intoxication of life is the absolute value' (Henry 2012: p. xv). Vigilance against ideologies and practices that jeopardize the value of life and imperil 'this incessant movement of self transformation and self-fulfilment' represent forms of barbarism, which therefore is 'a ruin, not a rudiment'. Resistance in the face of attempts to encroach upon spaces for self-transformation opens up possibilities within this conception. History is replete with experiences of such struggles.

However, Henry identifies the present conjuncture as one that is particularly threatening because it has at its core an ideology which replaces the real 'experience-in-life' with what 'corresponds' to it, its 'representational sensation', that is, the objective 'consciousness of' the world. What follows is the reduction of the lifeworld—not a world of intuition but of praxis or the exercise of it—to the world of science. It is the reduction of natural process to its abstract physico-mathematical parameters; it is the emergence and introduction of 'objectivity'. Science never exists alone but the 'world of Galilean science' makes 'it act as if it were alone.' (Henry 2012: p. 42) Technology, too, is transformed. 'The original essence of techne is the whole system formed by my body in movement and effort.' In the use of 'tools', we understand that 'Body and Earth are joined together by Co-belonging (Copropriation). It is so original that nothing can ever occur in a pure Outside, as an object, for a theoria, as something that would be there without us—except as the history of this Co-belonging (Copropriation) and as its limit mode.' So we begin to comprehend the sense in which 'initially the world is always a lifeworld ... before even being a sensible world' (Henry 2012: pp. 45–6).

The 'objectification' of techne results in converting technology into an instrument, the means by which the ends that it is competent to actualize, are achieved. Action is now apparently located outside of life, occurring as a function of machinery at sites that are other than the placement of praxis at the point of its real fulfilment so that techne is no longer simply the expression of life, its self-realization and self-growth. With praxis and knowing falling outside of each other, 'Action is ... but a sort of empirical curiosity ... Knowledge (identified with science) by contrast is everything' (Henry 2012: p. 49).

With this ontological reversal:

> one draws near to the essential point with Marx, when one can recognize the inversion of vital teleology that occurred at the end of the eighteenth and nineteenth centuries. The production of consumer goods that is characteristic of every society ceased to be directed by and for their 'use value' in order to then see the obtaining and growth of the exchange value, that is to say, money: When production became economic... when an economic reality took the place of goods useful for life and designated for it—the entire face of the world was changed (Henry 2012: p. 48).

This situation characterizes the 'current phase of world history. We can say that we are undergoing Modernity, if it is true that in Modernity, for the first time ever, life has ceased to dictate its own laws for itself' (Henry 2012: p. 42). The 'expert', the repository of the complete sway of scientific knowledge, dominates the intellectual landscape leaving no room for democratic questioning or conscience. 'Everything that can be done by science ought to be done by it and for it... Technology is its self-realization' (Henry 2012: p. 55). Production is similarly dominated by capital and an economic teleology, seeking the production of exchange values which is driven by consumerism with the stimulation of artificial consumption and artificial needs.

The cancerous spread of this ideology generates an abject feeling of helplessness among the cultured on the one hand, and on the other among those who either have been or are threatened with dispossession by contemporary market conditions and values—workers, peasants, petty producers, indigenous peoples, and marginalized communities. The deep descent into barbarism was initially signaled by Milton Freidman's Chicago School movement known also as 'neoliberalism' or simply 'globalization' (Klein 2007). Born of the belief that there is no alternative to combat, the 'stagflation' —deep recession accompanied by high prices—that afflicted the system in the 1970's, capitalism's response has been to

Commoditizing Higher Education... 81

aggressively use a variety of strategies to effect an even more radical extension of economic rationality to all spheres of life—cultural, social and political (Harvey 2005). The market is projected as the inevitable organizing and evaluative force in all areas of social life. 'In its capacity to dehistoricize and naturalize such sweeping social change ...neoliberalism reproduces the conditions for unleashing the most brutalizing forces of capitalism' (Giroux 2009: p. 32). Unionism, State intervention, and welfare action are decried as distortion, but state power is intact and encouraged to facilitate market creation and consolidation, corporatization, and multi-national support through trade pacts and regimes, and even military action, for advancing the needs of capital (Friedman 1962; Hayek 1944). As these ideas hegemonize and shape individual `common sense', a redefinition of the individual occurs from citizen to 'consumer', that is, an autonomous economic actor (Turner 2008). This is the epitome of ideology; neoliberalism defines not only the social, economic, and political institutions and policies, but also dictates the manner in which individuals make day-to-day decisions and structure their lives. There is a commoditization not only of goods, services, and labour, but also of culture, relationships, and social institutions, which had been anticipated as logical extensions of the free market economy. 'Instead of economy being embedded in social relations, social relations are embedded in the economy' (Polyani 1944: p. 60). Consequently, there is no distinction between society and the economy; everything is now economic. Distinctions drawn between market and state, between public and private, and between individual and social, lose their relevance (Lemke 2001).

It cannot be ignored, of course, that the range of these distinctions is itself a product of bourgeois society, which thereby allows the institutions of 'civil society' a more significant role in processes, which organize political control through consent. Ruling ideology, disseminated through the apparently autonomous structures of social life, becomes naturalized as custom, habit, or spontaneous practice (Gramsci 1971). In the political arena of bourgeois society, too, the abstract equality of citizens serves to veil their concrete inequalities within civil society (Eagleton 1991). However, the concomitant notions of secular identity and hence universal rights of citizens, and the obligation of the State, not merely to recognize but also to defend them even against itself (Dworkin 1977), create a legitimate space for the articulation of a plurality of contending ideologies to engage and for conflicting social interests to organize and struggle for their demands. Although the State is never neutral, 'it can be used as a site for struggle and can effect reforms' (Hill, Greaves and Maisura 2009: p. 115). This distinguishing characteristic of modernity *coupled with on-going struggles to reclaim and expand* the space to contest and combat exploitative hegemonies, defines modern society and opens up avenues for reversing the dehumanizing one-dimensionality being imposed on social life by the spread of contemporary neoliberal capitalism.

Living and Learning

This analysis profoundly influences evaluation of educational policy and the functioning of educational institutions in contemporary society. It also alters the approach to pedagogical methods and learning processes. Life as an irreducibly intrinsic value and learning as the praxis by which self-transformation and fulfilment either move ahead, or fail to do so, are vitally connected. The nature and range of knowledge represents the fullness of life and learning, and is thereby a continuing and reflective component of a meaningful, worthwhile life. The processes, structures and institutions through which the ability to know is socially actualized, should therefore facilitate and not hinder this essential quality of life/learning. It is imperative that academics, educationists, and students concern themselves with these issues now because radical changes effecting the nature and social relevance of education are being introduced under the pretext of 'reforming' the system.

Society educates its youth to ensure that intellectual and technological achievements are passed on to future generations and to equip them with the skills to lead a productive life in the community, but education cannot be reduced merely to instruction in the use of existing theories, methods, and practices. It has to encourage both competence and critical thinking. An instrumentalist approach to knowledge would obstruct even technological progress, which explores new ways to achieve existing goals, initiates new directions, and pursues novel ideas and purposes. Adaptation is a function of one's degree of intelligence and not only of the extent of one's mastered skills.

The ability to innovate, therefore, requires above all an *environment* that fosters the *fullest development of the personality*. That is why we most frequently describe learning as a process of 'educating oneself'. To learn is to change; to educate oneself is to become what one was not. This has consequences both for individuals and for the societies, which they constitute, for the *transformational* character of education lies at the core of the learning process itself. The freedom and autonomy to 'educate oneself' must characterize the entire learning life of individuals. In particular, it must be the foundation of *all* institutions of education.

The contribution made to universalizing education through the concept and implementation of common neighbourhood schools with equal access for *all* children has been an important part of modern education.

> [The] 'general education of all children without exception at the expense of the state—an education which is equal for all and continues until the individual is capable of emerging as an independent member of society... would be only an act of justice ... for clearly, every man has the right to the fullest development of his abilities and society wrongs individuals twice over when it makes ignorance a necessary consequence of poverty (Engels 1845/1975: p. 253).

The heterogeneous composition of students in the classroom and on the playing fields poses a pedagogical challenge that cannot be met by 'memorize and recall' modes of learning. Nor can the differences brought to the surface in classrooms be resolved by an enforced conformity to dominant response patterns. The mediocre state of India's highly stratified education system serves, by contrast, to make this evident.

Learning 'by rote' is the preferred method not only in substandard schools for the under-privileged which frequently lack even a full complement of trained teachers or adequate infrastructure, but also in well-equipped 'elite' institutions. Although presumed to provide 'quality' education, such schools cherry-pick students to preserve a homogeneous, 'anaemic' social character (Education Commission 1964–6), which is usually associated with a proficiency in limited learning skills. Elite institutions therefore are also unable to overcome the use of 'cramming' techniques, which are hurdles to true learning.

Within the heterogeneous learning environment provided by commonly accessible educational institutions, academic autonomy and critical freedom are transformed in a complex relationship. Intellectual autonomy, rescued from its 'ivory-tower' status as a privilege, becomes the *enabling condition* for engagement across and through diversities as the actual plurality of individual and social experience is present in such institutions. *Equality of access and free, critical thought require to be recognized as intrinsic components of the process of personal and social transformation at all stages throughout the education system.* This conception is, of course, significantly differentiated from an alternative modernist conception of universalizing education according to notions of 'integration', 'inclusion' or 'mainstreaming'. These entail the imposition of 'dominant' paradigms with the aim of producing uniformity and involve a conception of knowledge as primarily instrumental to productive needs and purposes.

The pedagogical challenge we are now faced with arises from the following issues: Is learning in our institutions taking place in an environment that is conducive to 'educating oneself'? Do institutions of mass education supported by policies and legislative frameworks actually further the democratic goals for which they are set up? Within the modernist framework of universal rights, access to education cannot be divorced from the democratic conception of the purpose and quality of education, which has to be provided as a fundamental right to all children. Quality has to be 'recognition of a large variety of competences *and the grant of equal status to them* will make "quality" compatible with both "equality" and "quantity" (Naik 1975: p. 50). Learning takes place everywhere in society and acquiring knowledge, skills and abilities to cope with life in ways that are varied and socially interactive reflect the reality that `educating oneself' is a social process. The classroom/ institution succeeds in being a significant contributor to the formal system of education only to the extent that it responds creatively to this situation.

From the early twentieth century onwards, when the spread of mass education reflected its recognition as a social necessity and a right for all citizens, radical theorists in the field of educational psychology have placed the origins of cognition in social interaction and demonstrated that social adaptation facilitated cognitive development. Lev Vygotsky showed how optimal learning occurred through a 'collabourative dialogue' between the 'self' and more skilful 'others', including peers, to effect the transition from other-regulation to self-regulation. (Vygotsky & Vygotsky 1978). Deeper thinking abilities were seen to develop among children as collabourators and creators of 'disequilibrium' amongst each other when they conflicted, disagreed, and persuaded one another (Piaget 1972). Despite fundamental differences in their approach, both Vygotsky and Piaget believed that young children are curious and actively involved in their own learning. The teacher was no longer seen to dominate the classroom as a central authoritative figure or the sole source of knowledge. It was acknowledged that learning did not rely only on individual effort or on pre-determined benchmarks of achievement.

The Common School System (CSS), with the *neighbourhood school* at its core, provides for facilitating conditions to be physically realized in the classroom. The didactic test is no longer about how 'we' go about dealing with 'them' because the altered environment makes 'how do we learn from each other' the fundamental question before both educators and learners. Conceptions of excellence, and consequently, goals for self-improvement are relative and depend upon social and individual choices. In a 'new milieu of emphasis on the abolition rather than on the continuation of privilege, a common school system would be regarded as providing "quality" education just as trends towards segregation would be regarded as undesirable' (Naik 1975, p. 61).

We have here grounds for developing and sustaining a *strong social consensus* in support of a nation-wide system of quality education through common neighbourhood schools, on the one hand, and a vibrant, expanding higher education sector on the other. The right to learn should be assured to every individual without discrimination and with full equality of opportunity throughout her life. Recognition of the entire education system as a 'public good', justifiably imposing constitutional and financial responsibility on the State, follows as a necessary consequence from such a consensus.

Lessons from History

Education, like all social activities, has historical dimensions. Reflective self-consciousness can be deepened and fresh insights arrived at through analysing the historical origins and evolution of the contemporary philosophy of education. (Carr 2004).

In India, the advance towards universalizing education was part of the struggle to create a modern, self-reliant nation by repudiating traditional hierarchies of caste/class on the one hand and, on the other, the 'elitism' that characterized the colonial policy and practice. The freedom struggle brought to the forefront the idea of the democratic rights of all citizens as movements of workers, peasants, Dalits, tribals, women, gained in strength and articulation. The cultural diversity of India was welcomed as the foundation of a vibrant democracy. The Constitution of the newly independent republic, adopted in 1952, was itself the culmination of a long struggle and set the standard for evaluating current policies, distinguishing between those that would strengthen and *advance* the freedoms it promised, and those that undermined its potential by compromise, infringement or direct violation.

Within the traditional Brahmanical system, caste determined access to education, the purpose of which was the inculcation of norms and practices appropriate to a pre-determined caste status in society. The '*guru-shisya*' tradition was a pedagogical method imminently suited to this goal but is out of place in a democratic conception of education. At best, it can be dismissed as a piece of traditional sentimentality; at worst, it signals the enduring failure to break with caste stratifications. The stability of the caste system even under the medieval and colonial regimes—although the Muslim elite and British imperialists had no cultural or religious empathy with the system—has been attributed to the ease with which surplus could be extracted as tax from 'isolated' village communities constituted through caste divisions (Habib 2009). In British India, although the railways represented the most significant step towards technological 'modernization' of the country, Dalits could not drink water from the 'common' facility provided at railway stations.

The East India Company's early educational initiatives at the level of higher education followed both caste strictures and religious divisions. It was only with the establishment of the Delhi and Agra Colleges (1823–4) that 'open' admissions were allowed. This apparently 'modern' feature, for the introduction of which colonial rule is usually credited, in fact continued a practice prevalent in madrasas of the region, (then still under the cultural influence of the Mughal court), where large numbers of Hindus from the Khatri and Kayastha castes in particular were drawn to these schools of Persian literature, science and jurisprudence. 'The Persian schools are the most genuine educational institutions in the country. They are attended largely by the Khatris, the Hindus forming a greater proportion than the Muhammadans' (Arnold 1922: p. 290).

The colonial policy for education, the first ever in the history of the subcontinent that was determined by a trading corporation and based on a functional, instrumentalist conception of knowledge, was communicated through a Despatch of the East India Company's Court of Directors of 29 September 1830. Inspired by the utilitarian concept of 'useful learning', aggressively promoted for the colonies by missionaries (Grant 1792), it contained in entirety the policy advocated in Macaulay's infamous Minute of 1835. Promotion of English as the principal medium of instruction was aimed at creating 'an elite class of learned natives' trained in European science and literature, who would 'communicate a portion of this improved learning to the Asiatic wider classes'. The government in India was instructed to use 'every assistance and encouragement, pecuniary or otherwise', including a declared preference in government employment, to further this goal. *'We wish you to consider this as our deliberate view of the scope and end to which all your endeavours with respect to the education of the Natives should refer'* [emphasis added] (Howell 1872: pp. 20–1).

The political strategy motivating this policy had extremely negative academic consequences. It, cut the links of the new 'educated class' instructed in English medium and curriculum from classical oriental learning and not just from the traditional feudal elite who had patronized it. The promise of jobs in the government as a means of promoting the new education succeeded primarily in promoting 'babu', that is, clerical, culture as these were the jobs open to 'natives'. Not surprisingly, a principal 'weaknesses of the native student' was soon identified as 'the strong temptation to lay aside his studies as soon as employment supplies his moderate necessities; the scanty inducement to fit himself for higher duties, — all help to dwarf the moral and intellectual growth ... His ambition waits upon his daily wants.' (Report of the Education Commission 1882: pp. 300–04).

Woods Despatch (1854) has been regarded as supportive of a system of mass education because it advocated elementary education in the 'vernacular'. However, its limited objective in systematically reforming the indigenous village *pathshala* and *maktab*, which had taught 'a little reading, chiefly a religious text in Sanskrit, Arabic or Persian, very little writing, and some elementary arithmetic', was the introduction of a new revenue system. This aimed at defining

> the nature and extent of many different kinds of land rights, and devise a system for their complete registration. The efficacy of this system depends on the ability of the people to comprehend it, and to take precautions that their interests are accurately shown in the registers. For this they should be able to read, write and understand the elementary rules of arithmetic. (Indigenous

Education Prior to 1854, North-Western Provinces: Government Measures 1791–1854, Report of the Education Commission 1882: pp. 18–20.)

In fact, Woods Despatch explicitly formulated the 'elitist' divide between this stage and the extremely restricted secondary and higher education, which were exclusively in English medium and taught a European curriculum. Ratified for implementation in 1859 following the crushing of the Revolt of 1857, it neither provided for the spread of primary education or for the development of any Indian language; nor was it able to reduce the gap between Anglo-vernacular and vernacular schools. Liberal funding for the three affiliating and examining universities set up in accordance with its recommendations led to the promotion of English language and the creation of an English-educated class among the 'native' population to serve the requirements of the colonial administration.

Dadabhai Naoroji in 1881 placed before the Hunter Commission (Education Commission 1882) the demand that four years of compulsory primary education, ensuring literacy, be provided to all children. Meticulously and persuasively arguing that poverty in India was the creation of British colonial policies, his demand was occasioned by the concern that it be substantially alleviated. The Commission only recommended that admission to existing schools and colleges should not be denied on grounds of untouchability, caste, religion and gender. However, as no attempts were made by British administrators to remove untouchability and caste prejudice in society, 'even when untouchable children were admitted to schools, they had to sit away from the other children (they were not even admitted into the school building if it happened to be a temple) and were not touched either by the teachers or by the other students.' (Naik 1975: p. 8)

Further, the formal structure of the colonial system of education—single-point entry, full-time instruction, annual examinations—became an instrument for *not* educating the poor, and for treating their socioeconomic handicaps as a measure of 'intellectual incompetence'. The insistence that students pay fees and that stipends be abolished ensured that access to education and retention of those who did enter the system was severely restricted. Non-fee paying and stipend-based education had been characteristic of the pre-colonial philanthropically supported madrasa system. It is unfortunate that we fail to draw upon the multiple traditions that have contributed to the intellectual and cultural history of the sub-continent. This failure afflicts the appropriation of our history and of the traditions that we seek to make our own. Rather than critically evaluating the rich and complex experience of heterogeneity that constitutes the historical past, the dominant tendency is to revert to colonial patterns as is evident in the currently prevalent association of learning with 'job opportunities' and of fee-paying with the quality of education.

In 1886, Jyotiba Phule upbraided the colonial government for financing education only for the Brahmins and the children of the rich while the masses wallowed in ignorance. Indeed, for all the claims of advantages supposedly accruing to India as a result of colonial education policy, as late as 1921, only 11 per cent of the population was even literate. In fact, during the latter half of the nineteenth century and in the early twentieth century, rulers of Indian states like the Maharaja of Baroda, the Begums of Bhopal, the rulers of Travancore-Cochin and pioneers like Savitribai Phule, were engaged in far more radical endeavours opening up education for lower castes and girls.

The idea that an education system providing for equality of opportunity could become an instrument for social transformation emerged as an integral part of nationalist thought. The colonial obsession with English was replaced by the demand that the mother tongue be used at the elementary level, and the idea that Indian languages become the medium of education at secondary and higher levels of learning was actively promoted. The neglect of science and technology was criticized as detrimental to developing the productive capability of the people. Patriotism instead of subordination to imperial ideology and policy was raised as the prime value to be inculcated by the education system, and the growing demand for compulsory elementary and expanding secondary and university education was perceived as the engine for 'modernizing' and constituting India as an independent nation.

In 1910, Gokhale moved a resolution reiterating Naoroji's demand in the Central Legislative Assembly, following it up with a Bill in 1912. The Nagpur Session (1920) of the Indian National Congress (INC) advised the withdrawal of children and youth from existing schools and colleges and the establishment of parallel nationalist institutions. The Wardha Conference on Education (1937) developed the Gandhian concept of basic education the content of which was defined as being 'equivalent to matriculation *minus* English *plus* craft'. (Naik 1975: p. 17) Gandhi made it clear that the 'plan to impart primary education through the medium of village handicrafts... is thus conceived as a silent revolution fraught with the most far-reaching consequences.' (Acharya 1997: p. 604). The colonial education system was opposed because of its inherently elitist character and '...through craft, [Gandhi] wanted to impart knowledge on all important branches of knowledge.' (Biswas and Aggarwal 1994: p. 90). The Wardha deliberations were elabourated and advanced by the Zakir Husain Committee Report on *Nai Talim* (New Learning), which recommended nation-wide provision of free and compulsory education in the mother tongue for a minimum of 7, later 8 years, that is, up to 14 years of age for all children. These developments formed the basis for the resolution 'to build national education on a new foundation' which was passed at the February, 1938 Haripura Session of the INC.

Nationalist resistance compelled the colonial administration to overturn the goals of its own policy. The 1944 report of the Central Advisory Board of Education led by John Sargent, *Post-War Plan of Educational Development in India*, declared that 'the minimum provision which could be accepted as constituting a national system postulates that all children must receive enough education to prepare them to earn a living as well as to fulfil themselves as individuals and discharge their duties as citizens'. The report argued that

> if there is to be anything like equality of opportunity, it is impossible to justify providing facilities for some of the nation's

children and not for others... a national system can hardly be other than universal. Secondly, it must be compulsory, if the grave wastage which exists today under a voluntary system is not to be perpetrated and even aggravated. And thirdly, if education is to be universal and compulsory, *equity requires that it should be free and common sense demands that it should last long enough to secure its fundamental objective* [emphasis added]' (Government of India 1944: p. 3).

The emergence of the demand for education as a right is firmly grounded in this history. Article 45 of the Directive Principles of State in the Constitution obligated the State to universalize free and compulsory early childhood care and elementary education in regular full-time schools of comparable quality for all children up to 14 years of age by 1960. Nationalist opinion also favoured a rapid extension of universal free and compulsory secondary education, and access to higher education as the next steps in the establishment of a complete system of national education.

Independent India's first Education Commission (1964–6), the D.S. Kothari Commission, examined the inadequacies of the existing educational infrastructure when it failed to universalize elementary education within the constitutionally specified period. It recommended far-reaching structural changes to place the system on the right track. The target was the setting up of a national system of publicly funded compulsory and free education through a network of government, local bodies, and government-aided schools of comparable quality. Noting the presence of what was then a small stream of elite 'public' schools (a nomenclature used for private institutions in India), it stated: 'The so-called Public Schools... system was transplanted in India by British administrators and we have clung to it so long because it happened to be in tune with the traditional hierarchical structure of our society. Whatever its place in past history maybe, such a system has no valid place in the new democratic and socialistic society we desire to create' (1.38). In contrast, the report analyses, extols and strongly advocates the role of public funded common neighbourhood schools with a socially, culturally and economically diverse student body as the authentic institution of a pedagogically sound and egalitarian national system of education (1.36–1.38 and 10.19).

The Commission's report acknowledged that political will and decisive legislation were needed to put such a system into effect. It anticipated that objections to CSS would come primarily from the well-off sections of society as common neighbourhood schools would satisfy the hunger of the deprived for education and for equality. Only those with the status and income to access elite schools would claim that they were being deprived of the 'democratic' right to choose a school for their children. Even today, the School Choice Campaign in India, inspired and guided by World Bank (WB) advisers, demands that government should not fund 'schools' but 'children' through vouchers that would transfer public funds to privately owned elite and low-budget school managements alike (School Choice National Conference, New Delhi, 4 December 2012).

The Report of the Committee of Members of Parliament on Education (1967), rejected persisting inequalities:

> the unhealthy social segregation that now takes place between the schools for the rich and those for the poor should be ended; and the primary schools should be the common schools of the nation by making it obligatory on all children, irrespective of caste, creed, community, religion, economic conditions or social status, to attend the primary school in their neighbourhood. This sharing of life among the children of all social strata will strengthen the sense of being one nation which is an essential ingredient of good education (Government of India 1967: p. 2).

The 1968 National Policy of Education (NPE) still looked to the CSS as the vehicle for establishing equality of educational opportunity and social cohesion.

However, the consensus at the level of policy was not reflected at the institutional level. Innovative policies with full financial support from the State were required to effect a transformation of the structure and content of the education system to facilitate achievement and progress of the marginalized. Caste and class prejudices remained intractable leading to a failure to break the linkage of 'privilege' with 'quality' that was inherited from the past and cast into its distorted 'modern' form through colonial policy and practice. The attempt at the elementary level, 'to extend to the poor people an education system basically meant for the well-to-do middle classes did not succeed and the rates of stagnation and wastage became disturbingly high' (Naik 1975: p. 47). The poor and the marginalized lacked not only the economic but also the socio-cultural wherewithal to take advantage of such a system. The diversity of the life experience of India's children became the stumbling block, rather than the failure of the system to meet the challenge of this diversity.

By 1986, indicating a withdrawal from the State's constitutional commitment to provide quality education and equality of opportunity for all from school to higher education, the National Policy on Education (NPE), its companion Programme of Action, together with their modified versions of 1992, *converted the idea of a national system of education, evolved through the freedom struggle and reflected in Constitutional goals and provisions, into a series of missions and campaigns to impart market-oriented 'skills'* beginning with the lowliest one of 'functional literacy'. This led to a conceptual and curricular de-linking of cognitive and aesthetic accomplishments from the acquisition of practical skills now claimed to be sufficient for making the mass of citizens employable. *The most negative feature of the NPE was a direct consequence of this approach.* It was the policy provision for low-cost, poor quality non-formal education (NFE), which was to be treated as 'equivalent to schooling' for those children who could not 'be expected to attend a full day at school'. Children living in habitations with no educational facilities, working children including boys and girls with household responsibilities, children from marginalized groups, who even now constitute over 80 per cent of children in the relevant age-group, could now legitimately be excluded from the formal system of education. NFE introduced the policy of multi-track, discriminatory streams of education and legitimized the denial of education of comparable quality to all India's children. Throughout the 1990's, low-cost practices began to infiltrate the government school system as a whole. Infrastructural inputs, urgently required as the pressure to provide access increased, were neglected. Recruitment of full-time, trained teachers was severely affected. Para-teachers, *shiksha mitras*, *acharyas* in Education Guarantee Centres, and multi-grade teaching were used to cut costs of trained teachers particularly after the Fifth Pay Commission. By 2003, NFE extended to 25 states covering 7.4 million children. Worked by state governments with the aid of thousands of voluntary groups, it became the most powerful obstacle to the struggle for realizing the constitutional directive of quality education for all.

The approach of the NPE 1986 ultimately came to fruition in the Right to Free and Compulsory Education Act (RTE 2009) which legalized a highly inequitable and discriminatory 'fundamental' right to education as it excluded from its purview private unaided schools and also the 'special' public funded schools such as the Kendriya and Navodaya Vidyalayas and the Saink Schools. With the passage of the RTE 2009, the very idea of a national system of public funded education for which the State would be both responsible and accountable has been given up. The results have been as expected. After completion of the 31 March 2013 deadline for meeting the infrastructural requirements stipulated by the Act, less than 10 per cent schools RTE-compliant. Quoting government data, the NGO Pratham's Annual Status of Education Report (ASER 2012) finds that 29.8 per cent primary (Std I – V) students attended private schools in 2010–11. In just two years after the implementation of the RTE Act, there has been a 5.8 per cent point increase in private school enrolment. By 2020 the report estimates that over 50 per cent students will be paying for primary education (*The Times of India*, 22 January 2013).

Higher Education and the advent of a modern society

Up to the 1970s opinion among academicians, policymakers and major political leaders appeared to be fairly harmonized on the importance of higher education as a channel for promoting chosen social values, and the objective of creating a democratically unified but plural polity and society was clearly expressed in educational policy. This encouraged the academic community to regard the values on which society was based as being 'properly open to questioning and that they have some responsibility for choosing which values they adopt' (Winch 2005: p. 68). The 1948 *Report of the Radhakrishnan Commission on Higher Education* affirmed that 'Education is not a discipline imposed from above on an apathetic if acquiescent nature... All true development is self-development' (p. 37). It drew attention to the fact that the academic community constituted an important section within the wider society, a section that was *trained* to reflect upon and critically respond to the latter and acknowledged that while 'universities should be sensitive to enlightened public opinion, they should never let themselves be bullied or bribed into actions that they know to be educationally unsound or worse still, motivated by nepotism, faction and corruption' (p. 406).

Critical freedom was identified as the prime enabling condition for independent inquiry and self-development which allowed such institutions to properly perform their important social role. 'The function of the universities is not only to preserve, disseminate and advance knowledge but to furnish intellectual leadership and moral tone to society', and while 'an autonomous university may not always achieve these ideals; but it is certain that a university which is not autonomous, is hardly likely ever to achieve these great objectives' (Report of the Committee on Model Act for Universities, 1961–4: p. 5).

The report of the Kothari Commission displayed a remarkable awareness of the risk posed to academic freedom by organizational structures that were not adequate to its requirements and goals. It asserted that principles of administration or governance (clear chain of responsibility, delegation of function and authority, economy and efficiency) only appeared to be common to all good organizations. In fact, the specific nature of the activities would determine how and through what measures these could be realized in particular fields.

> The character of a university as a society of teachers and students engaged in the pursuit of learning and discovery, distinguishes fundamentally the regulation of its affairs from, say, the profit-

motivated management of commercial or industrial concerns or the administration of a government department or municipal corporation, or a unit of the armed forces... Rules, regulations and techniques that hamper the achievement of the real purposes of the university should be modified or scrapped—they should not be allowed to become strait-jackets into which all university activities must be fitted (p. 299).

Highlighting the *shared goals of the teachers and students who constitute the academic community*, it drew an important distinction between mere 'institutional autonomy' and 'academic freedom'. Teachers and students must have the freedom 'to hold and express their views, however radical, within the classroom (and outside) provided they are careful to present the different aspects of a problem without confusing teaching with "propaganda".' The Commission recommended that a teacher (or student) 'should receive all facilities and encouragement in his work, teaching and research, even when his views and approach be in opposition to those of his seniors and the head of his department or faculty' (p. 300). *The Report of the Committee on Model Act for Universities* (1964), emphatically stated that:

> the proper functioning of a university depends on the all-round acceptance of two basic principles... autonomy for universities from external controls together with a democratic administrative system, and effective participation of the academic community in the formation and implementation of university policy and programmes ...*If such a community (teachers and students) is to discharge its duties to itself and to the nation, its governance of the university must essentially be in its own hands.* The teachers should have in practice an effective voice in the determination of the policies and the management of the affairs of the university; their participation should be real and meaningful and not merely formal and constitutional (p. 8).

The Commission's report asserted that the *democratization of structures of internal governance* went hand-in-hand with the increased responsibility of the University Grants Commission (UGC) to support and strengthen the independence of the universities precisely as the *quantum of public funding* of the system of higher education *increased*. As a step in this direction and in order to attract and encourage competent faculty across different types of institutions, the Commission strongly recommended that undue hierarchies should be removed so that 'the "gap" in conditions of service (including salary scales) of teachers (with similar qualifications) in the affiliated colleges and the university departments should be reduced' (p. 30). The report of the Gajendragadkar Committee on Governance of Universities and Colleges (1971) not only endorsed this demand, it also recommended student participation in academic and administrative decision-making to enhance the 'sense of belonging' within the academic community.

The responsibility and relevance of the academic community and of higher education for society were seen as resting firmly on this foundation. The perception of higher education as a public good formed the basis of its relationship with the State. Institutions of higher education were seen as being sufficiently responsive to societal needs to merit governmental support, yet they were to be adequately protected against external pressures, including political, bureaucratic, and market pressures, to safeguard their societal critique.

The significance of the separation of the university and protection of its 'autonomy' against interference by political structures of power and market forces within bourgeois society is based on two considerations. The recognition of the specificity of functions performed by the university and the divergence between these and the functional characteristics of the political and economic spheres is primary. Where creative and critical thought distinguish the former—despite the demarcations of disciplinary boundaries—the latter under modern conditions are marked by routinized mass processes of administrative governance and productive efficiencies. The other feature of universities is the existence of rules and norms favouring self-regulation by academics. Although conservative and even State-supportive views flourish under these conditions, it is also the case that the `independence' of the university facilitates the articulation of effective challenges as it creates space for the rise of critical knowledge, for dissent and even confrontational engagement. In contemporary neoliberal conditions this academic autonomy is sought to be eradicated as it acts as a barrier to the conceptual hegemony of neoliberal perceptions which reduces the capacity of post-secondary institutions to teach and research outside the market logic of corporate power. The withdrawal of public funding is a major step in this direction as the need to generate their own resources facilitates the conversion of the universities into extensions of capitalism.

In India, the protective barrier is being rapidly dismantled under the neoliberal assault. Failure to universalize elementary and secondary education provided a 'privileged' status to the approximately 10 per cent of the relevant age group who were, until a few years ago, able to benefit from higher education. This was disingenuously used to propagate the idea of privatization of higher education as it was argued that there could be no justification for burdening the taxpayer with the cost of providing higher education as its benefits accrued only to those who received it. Eventually, the Minister of Human Resource Development, Murli Manohar Joshi, advised institutions of higher education to 'raise their own resources by raising the fee levels, encouraging private donations and by generating revenues through consultancy and other activities' (Address to the UNESCO World Conference on Higher Education, 1998). The lack of political will shown by successive governments to address the cause of low access to higher education finally resulted in a strategy, which aggravated the problem by recommending the *commercialization* of higher education.

Influence of the World Bank

The impetus for the strategy owed much to policy prescriptions from the World Bank and other international donor agencies that argued against the use of public funding for an expansion of higher education. 'Higher Education: The Lessons of Experience' (WB Report 1994) termed higher education a private or quasi-private good which allows the student-consumer to command a better market value for her skills. Thus public investment in universities and colleges magnified income inequality as the elite dominated higher education. Hence, governments were justified in leaving this sector in private, that is, commercial hands. By 1997, India's Finance Ministry was aggressively advocating cuts in the `subsidies' given to higher education as it was a 'non-merit good'. Although this categorization was revised in 2004 with higher education being termed a 'merit 2 good', which could be provided subsidies although at a reduced level, the conception of higher education as a public good had been dealt a fatal blow (Tilak 2004).

The pressure exerted by WB prescriptions in determining shifts in India's education policy can be seen to correspond with the introduction of the New Economic Policy (NEP) in 1991 and the neoliberal economic reforms and structural adjustments. This influence has been exerted with the willing collabouration of India's political class, a largely supportive media, and sections of the intelligentsia and civil society that have either aspired to the allurements held out for the elites by accommodating national democratic interests to the requirements of the current global economic order, or have not been sufficiently vigilant against the implications of this accommodation. The consequent alienation of these sections from the demands, hopes and aspirations of the people reversed the process which was seen during the freedom struggle and the early decades of the post-Independence era.

The millennium year 2000 brought with it policy initiatives that represented a complete reversal of fortunes for the higher education sector in India. The WB now pressed for 'urgent action to expand the quantity and improve the quality of higher education' because without the 'specialized skills... increasingly in demand in all sectors of the world economy' developing countries would find it increasingly difficult to benefit from the global knowledge-based economy' (World Bank 2000). Conceding that profit driven market forces were not adequate for devising an appropriate system, it argued that the state should 'concentrate on establishing the parameters within which success can be achieved'. Funding models were advocated to allow for consistent and productive input of public finances to promote maximization of the 'financial input of the private sector, philanthropic individuals and institutions, and students.'

The results were quickly seen. Firstly, the Ambani-Birla Report, *A Policy Framework for Reforms in Education,* was made public. It was not the analysis of any committee of academics, but was the creation of two of India's leading industrialists commissioned by the Council on Trade and Industry of the Prime Minister of the National Democratic Alliance (NDA)! It explicitly stated that corporate investment could double the number of postsecondary institutions by 2015, and that privatization and commercialization were the chief instruments for reform in higher education. It wanted the 'user-pays' principle, with loans and grants for the needy, to be the means for making investment *profitable for investors.* With its companion Model Act for Universities 2003, prepared by the UGC, it recommended restructuring of higher education on the *model of market-oriented enterprises promoting corporate values.* It was shelved because of strong opposition from academicians and teachers unions, the report's basic features have provided the changed environment within which higher education policies are conceived and debated today.

Secondly, the World Trade Organization (WTO) and the General Agreement on Trade in Services (GATS) made an entry into the arena of higher education in India. In 2000, the WTO considered a series of proposals to ensure that the import and export of higher education was brought under WTO protocols. Nigvekar, then UGC Chairperson, presented the position paper, 'Trade in Higher Education: Impact of GATS on Higher Education, Research and Knowledge Systems in Selected Contexts in Asia and the Pacific Region', at UNESCO's second regional meeting. As the UGC website posted it, 'the overall thrust of the presentation was that higher education itself has become a tradable product and knowledge has become commodified. The important point was made that as yet, there is little, if any, empirical evidence that GATS and the trade in education service per se is compromising national systems of higher education.'

Both conclusions were problematic. Commodities are produced primarily for exchange for profit rather than for their intrinsic use value. In a highly developed system of commodity production like capitalism all exchanges are market exchanges, which will be affected by scarcities, monopolies, manipulated tastes, and more or less accidental variations in supply and demand. Therefore, the idea of the 'commodification' of knowledge appears to be a contradiction in terms, *unless one is prepared to seriously degrade the concept of knowledge to mere instruction and acquisition of skills for the market*. On the issue of compromising national interests, education ministers from the states of the Union in 2005 expressed concern that 'the national values and concerns of the host country may be undermined by the presence of foreign providers not sharing such values' (background paper prepared by the National Institute of Educational Planning and Administration (NIEPA) for the Conclave of State Education Ministers, held at Bangalore, 10–11 January 2005). Yet, the offer to put higher education on the WTO table as a tradeable commodity was endorsed by the United Progressive Alliance (UPA) government in 2005. The Commerce Ministry felt that 'service negotiations (in WTO) could be used as an opportunity to invite foreign universities to set up campuses in India, thereby saving billions of dollars for the students travelling abroad'. Therefore, it identified a need 'to strike a balance' between 'domestic regulation and providing adequate flexibility to such universities in setting syllabus, hiring teachers, screening students and setting fee levels' (*Higher Education in India and GATS: An Opportunity*, consultation paper on trade in higher education circulated by Commerce Ministry, 2006). Despite sharp criticism by teachers and students organizations, government seems headed towards binding higher education in perpetuity within the strictures of the WTO regime.

By 2005, a new mantra for reform of the higher education sector identified structures of regulation and cooperation between investors and governments in Private Public Partnerships (PPP) (Dahlman and Utz 2005). To create a sustained cadre of 'knowledge workers', India required to make its education sector more 'demand driven' by 'relaxing bureaucratic hurdles' to allow the private sector to meet the burgeoning demand for higher education and increasing industry-university partnerships in research and application including use of learning technologies for providing distance education across the board for lifelong training and upgradation of skills. The system was to be facilitated by putting in place accreditation systems for private providers.

National Knowledge Commission's (NKC) recommendations, haphazardly presented a Report to the Nation 2006, which was not based on any exhaustive review of the state of higher education in the country but was guided by WB suggestions. Far-reaching and sweeping they continue to resonate in later documents including the Yashpal Committee Report and in the higher education reform Bills pending before Parliament or being implemented in the form of UGC regulations.

The major constants can be identified:

- establishing a single, independent regulatory authority for Higher Education to replace the regulatory functions of the UGC, AICTE, MCI, and BCI which reflect the diversity of higher education. Insulated from executive structures, such as the MHRD, which are answerable to Parliament and 'other stakeholders' in the final analysis, this neoliberal 'single-window access.' facilitating the entry of domestic and international capital to the higher education 'market' is a dominant feature. Currently on hold due to opposition from the Medical and Bar Councils, it will no doubt reappear in some new *avatar*;
- concentrating 'excellence' in pampered enclaves which results, on the one hand, in creating mediocrity in existing neglected institutions outside the 'circle of excellence', and on the other, produces intellectuals who are distanced from the conditions and problems of a developing society;
- pegging fees to 'quality' so that the 'user pays' principle, adequately rewards investors. This travesty of constitutional and pedagogical wisdom is sought to be made acceptable on grounds of 'economic' efficiency. It ensures that the rich and the privileged retain their hold over the gateways to power;
- creating hierarchies to foster cut-throat competition

between institutions and among faculties through a system of rewards and punishments.

Assault on Democratic Decision-making Processes

The WB report, which identified the Prime Minister's office (PMO) as most 'appropriate champion to coordinate and orchestrate the necessary knowledge-economy related actions across the various domains', and lauded the formation of the NKC initiative for making timely recommendations for implementation to the PMO, also had a very negative impact on decision-making processes in higher education. Democratic structures of policymaking and accountability are being ignored in favour of committees of 'experts' who advise government directly. Over the past few years this has been reduced to caricature as education is being 'reformed' through press statements and interviews. The higher education reform bills were brought to Parliament with little prior information and no national debate over their contents. The situation has degenerated so much that even Vice-Chancellors bypass statutory academic and administrative decision-making bodies to function through the exercise of 'emergency powers'. The case of Delhi University colleges being *forced* initially to change their undergraduate program to semester mode, and now to adopt a Four Year Undergraduate Program is only the most prominent and blatant example [Prasad 2013: pp. 19–34]. The UGC has set up a review committee to see how these changes can be implemented nationwide.

The crisis in higher education in India is chronic and affects lakhs of students enrolled in the country's 34,000 odd colleges and hundreds of universities. State financed or subsidized universities and colleges suffer from chronic under-funding and the vast majority of fee-charging private 'teaching shops' exploit the promise of providing market-oriented courses without making available even the barest facilities. The demand for reform including rapid expansion of access particularly for the marginalized sections, improvement of quality, and imposition of strict curbs on the trend towards commercialization has been a major feature of the contentious academic debate over higher education reforms and a prominent demand of students, teachers and people's movements. However, the neoliberal conception of higher education as a 'private good' and a tradable commodity directs the policies being pursued by successive governments. Opposed to the Indian Constitution's vision of education as the primary vehicle for promoting equal opportunity, social justice, and an economic system that does not result in concentration of wealth, these policies remain indifferent to the plight of existing universities and colleges and the fate of their students, while government aggressively proceeds to privatize and commercialize higher education. In fact, the pending bills aim at putting in place laws to the entry of national and foreign capital in higher education and meet the conditions required for the implementation of GATS regulations. The creation and securing of this 'market' in higher education—a market, which it is estimated will reach $50 billion by 2015—is in the forefront of current policies and initiatives. These bills the National Accreditation Regulatory Authority for Higher Educational Institutions Bill, 2010, the Educational Tribunals Bill, 2010, the Foreign Educational Institutions (Regulation of Entry and Operations) Bill 2010, and the Prohibition of Unfair Practices in Technical Educational Institutions, Medical Educational Institutions and Universities Bill, 2010 and the proposed bill to establish a highly centralized National Council for Higher Education Research (NCHER)—will alter completely the academic thrust, the structure and administration of higher education in India.

Unfortunately, the change would not be in the direction of democratizing the spread and content, or improving the quality, of higher education. For it is the familiar neoliberal norms which are being set to work in many developing countries (Varghese 2004): easy entry and mobility for national and foreign capital in higher education; homogenizing criteria and methods of evaluation and grading across disciplines, institutions, and culturally diverse regions; substituting 'transparency' of increased costs of education for regulation and rationalization of fees; and the introduction of an arbitrary grievance redressal system that ends students, teachers and employees unions, and makes recourse to courts of justice almost impossible.

We need to pay closer attention to the Foreign Educational Institutions (FEI) (Regulation of Entry and Operations) Bill, which opens the door to 'foreign education providers', with at least twenty years experience as a provider in, and with accreditation from, the country of its origin, to a fast track entry into the Indian higher education market. Complete advertisement of fees and development charges, of syllabi, faculty, and facilities is the only requirement to be met by the provider. Violating constitutional provisions, there is no provision for providing reservation for Scheduled Castes, Scheduled Tribes and Other Backward Castes. In case the recognition of an FEI is withdrawn for whatever reasons, the erstwhile provider can no longer give 'a degree or diploma or equivalent qualifications', but is free to continue operations by giving a 'certificate'! Penalties imposed on violators can, in view of the 'reputation' of the Foreign Education Provider (FEP), be waived or altered by the Central Government. Since FEP's are not required to send reports either to the central government or the UGC, the task of detecting violations would become almost impossible. The failure to implement All India Council for Technical Education (AICTE) Regulations (2005), now replaced by the AICTE (Grant of Approval for Technical Institutions) Regulation (2010), prohibiting such violations under Cr PC or to prevent 'unrecognized' but prominent institutes collabourating with foreign providers to continue to ruthlessly exploit students does not inspire confidence that the much 'softer' approach of this Bill would enable effective monitoring of FEIs.

The Universities for Research and Innovation Bill 2012 for setting up 14 innovation universities has also been found wanting on almost all its provisions by the Parliamentary Standing Committee (PSC). To be funded, staffed and managed completely independently by 'investors' with only the stipulation that 50 per cent of their students should be Indian citizens, the PSC has objected to the absence of regulatory and accountability mechanisms for such universities and has opposed the surreptitious entry of foreign universities and private players through this route. The proposal to set up these universities through a Memorandum of Understanding with the Central Government and not through an Act of Parliament has also been criticized. But again, MHRD is trying to circumvent parliamentary scrutiny through regulations, recently passed by the UGC. The UGC will grant funds—from 25 to 300 crores—for innovative projects, research and governance ideas to central and state universities of 10 years standing and with A level accreditation. Such projects could of course involve collabouration with private players, both national and foreign.

The academic consequences of this 'reform' package will be catastrophic. Worldwide experience has shown that nationally advanced systems of education attract engagement and competition with other advanced systems. Instead of concentrating on improving the hundreds of universities and thousands of colleges in India, the government wishes to open the doors to corporates and FEPs to do the job. The former are in the market to do business, and FEPs are certainly not motivated by the zeal to reform higher education in other countries. The increasingly competitive and fast moving global higher education scene is already dominated by the universities and research facilities of the industrialized countries, which are also home to the multinational corporations, which have become powerful in the new global knowledge system. It is the funds crunch they are facing in the current world recession that lies behind the pressure on countries like India to open up and restructure higher education to privatization and the entry of foreign capital.

The privately-borne high cost of education will adversely affect the pursuit of knowledge itself. It will put a premium on disciplines and courses that are directly linked to the demands of national and international capital markets. That is why, the world over, disciplines and areas of research that are foundational to dynamic and innovative systems of higher education depend significantly on state funding and philanthropic support. Replacing this with profit-oriented enterprise would mean that these disciplines will suffer an inevitable decline. As a consequence, the critical and transformational purpose of institutions of higher education will recede into the background.

Privatization and commercialization of higher education provide autonomy to capital—opening up captive markets for investment and profit-taking as knowledge is now a key component in economic development—but its impact on the academic community is decidedly anti-democratic and has grave consequences for the very conception of higher education as a *public good*. Higher education is perceived merely as 'a producer of graduates and research outputs' (Bleikei and Vabo, 2000). But students are not products, nor are they 'consumers' or 'clients'. Academicians are not part of a delivery service and universities are not businesses. 'Knowledge and thought are not commodities... [Education is] the very anti-thesis of a commodity.' (Campaign for the Future of Higher Education 2003). Studies relating to postsecondary institutions across developed and developing economies show that as universities become financially autonomous institutions, their academicians are increasingly less able to direct their own working lives. (Perry et al 1997). Workplace knowledge is, in the first place, transferred to the control of administrators, and within administrations, to financial experts, not to those who excel in their disciplines. With privatization, there is a transformation of academic institutions into 'entrepreneurial universities' and 'commercial institutions', whose single most important objective seems to be the mobilization of greater resources. In the view of neoliberal capital higher education has become too important to be left to the academicians.

Unregulated Privatization

Significant changes are occurring in higher education in India today. A recent analysis indicates that the country is currently devoting a very high proportion (3 per cent) of GDP to this sector. The gross enrolment rate (GER)—the proportion of the age group accessing higher education—at 18 per cent is up by 6 per cent from the 12 per cent GER at the start of the 11th Five-Year Plan. The 12th Plan aims at raising it to 25 per cent by 2017[1]

(Altbach and Aggarwal 2013). However, after the adoption of the neoliberal reforms program in 1991, 'private sources' are now contributing a higher proportion (1.8%) of this investment than public ones (1.2%). In 1990, public expenditure on higher education and technical education respectively as percentage of GNP and as budgetary expenditure was 0.46 and 0.15 (% of GNP) and 1.58 and 0.51 (% of BE). By 2002–03 it was down to 0.40 and 0.13 (% of GNP) and 1.31 and 0.42 (% of BE). This represented a cumulative decline in budgetary expenditure from 2.09 per cent to 1.72 per cent, which by 2004–05 was further reduced to 1.60 per cent. In higher education alone, the decline as a percentage of GNP was down to 0.34 per cent (2004–05) from 0.46 per cent (1990–01) [Source: GOI. Analysis of Budgeted Expenditure, various years].

The consequences of this trend are disturbing. With private funding being increasingly 'investment' oriented, a greater proportion of students constituting the increased GER is already paying and will be paying higher costs for their education. Education is becoming a means to profitably recoup, through market mechanisms, the investment made either in providing or acquiring it. Choice of courses and course content are also being determined by market requirements. Like policymakers, the media and society at large, even students and their parents, no longer regard higher education as an intrinsic value with significant personal, social and civilizing worth, but as a 'private good' where the 'user-pays' principle of market exchange, however painful, seems appropriately applied.

These are serious issues. Allowing market forces to determine the value of higher education on the one hand, and on the other limiting access to those who can afford it, endorses an instrumentalist view of knowledge which directly impacts the character and structure of higher education. Historically, modern universities have served a broad public purpose as sites for critical conceptualizing of values and goals for national development and for strengthening civil society. Both are necessary components of India's unfinished agenda of democratic transformation. If this role is undermined, the assault of neoliberalism on higher education would be destroying a valuable institution for the transformation of contemporary Indian society.

Yet, current policy perspectives appear indifferent if not hostile to this understanding. It has been argued that the State lacks funds for universalizing free and compulsory school education and must depend on the private sector. The responsibility for declining standards in higher education is asserted to be a consequence of opening the doors of academia to the less privileged through fee regulations and reservation policies. The bogey of regulation by the State is said to be the major obstacle to individual and institutional achievement. The solution being offered by policymakers, media pundits, and even sections of the intelligentsia is that the 'market' alone can pull the education sector out of its present crisis. Hence, not merely private investment, but *unregulated privatization* of the entire education sector is emerging as the central feature of the 'reforms' process.

Reclaiming Education

'To limit knowledge to what will actually be put into practice... is the deliberate reduction of one's being to the condition of a cog in the techno-economic machine' (Henry 2012: p. 121). Preparing persons for jobs and for entering into society can have very different meanings particularly when the growing hegemony of neoliberal ideas and practices has extended economic rationality to the cultural, social, and political spheres. Jobs require actualization of certain potentialities of individuals but remain indifferent or may even be opposed to the general development of their personalities. However, with the neoliberal redefinition of the individual from a social being or citizen to an autonomous economic actor becoming today's 'common sense', this obvious truth is blurred.

The impact of this neoliberal 'barbarism' on educational institutions in general, but particularly on institutions of higher education, threatens their very existence as environments that foster the process of 'educating oneself'. Now, only that education is said to have value that allows the student-consumer to fetch a good market price for the skills she has acquired. The 'excellence' of institutions providing education must now be commensurate to the fees charged so that those who pay more, get more and those who pay less, should expect less. Those who lack resources get nothing and are brushed aside as failures (Bauman 2004). In India's highly stratified society, government data itself reveals that 78 per cent of the people live on less than twenty rupees a day (GOI 2007: p. 6), it is evident that the creation of such an 'education market' could make no contribution whatsoever to universalizing school education and ensuring access to higher education.

Social accountability cannot be restricted to a function purely of matters of finance. As a contemporary social philosopher has argued, 'our interests in our fellow citizens extend beyond our concern as to how they spend their money; their behaviour in other respects effects our well-being. If others in our society fail to flourish or flourish in an inappropriate way, then this has repercussions for us. The interests of others affect us more directly as well, through the allocation of positional goods...' (Winch 2005: p. 65). These interests and concerns, this call for recognizing the inter-connectedness of human lives in society, and hence the need for social justice, as the condition not only for social transformation but also for the continuing self-development of individuals, constitute the grounds for mounting a determined resistance to the degradation of life and knowledge under neoliberal dispensations. Education, so vital for life, dignity and development of the personality, lies at the heart of this struggle to reclaim the value of life itself.

REFERENCES

Acharya, Poromesh (1997) 'Educational Ideals of Tagore and Gandhi—A Comparative Study', *Economic and Political Weekly*, Vol. 32, No. 12

Altbach, Philip G. and Pawan Aggarwal, 11 February 2013, 'Scoring Higher on Education', *The Hindu*

Arnold, W.D. (1922) 'First Report' 1857, in *Selections from Educational Records*, Part II (ed) J. A. Richey, Superintendent of Government Printing: Calcutta

Biswas, A. and S.P. Aggarwal (1994) *Development of Education in India: A Historical Survey of Educational Documents Before and After Independence*, Concept Publishing Company: Delhi

Bleikei, I.R. Hostaker and A. Vabo (2000) *Policy and Practice in Higher Education: Reforming Norwegian Universities*, Jessica Kingsley Publishers: London

Campaign for the Future of Higher Education (2003) htpp://www.cfhe.org.uk

Dahlman, Carl and Anuja Utz (2005) 'India and the Knowledge Economy: Leveraging Strengths and Opportunities.' Finance and Private Sector Development of WB's South Asian Region and the WB Institute

Dworkin, Ronald (1977) *Taking Rights Seriously*, Harvard University Press

Engels, Frederick (1845/1975) 'Speeches in Elberfeld, February 8, 1845', *Marx–Engels Collected Works*, Vol. 4, 1844–45, Progress Publishers: Moscow

Feierman, S. (1993) 'African histories and the dissolution of world histories' in Bates, R., V.Y. Mudimbe and J.F. O'Barr (eds.) *Africa and the Disciplines*, Duke University Press: Durham N.C.

Friedman, M. (1962) *Capitalism and Freedom*, University of Chicago Press: Chicago

Government of India (2007) *Report on Conditions of Work and Promotion of Livelihoods in the Unorganized Sector*, National Commission for Enterprises in the Unorganized Sector: New Delhi

Gramsci, Antonio (1971) *Selections from the Prison Notebooks*, ed. and translated by Quentin Hoare and Geoffry Nowell Smith, International Publishers: New York

Grant, Charles (1792) *Observations on the State of Society among the Asiatic Subjects of Great Britain*

Habib, Irfan (17 March 2009) *Economics and the Historians*, Krishna Bharadwaj Memorial Lecture, Jawaharlal Nehru University, New Delhi

Hayek, F.A. (1962) *The Road to Serfdom*, Routledge: London

Henry, Michel (1987/2012) *Barbarism*, trans. by Scott Davidson, The Continuum International Publishing Group Pvt. Ltd.

Howell, Arthur (1872) *Education in British India: Prior to 1854 and in 1870–71*, Superintendent of Government Printing: Calcutta, pp. 20–1

Indigenous Education Prior to 1854, North-Western Provinces: Government Measures 1791–1854, *Report of the Education Commission 1882*, pp. 18–20

Lenin, V.I. (1917/1976) 'Imperialism, The Highest Stage of Capitalism', *Selected Works*, Progress Publishers: Moscow
Luxemburg, Rosa (1916) *The Junius Pamphlet*
Marx, Karl (1844/1975) 'Economic and Philosophical Manuscripts of 1844'. *Marx-Engels, Collected Works, Vol. 3, 1843-1844*, Progress Publishers: Moscow
Marx, Karl and Fredrick Engels (1848/1976) 'Manifesto of the Communist Party', *Collected Works, Vol. 6, 1845–1848*, International Publishers: New York
Marx, Karl (1853/1978) *The Future Results of the British Rule in India, On Colonialism*, Progress Publishers: Moscow
Naik, J.P. (1975) *Equality, Quality and Quantity: The Elusive Triangle in Indian Education*, Tagore Memorial Lectures, Poona University, 23-25 August 1975, Allied Publishers: New Delhi
Perry, R., V. Menec, C. Struthers, F. Hector, D. Schonmeter and R. Menges (1997) 'Faculty in Transition: A Longitudinal Analysis of the Role of Perceived Control and Type of Institution in Adjustment to Postsecondary Institutions', *Research in Higher Education*, 38(5), pp. 519–56
Piaget, Jean (1972) *The Psychology of the Child*, Basic Books: New York
Polyani, K. (1944) *The Great Transformation: The political and economic origins of our time*, Beacon Press, Boston
Prasad, Madhu (2013) 'The Decimation of a University', *Social Scientist*, Vol. 41, Nos. 7–8
Tilak, J.B.G. (2004) 'Public Subsidies in Education in India', *Economic and Political Weekly*, 24 January 2004, pp. 343–59
Varghese, N.V. (2004) 'Incentives and Institutional Changes in Higher Education', *Journal of the Programme on Institutional Management in Higher Education*, Vol. 16, No. 1, OECD, pp. 27–40
Vygotsky, L. and S. Vygotsky (1978) *Mind in Society: The Development of Higher Psychological Processes*, Harvard University Press: Cambridge, MA.
Winch, Christopher (2005) 'Autonomy as an Educational Aim' in Wilfred Carr (ed.) *The Routledge Farmer Reader in Philosophy of Education*, Routledge: London, pp. 65–73
World Bank (1 March 2000) 'Peril and Promise: Higher Education in Developing Countries', Summary of Findings by the Task Force on Higher Education and Society.

5

Caught between 'Neglect' and a Private 'Makeover': Government Schools in Delhi

Radhika Menon

Introduction

Neoliberalism as a word, may be unknown to the vast mass of people in the country that it affects, but media, the State and the market have worked extensively since the Bretton Woods Institutions prodded the structural adjustment policies to create a 'common sense' of the market with 'manufactured consent' (Herman et al 1988)[1] and the centralized role of big capital and corporations in economy and society. McChesney (1998: p. 7)[2] points out that for the 'public at large', neoliberalism becomes known through its 'free-market policies', 'consumer choice', and its 'near sacred aura', all rolled out by 'corporate financed public relations'. This 'capitalism with gloves off' (p. 8) approach is aggressive in its announcement that there is no alternative to free market principles. Ultimately, all forms of social life is invaded, 'not just by the accumulation of capital, but also by an ability to reproduce itself' and by 'commodifying all aspects of social and cultural life' (Giroux 2009: p. 30).[3]

Schools and education, like other aspects of social life are also becoming structured and ordered under market assumptions. In India, market inroads and privatization has not only been in new areas of educational demand but also in existing areas of State entitlement. Annual Status of Education Report (ASER), a report by an organization of the same name and which is funded and advised by those believing in the principles of 'efficiency' and the market,[4] has claimed through its surveys (ASER 2012)[5] that private school attendance is increasing across the country. In 2006, 18.7 per cent of students were going to private schools, while in 2012, this had increased to 28.39 per cent. The Economic Survey of Delhi (2012–13)[6] also declared that in 2010–11, 28.24 per cent of primary and middle level students were in private schools, while in Secondary and Senior Secondary, this was as high as 42.71 per cent. The shift towards private schools is visible, but the private sector is also entering the Government schools. In Bombay, the Municipal schools are already facing takeover by private organizations through public-private partnerships. The ASER Report (2012–13: p. 5) endorses this direction of private takeover of public schools with the declaration by its CEO: 'Government funded and regulated, but not controlled, private schools—like the aided or "charter schools"—replacing Government-run schools seems to be the way of the future.'

The takeover of public schools has, however, been happening for a while in the country. The educational policies, Sadgopal has argued (2006a and 2006b),[7] facilitated this process through 'distortion' and 'dilution' of norms and recommendations. The funding has been below what is required, making it hardly 'free' for the students (Tilak 1996),[8] and it has also been going down steadily with reduction in non-plan expenditures for existing Government programmes and reliance upon private sector for its plan activities, like that of setting up model schools (Tilak 2010).[9] The public-private partnerships have led to 'the private permeating the public education system' and 'gradually taking it over, administration, academics, assessments, examinations, everything' (Menon 2008).[10]

The State's attempts at privatizing itself is for what Sears (2003: p. 2) calls, a conversion to a 'lean State': 'reducing wastage' and effecting the efficiency of making itself as small as possible, where 'workers are flexible' and there is a 'demolition of the entitlements of the social welfare State'. The teachers, the main workforce of schools, have been posed as the main impediments in this process and State programmes, promoted by World Bank, have recruited para teachers in their place (Kumar et al 2001).[11]

In this paper, I examine processes and aspects of private expansion in public schools of Delhi to see, what it has to offer for those from among the disadvantaged sections. I draw upon my ethnographic fieldwork conducted in 2005–06, 2010 and 2012, in a predominantly working class settlement of South Delhi[12] and the schools they attend. Further, an examination of judicial, policy, and academic records of Delhi's pace setting schools (the Rajkiya Pratibha Vikas Vidyalaya (RPVV)), and web and media campaigns for a corporate-NGO intervention in schools, called the Teach for India (TFI) programme is done.

In Part 1, I discuss the neglect of the public schools of Delhi based on ethnographic fieldwork. Part II discusses the nature of private schooling in Delhi. Part III presents the private 'makeover' of public schools, with the case of RPVV and the TFI programme. Finally, in this scenario of 'neglect' and 'makeovers', I discuss the possibility for transcending the neoliberal common sense and consent.

PART 1: 'The Neglect'

Rohit's Schooling

In South Delhi, adjacent to an industrial area, exists 'Morpur',[13] a rapidly urbanizing fringe of rural Delhi. It is an area consisting of three Census towns and is a vast settlement resided mainly by those working in the factories. Most of the residents in this colony are first generation migrants. Rohit, a 13-year-old, stays on rent in a one room tenement here with his sister and parents. His father is an unskilled factory worker and his mother is ill with a chronic respiratory disease and confined to the house. Rohit's sister completed her senior secondary school, but abandoned the idea of further education in order to support her family. She worked first in a cable-packing factory and then moved to a garment factory. The work is tedious, low skilled, and the working hours are long and leave her with little time to study further. Though nursing ambitions of finding a profession, she is worried that if she doesn't work, Rohit, may quit studies and start working in the factories himself.

It was while Rohit was in class VII that the family's financial situation started spiralling downwards. The family fell into debt for an elder daughter's wedding and treating the health problems of Rohit's mother. At this time, Rohit was in a small elementary level private school near his house, which the ASER Report calls 'affordable schools'. It is one of thousands of such schools in Delhi that have faced de-recognition for not fulfilling infrastructure norms by 31 March 2013, as per RTE Act (2009). He had been studying in this school ever since the local MCD school turned him away even after repeated visits for admission by his mother for want of affidavits, ration card, and certificates. A teacher in the school later explained to her that there was no place in the school for any more children.

In the private school, he knew the teachers, most of them were young women who lived around his house. His mother felt, 'it is good that the boy is going to a private school. They pay attention in these schools and by Class V he will be as good as X in the government.' In the private school, Rohit had no time, first studying in the school and then attending tuitions where the teacher helped him finish school homework. Rohit, unlike his other classmates, managed not to be failed or detained. He 'memorised lessons' and 'learnt answers to the given questions'. The family's financial crisis changed all this as they could not continue tuitions and fees for the school. So they continued his tuitions and shifted him to the Government Senior Secondary School in Class VIII.

Rohit found himself in a school situated within a school complex, which has an upper primary, secondary, and senior secondary schools. Several thousand students from three census towns and several villages of the surrounding areas studied here. The schools were double shift schools, and the three school buildings housed a girls' school in the morning and a boys' school in the afternoon.

Rohit became ill, cried, and avoided the school, after a month. His sister found out that he had no place to sit in the crowded class. His class had 74 students, while the classroom could accommodate only 35 students. The gates of the school would be closed, but soon after attendance, students jumped out of the windows, scaled the wall and attempted to escape. The days he was in the class, he was unable to hear the teacher —'there is so much noise.' He was also finding it difficult to follow Maths and Science as it was taught in Hindi medium, while he had been taught in English medium. The teachers were in a hurry to finish the syllabus as per the weekly plans dictated by the Directorate of Education and kept records to show that they were following the schedule. He continued to 'memorise lessons' and 'learn answers to the given questions' at home.

The schools itself were collapsing to worry too much about Rohit or others like him. In its 40 rooms, 12,064 students were expected to study.

Table 1: Overview of the Morpur's Government Senior Secondary School

	School shift for boys		School shift for girls	
	2005	2012	2005	2012
Students	2370	5097	3081	6967
Rooms	19	19 *pucca* rooms	37	37 *pucca* rooms
Teachers	44	86	61	72
Student-Teacher ratio	54:1	60:1	51:1	97:1
Ratio of students to class rooms	85:1	268:1	84:1	188:1

Calculations based on information provided to Radhika Menon by the schools and observations undertaken. Teachers in 2012 show an increase not because of the students but because of introduction of Science and Commerce in the schools and the induction of Urdu teachers.

On hoardings kept all over the city, the Government claims that schools are improving. However, neglect is stark. In 2005, the teacher-pupil ratio was 1:54 and classroom-student ratio 1:85 in Rohit's school, while in the girls' school it was 1:51 and classroom-student ratio 1:84. Instead of improvements, the situation has been worsening. In 2012, for one room there were 268 boys and 188 girls, while the teacher student ratio stood at 1:60 boys and 1:97 girls. Enrolments have surely been rising, but as a teacher in Rohit's school pointed out, they were now 'herdsmen'.

The school does not have drinking water, the toilets overflow, the library has far too few books to be issued out to students and is only a small room, where not all students in a class would be able to visit even if they wished.

In the meantime, two private schools near Rohit's house have added classrooms, for 'secondary classes'. They lay vacant in 2012 as they were still seeking permissions and clearance for starting secondary classes. Rohit's father observed, 'He wants to study in a school where they would pay some attention to him. But he won't say so. In this age of *mehengayi* (price rise), children also know we can't afford it, never mind how many rooms they build.' Rohit's sister, however felt, 'If they have built classrooms they must be lying in wait for the children. It may not lie vacant for long.'

Rohit's school and his experience with denial of admission in elementary public school, resorting to private schooling, tuitions, the deteriorating financial condition of his family in the face of low social security and price rise, dismal condition of school knowledge in both private and Government schools dependent as they were upon rote learning, his becoming a part of a 'herd' that had to be controlled, even as private schools waited with empty classrooms for students, who were being expected to leave the Government schools, all represent the story of schooling in Morpur and the crisis of school and people caught between the State's neglect and private solutions.

Manufacturing Neglect within the Government Schools

There is no dearth of schools such as the ones in Morpur in the city. Studies have found Government schools in the city wanting in infrastructure and teaching aids (Mooij and Jalal 2009).[14] In another part of South Delhi, the situation forced students to write to the Delhi High Court to point out that in their classes, 150 students were sent to rooms with 20 to 30 benches, where rainwater flooded in, walls gave off electric shocks and teachers ill treated them.[15] In a recent school survey, it was found that 61 per cent of school toilets were cleaned only once or twice a month, posing health hazards to children.[16] The schools are short of not only non-teaching staff like sanitation workers but teachers also. Though the Government claims that it has a student-teacher ratio of 33.95:1 in its schools (Economic Survey of Delhi 2012–13), the gap between sanctioned strength of the teachers and the situation at hand is such that, thousands of principals, teachers, and labouratory assistants posts in schools have been vacant, forcing the Supreme Court to question the Government.[17]

It is not as if oversight led to neglect of the schools and the deteriorating physical and academic infrastructure. Enrolments have been the over riding concern rather than quality of education in the schools. This is reflected in the way policy has short changed schools with the RTE Act (2009) by giving the Sarva Shiksha Abhiyan norms, which are below what is required. Sadgopal (2010: pp. 40–1)[18] has estimated that by maintaining the norms of Sarva Shiksha Abhiyan, the Act, when fully implemented, would still leave about 67 per cent of the primary schools without a separate teacher/classroom per class, 75 per cent of primary schools without a Head Teacher, more than half of the upper primary schools without a Head Teacher, and more than half without even a part-time teacher for art, health, physical education, and work-based education.

The Governments at the Centre and State, however, have been unwilling to provide even the reduced norms, after rounds of self congratulation at implementing the Act. One of the richest states in the country, Delhi has not even contributed its share to RTE funding (Chopra 2012).[19]

In the coming years, as the funding from the states is expected to increase, the situation is headed for worse times ahead.

Public expenditure is being reduced as part of the 'lean State' measures and the Capital city of Delhi is showing how neglect can be publicly manufactured. The city which already has a population of 1.38 crores persons and a decadal percentage growth of 20.96 per cent, is a rapidly growing city with migration and increasing educational needs (*Directorate of Economics and Statistics*).[20] Instead of matching or attempting to catch up in provisioning, educational expenditure has seen a decline and stagnation, as the percentage of Gross State Domestic Product public expenditure on education fell from 1.67 per cent in 2004–05 to 1.36 per cent in 2007–08. The brief climb upto 1.63 per cent in 2009–10 has since fallen and remained stagnant at 1.60 per cent since 2010–11 (Economic Survey of Delhi 2012–13).[21]

Consequently, fewer public schools are opening up (see graph 2). Despite RTE (2009) and the cess levied by the Government, only 98 more primary schools added up, while at the middle (upper primary) and secondary level, 71 schools closed. At the senior secondary level, 184 schools increased but through mergers and upgradation of middle and secondary schools, rather than through opening up of new schools.

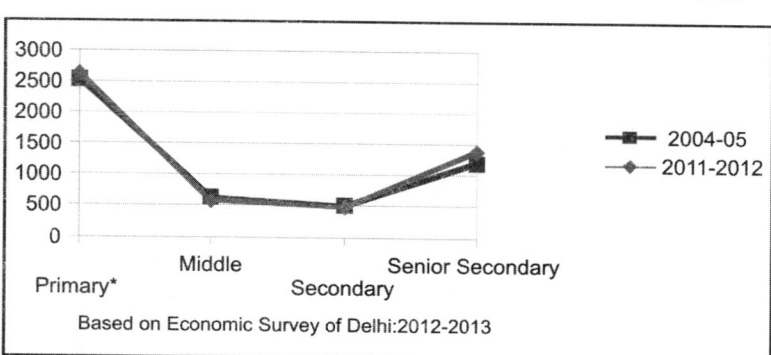

Chart 1: Number of schools in 2005-06 and 2011-12: Delhi

[Chart showing number of schools by level (Primary*, Middle, Secondary, Senior Secondary) comparing 2004-05 and 2011-2012. Based on Economic Survey of Delhi:2012-2013]

The institutional figures need to be seen in the backdrop of rising number of students who have expressed inclination and persistence in wanting to go to school. The enrolment figures show increase at middle and secondary levels, while the number of these schools were actually going down. The increased enrolments are being adjusted in the senior secondary schools, but then these schools have started looking like Rohit's school in Morpur complex.

Chart 2: School Enrolments 2004-05 and 2011-2012: Delhi

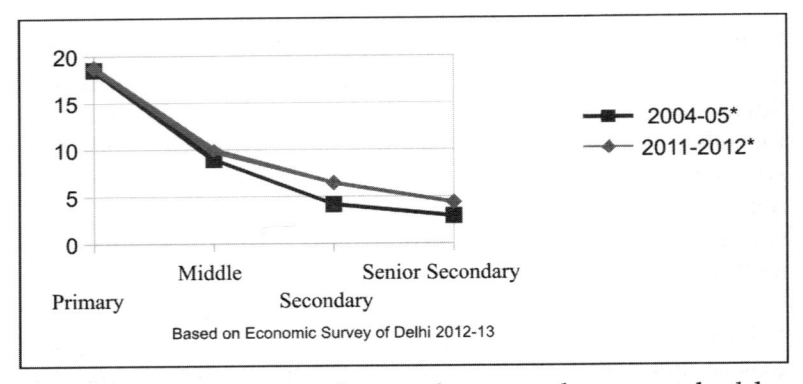

Based on Economic Survey of Delhi 2012-13

The increase in enrolments have not been matched by teacher recruitment either, and those who remain have become 'herdsmen' minding children and preventing their escape from school premises as they hurry through the course schedules. Corporal punishments have not stalled and students unable to deal with the school are left to their own and family's devises.

'Neglect', however, could lead to terrible tragedies for its students. Students have got molested and assaulted, gang fights and bullying are rampant, and only the 'herdsmen' teachers are pulled up for not policing enough, while systemic causes thrive. In September 2009, a stampede killed and injured several girl students on a rainy day in a North East Delhi school. The girls were engaged in an exam, the school was dark, there was no electricity supply to the school and several ground floor classrooms had got flooded. When a few hooligans entered school premises and misbehaved with the girls, they panicked and rushed out, only to be caught in a stampede in the dilapidated stairwell.[22] Four years after the tragedy, the condition of girls' schools remains more or less same with more girls in worse buildings.

As the State abdicates its responsibility with a 'neglect' manufactured by policy and financing, families are left with little option, in spite of dire financial condition and indebtedness, in the hope of a different future.

PART 2: The Private Schools

In the given situation where the schools they attend become less and less like schools, the private school gains the aura of an 'ideal school'. Balagopalan (2005)[23] narrates how this ideal of the school develops even among those in extreme margins of society, especially as they start comparing the differences between their own 'school for poor children' that is, non formal schools and the regular private schools in poor Kolkata settlements.

Yet, in the private school that Rohit attended upto class VII, the nature of learning was hardly different. The school, too, was of questionable quality and the absence of regulation has helped these schools grow in numbers (Mooij and Jalal 2009). As far as infrastructure was concerned it did not meet the minimum norms of RTE (2009) and was among the 2200 'budget' schools in Delhi that faced closure in March 2013.[24]

In the Morpur area where this researcher did fieldwork, these small private schools thrive because there are not enough Municipal and Government schools. These schools also do not take enough students on some pretext or the other, to keep out the numbers. In addition, for parents engaged in labour, immediate neighbourhood schools mean that they cannot go out for work and hope for a neighbour who can watch over the child, while they are away. The English medium school, and the hope that the private school will quickly get things done— ('by Vth he will be as good as X in the government'), has as much to do with the difficult financial situation they face as the uncertainty of being able to afford educational expenditure in future.

The teachers in these private schools were mostly girls, who had completed class XII from the Morpur Senior Secondary Government School morning shift. They did not have more than 30 to 35 students in their classes. They had difficulties in managing the classes but the numbers were less than that in the MCD schools in the area, where 60 to 70 students studied in each class. The girl teachers had younger relatives from their families studying in the school. As they stayed in the area, they also encouraged parents in their neighbourhood to send their children to these schools, and taught them through tuitions in the evenings after they returned home. They also felt endowed with a sense of respectability. However, they were paid only Rs 900-1100 in the schools, making it an educational sweatshop, maximizing surplus out of their work. The low payments made girls like Rohit's sister not consider this kind of work and turn to the factory. Though such teachers have been celebrated by neoliberal promoters, the 'teaching effectiveness' of these schools is certainly very uncertain. Nawani (2013: p. 20)[25] comments that since such teachers have little training, limited experiences, and a rudimentary 'repertoire of skills and knowledge required to transact the prescribed curriculum meaningfully', they are unable to take their students to higher pedagogic levels.

In Morpur, though most of these 'budget' schools are managed by people who live around the area, they have found larger advocates in their favour (such as Centre for Civil Society in Delhi) who have been advocating choice of schools to poor parents with Government support. The votaries of the 'budget' schools, however, themselves operate on large budgets and as Nambissan et al (2011)[26] map out, are internationally networked as well. They are actively engaged in making money out of poor parents (Nambissan 2012).[27]

In contrast to the budget schools, the elite and middle level private schools of Delhi have closed ranks against the poor. They have instead cultivated exclusivity to brand themselves and the parents of these schools go to great extent to ensure competitive success of their children (Vincent and Menon 2011).[28] Social networks, costs, student selection, and parents' interviews keep their schools homogenous as well. They have also been highly reluctant to implement 25 per cent reservation as per RTE and have also approached the court for relief from the poor as 'the gap is just too wide' (Manju Bharat Ram, founder of Shri Ram School quoted in Anand 2011).[29] This has also been accompanied by intensely discriminatory attitudes towards children and their parents who do manage to find their way in. Though the Government does reimburse private schools for taking in students from economically weaker sections, these reimbursements have been 'too low' for the elite and middle level private schools, thus leaving these schools to stage their charitable acts on occasions, even as resources are drained from Government coffers for funding discrimination. While the 25 per cent reservation clause for economically weaker sections in the RTE Act, has hardly opened up the elite schools for the poor, what it has opened up as choice are the 'budget' schools of doubtful quality that have been eager for Government funds for their business models. Thus, what is available for the poor in the private schools is a fundamental right towards a duality, where choice is not towards a private exclusive ivory tower but to a lowbrow educational sweatshop.

PART 3: The Private 'Makeover' of Public Schools

Neoliberal policy measures, having reduced schooling to a market, are now giving the public school system a private system-like 'makeover'. 'Makeover' is among the new[30] words that have got popularized by the media through its various serials, indicating attractiveness based on 'cosmetic change' and acquiring a different 'look'.

The bettering of the 'look' of Delhi's State schools is through an imitation of the dual model of the private school system. In this part, I present the case of the pace setting Rajkiya Pratibha Vikas Vidyalayas and the vast mass of Government schools that have opened up to numerous NGO interventions, and the agenda of one such programme, called Teach for India. I focus mainly on the impact of duality emerging in the public school system.

The Rajkiya Pratibha Vikas Vidyalaya (RPVV)

The RPVV are modelled after the pace-setting schools, like Navodaya Vidyalayas, envisaged in the National Policy of Education 1986. The Jawahar Navodaya Vidyalayas were set up to promote 'quality' education for 'talented' rural children in residential set-ups, after having identified them through entrance examinations. The studies by these Vidyalayas[31] have shown that, given the facilities in these schools, students perform well in public examinations. The RPVV, unlike the Navodayas, are non-residential urban schools. There are 19 Rajkiya Pratibha Vikas Vidyalayas in Delhi, which admit students in class VI, IX, and XI on the basis of stipulated marks obtained in the previous classes, following which they become eligible to sit for entrance examinations. It specifies that students from Government/Government Aided/MCD/NDMC/Cantonment Board schools can appear for the examinations.

Pace Setting or 'Escape' Setting?

The RPVV, however, is not based on nurturing specific unusual 'talents' as much as it is, for allowing a small section of students from amongst the various Government schools, to escape its dismal conditions as evident from a Cabinet note by the Government contextualizing the need for such schools:

> The schooling pattern in Delhi is clearly divided into two streams. On the one hand we have the so-called public schools, which charge high fees, and on the other hand, we have the Govt. and aided schools, which provide free education. Those who are being deterred by the poor standard of education in Govt. schools are forced to send their wards to high fee charging schools. The poor are also forced to send their wards to Govt. schools. In such a situation, very bright children are grouped with less than average children. Consequently, even bright children having potential suffer. This situation has to be corrected. Majority of the people are not bothered about status symbols and shall willingly prefer Govt. schools provided good education is available there. A Govt. school or a public school should be a matter of choice not of compulsion, as it is today. (Cabinet Note No.F.DE-15/Act/140/97 dated 27.03.1997)[32]

The Cabinet note thus decides that the public school system should incorporate choices for those 'deterred by the standards in a government school' and for a small section of its 'bright' pupils, even though 'bright' itself remains unspecified. It also lays ground for a stratified school order within the Government schools of Delhi and possible escape routes for some parents and children.

This logic of some pupils suffering as a result of being with others has also been raised by elite private schools to oppose induction of poor children within their schools under the RTE. The principal of Shri Ram School in Delhi has been quoted as saying, 'Teachers have come into my office and broken down. They say, "Help us. There is no learning happening for the other children. What we achieved in one week with kids before is taking three weeks"'(Anand 2011).

The Cabinet then decided to make a few islands of quality education for a few children, that fulfil minimum norms of schooling in terms of teachers, infrastructure, and curricular activities:

> Directorate of Education has given serious thought to this situation and has decided to make de-novo efforts to raise the standard of education in Govt. schools to a level acceptable to most of the parents. It has been proposed to select certain Government schools in different areas of the National Capital Territory of Delhi for upgrading to this level by making necessary addition to the school, making changes in the staff, *selection of good principals* and giving them certain more powers within the existing framework. *For giving good educational facilities, emphasis will be given on the selection of the teachers, the head of school, the students, the quantum of autonomy and system of achievement evaluation.* These schools *will also be provided extra facilities* for co"curricular activities and for inculcation of values. It is because of the *lack of these ingredients that the majority of the Government schools are not able to provide quality education.* [Emphasis mine] (Cabinet Note No.F.DE-15/Act/140/97 dated 27.03.1997)

Selection, as against universalizing opportunities, is presented as the key element for making the Government schools good enough to be considered as a choice. This includes selection of principal, teachers, students, and schools too.

A school becomes an RPVV 'on the basis of current achievement' and its teachers' 'ability to build up an institution.' Adequate and necessary funds are offered to a school thus, on the basis of school ranking and performance of the pace setting schools and the looking-like-private efforts begin not by ensuring minimum norms and providing a holistic curriculum, but by introducing the principle of competitiveness, and the 'micro efficiency' of the lean State. By linking micro-efficiencies and school ranking to allocation of budgets, the school's future is ensured. The neoliberal turn to performance linked plans and school financing gets into motion.

The neoliberal logic of the impossibility of school financing through any other means also gets rapidly unveiled. This permeates to all levels, and a Delhi High Court that was hearing on the validity of the selection of class VI children (which both National as well as Delhi Child Rights Commission had contested as being against the RTE Act (2009)) favourably responded to submissions of 'scarce resources' and dismissed it as a 'utopian state of affairs' that 'all schools can be raised to the level of RPVV'. It further went on to observe that in 'this unequal world the proposition that all men are equal has working limitations, since absolute equality leads to Procrustean cruelty or sanctions indolent inefficiency' (Delhi High Court judgement of 13 July 2012, Social Jurist vs GNCTD: p. 25) for continuing entrance examinations and the principles of selection for 10 to 11-year-olds in class VI in RPVV.

Assumptions of inefficiency override all other conditions afflicting the school and 'sanctions against indolent inefficiency' gets replaced as a greater virtue of schooling.

Towards Greater Educational Inequalities

The RPVVs, in the meantime, have been doing very well in public examinations, and been among the top performing schools. The analysis done by the Directorate of Education (Analysis class X and XII 2010–11) also shows 'sanctions against inefficiency' works as there is marked difference between the averages of the school that it calls Pratibha schools and 'Non-Pratibha schools'.[33]

It is a feature that brings in celebration among the Government and administration facing flak for the general condition of its schools. But the differentials between the two sets of schools have been widening, with a differential of almost 200 marks between them. It is a reminder to Saxena's (2012) pointers on Kasturba Balika Vidyalayas, that such excellences are actually privileging a few to subvert equality.[34]

In the meantime, the RPVVs are apparently becoming choices for those willing to consider between Government and private schooling as hoped by the Cabinet note:

> Even economically well to do parents were coming forward to get their children admitted in government schools in order to gain admission to RPVVs (one of the submissions by the Directorate of Education considered in the 13 July 2012, Delhi High Court Judgement: p. 20)

The economically well-to-do may get to choose these 'merit' schools but its selection procedures are such that those from labour households such as Rohit, find it far more difficult. Educational strategizing are best made by the middle classes (Vincent and Menon 2011) and entrance examinations require preparation and strategizing, but stuck as these students are in doubtful 'budget' schools, they are more likely to go to secondary schools at the bottom of the school ranks, as in his case.

The RPVVs, thus, with their selection process and exclusionary principles, are a 'makeover' for the Government schools so that they may look like the 'big and better' private schools. All this happens even when there is nothing established to claim that private schools are socially superior. The imitation adopts the private model of selection-based exclusivity, the market logic of resources being scarce-inadequate, the myth of inefficiencies, and financing based on school ranking and competitiveness among schools for ensuring that minimum norms are fulfilled. Or else face decay.

State Schools as a Platform for Market Expansion: Teach for India

The schools condemned to decay are also offered means, for a private 'makeover' by the educational market. But, the permanent teachers of the Government schools have been posed to be the biggest hindrance to this 'makeover'. Their reduction is part of making a 'lean State'. However, a lean State can only emerge from within the State and State schools.

Doing Away with Teachers and Teacher Education

The teachers, as the face of authority within schools, undoubtedly have a lasting impact on students. And bitter experiences based on misdemeanours and discrimination, can put a child off school and school learning. But this is not the domain of Government teachers alone, and could be rampant in private elite schools as well: the Shriram principal conveyed her biases to the press, 'I can't sit across the table from someone who sweeps my floors' (quoted in Anand 2011) when asked about students from economically weaker section in her school.

Instead of dealing with such attitudes of the teachers, neoliberal prescriptions have been for removal of professional teachers and their substitution with para teachers and their likes, as has happened through District Primary Education Programme (DPEP) and other NGO measures (Kumar et al 2001). NGO interventions in schools are part of the neoliberal governance model. Mooij and Jalal (2009), have found that in Delhi, this form of educational governance (which is based on principles of neoliberalism) has happened through established non-governmental institutions, but in other states they have come through corporate led NGOs.

One such organization working in Delhi is the Teach for India group. TFI is aligned in name and content with the 'Teach for America (TFA) Corps'—known for its stout stance against public school teachers. It has been advocating charter schools in USA and has pushed for undermining the long established public funded system of common schools (Miner 2011).[35] It became operational through an Indian NGO from December 2008, after a study by McKinsey and Company, and has since then undertaken a relentless media campaign along with media houses and celebrities to start working in schools across the country. In Delhi schools, they have been working since 2011. TFI, like its mother organization TFA, thinks it is not possible for certified public school teachers, to become engaged teachers. The organization thinks what it has on offer is far superior to what State schools have on offer. A TFI press note from Mumbai says,

Normatively, attending a BMC primary would have condemned her (a 12-year-old girl) to a rudderless, rote memorisation-driven education delivered in the vernacular Marathi or Urdu languages by unmotivated, inadequately trained teachers — to a life marred by unrealised academic potential. Instead Asira and her 30 classmates study a joyful, holistic, practical, and skills-based curriculum taught in English by (a TFI volunteer).[36]

Though a press note, what it does is to communicate the ideological nature and purpose of its programmes by demolishing the relevance of the State school system, trashing without any basis mother tongue education, and vilifying teachers. Attending a BMC school is equivalent to being 'condemned', vernacular learning is being 'rudderless', and Government teachers are apparently 'unmotivated, inadequately trained teachers'. Instead, it suggests a set of volunteers who would become not only teachers but leaders after a five-week crash course along with some mentoring while they learn hands on in the classroom.[37]

Along with teachers, professional teacher education is also made to appear redundant. This is overlooking the specialized nature of preparation required for elementary and secondary level teaching. Teacher training, as it exists, does have several problems. However, it is not as if better models of teacher education do not exist in the country (Batra 2005).[38] But 'neglect' of teacher education, too, becomes a reason for propagating logic of redundancy.

Disassociated Classrooms and Expanding the Market

The TFI training focuses on skilling the volunteer to manage the classrooms rather than engage with educational issues and its context. The context of the school is strongly disassociated from the classroom as emphasized by a TFI fellow working in a classroom in Delhi, in a video. He expresses his shock at the condition of schooling, claims that it is a problem of students imitating the community, and declares that he had set about '...segregating the school environment from the environment in the community' and '...tried teaching them values'.[39]

The values that he was talking about included that of

'generosity'. Many activities are done to teach the students the same. It is a sponsored class, and organized by Acumen Fund. This organization is a non-profit company that raises charitable donations for 'long-term debt or equity investments in early-stage companies' including education, to 'low-income customers'.[40] In the class, thus, while 'generosity' is taught, it is linked to venture capital of the sponsor, which promotes 'budget schools'. The classroom time, content, and students have been engaged on an agenda of a company that offers venture capital for tackling poverty. It is truly as the Acumen CEO announces in the manifesto that their mission is to reach where 'markets have failed and aid has not reached'.[41] The students have been approached and entitlements to education as a fundamental right have been replaced with notions of it being something you earn for yourself and also give. TFI and Acumen Fund demonstrate that they have successfully used a public school classroom in Delhi to expand the market a bit more. The 'budget school' finds a platform to launch itself in a State school camouflaged as a lesson for students.

Bound Futures and Pathways

The volunteers are selected from amongst 'outstanding' graduates and young professionals who are expected to work in under-resourced State and 'budget' schools for at least two years, before they embark on their regular lives and careers and assume 'leadership' roles. These volunteers with a few weeks' training become the antidote to what they project as the 'inadequately trained teachers'. But they are similar to para teachers in that they are flexible workers on a volunteer's salary, and are being groomed for leadership and as advocates of the neoliberal philosophy. Reports by volunteers and self-disclosures suggest that, this could mean remunerative corporate careers or degrees from Ivy League American Universities.

On the other hand, in sharp contrast, what is on promise for the children from socially and economically disadvantaged families, who go to the under-resourced State schools, is not clear. Perhaps, the volunteers on their two-year stints would know.

Caught between 'Neglect' and a Private 'Makeover'

Their emphasis upon a 'skills-based English curriculum', however, does not necessarily offer much hope for the students. The skills-based curriculum that it suggests for poor children from socially and economically disadvantaged backgrounds is not towards jobs and futures like the middle-class students and professionals who could become 'leaders', but more towards filling the skill needs of the country in lower level jobs as highlighted by it in another advertisement in *The Times of India*, which called for volunteers to teach English. It carried a photograph of a sad-looking boy in faded shorts, serving tea in a stall juxtaposed with another picture of a grown up boy wearing a smile and a uniform at a pizza joint. The text of the advertisement (see Chart 3) declares that the tea stall boy is on the 'edge of his opportunity' for a dream (pizza joint) job, if only, he had learnt some basic English lessons from the volunteers.

Chart 3: TFI advertisement calling for volunteers

THE TIMES OF INDIA

ENGLIS AATA HAI KYA?

He stands alone.

At the edge of an opportunity that could transform his life. A sharp, agile mind searching for an opening in the wall that stands between him and his destiny. Quietly sensing that this could be his big chance to get a job he's been waiting for.

When he's asked that one question.

Englis aata hai kya?"

"What will his answer be? "Yes" or "Nahi saab"?

And the fact remains, that even a basic familiarity with this potent communication tool can change livelihoods and transform lives.

Precisely why, Teach India moves on to an even more focused thrust this year. With a Spoken English Program developed in collaboration with The British Council and India's most dedicated NGOs, it aims to empower the less privileged with a working knowledge of English.

Which in turn will open up many little career opportunities in malls, sales teams and small offices across the new face of India. Because honestly, if we have to go any further as nation from here, every Indian has to be a part of the big surge forward.

So we're seeking a much stronger commitment this time round. Two hours, thrice a week for 3 full months.

It is more than we've ever asked for before. Because the simple truth is, many destinies will depend on you.

Question is, do you have it in you?

Spoken English Programme **TEACH INDIA**
OPENING JOBS.

BRITISH COUNCIL

If you believe you have it in you to empower livelihoods and transform lives, log on to www.teachindia.itimes.com

The futures are decided and planned for each class of pupils even as they are enrolled in the elementary schools. The opportunity chart of possibilities from education is strongly bound to their class origins. The middle-class volunteers could become 'leaders' propagating neoliberal philosophy, while the disadvantaged children from underprivileged backgrounds can find 'many little career opportunities in malls, sales teams and small offices across the new face of India' (see chart 3).

In the name of improving schooling through a TFI-like 'makeover', the under-resourced public school is made into a platform for undermining teaching as a professional career, discarding the need for rigorous teacher education, bringing the market into the classroom of the poor to promote new ideas of market expansion, and redrawing opportunity possibilities for people from different classes, yet keeping things confined to what the market has to offer. Surely, this is not the agenda of public schooling.

Conclusion

Bankruptcy is a neoliberal ploy for public sector disinvestment. It has been declared abundantly in India. In the case of schooling, bankruptcy has arrived through neglect, through the dilution of the norms around physical and academic infrastructure, stratified sets of schooling that have perpetuated educational inequality, and reduced the purpose of holistic school education to 'skilling'. In this paper, I have argued that public schooling in Delhi has certainly not been acceptable and that Delhi public expenditure has gone down, affecting the physical and academic infrastructure in the public schools where ordinary working, people of the city send their children. Their desperation for education is then diverted to the ideal of the private school. However, the private schools are both elite as well as inaccessible for the poor. The Government, when it decided to 'reform', has gone in for the dual private model. The imitation has meant sort-of-exclusive *pratibha vidyalaya*s or corporate NGO interventions, (the likes of TFI model in public schools for the poor). The 'private makeover' brings in the logic of the market in both places, leaving no one outside the domain of the neoliberal logic. However, this 'makeover' is socially diabolical as they repackage existing inequalities. Thus, a common school ideal (see Patnaik in this volume) has to be asserted and established for a real exercise of democracy and equality. This ideal—and it is indeed an ideal, because the existing public schools are neither neighbourhood schools nor common schools —has to be asserted. It involves 'going beyond the common sense' (Gramsci 1996: p. 420) of the market and would require us to make sense of the 'chaotic aggregate of disparate conceptions',[42] which the market poses.

Notably, when Rohit and Rohit's sister were asked what they wanted to do after getting educated, both in separate conversations had said '*samaj ke liye kuch karna hai*'—they wanted to serve the society. There is no consensus in this country that education and people are for 'makeovers' to serve the market.

NOTES

1. Herman, E.S. and N. Chomsky (1988) *Manufacturing Consent*, Pantheon Books: New York
2. McChesney (1998) 'Introduction' in Chomsky, Noam *Profit Over People: Neoliberalism and the Global Order* (1999), Seven Stories Press: New York
3. Giroux, H.A. (2009) 'Neoliberalism, Youth, and the Leasing of Higher Education', in Hill, D. and R. Kumar (eds.) *Global Neoliberalism and Education and its Consequences*, Routledge: New York, Oxon, pp. 30–53
4. ASER announces in its website its concern: 'Large sums of money are channelled into social sector programs: education, health, nutrition, and livelihoods, among others. Lack of information on how these investments translate into outcomes on the ground is a major barrier to evaluating their effectiveness and determining whether taxpayers' money is being well spent.' It is advised by those in World Bank, and is funded by big corporates and foundations initiated by the corporates working in education. http://www.asercentre.org/NGO/assessment/learning/education/outcomes/primary/reading/p/133.html, accessed 31 March 2013
5. *ASER (Rural)* (2013) ASER Centre: Delhi
6. Government of National Capital Territory of Delhi, Economic Survey of Delhi 2012–2013, available for download http://delhi.gov.in/wps/wcm/connect/DoIT_Planning/planning/

misc./economic+survey+of+delhi+2012–13, last accessed 2 April 2013
7. Sadgopal, A. (2006a) 'Dilution, Distortion and Diversion: A Post-Jomtien Reflection on Education Policy', in Kumar, R. (ed.) *The Crisis of Elementary Education in India*, Sage Publications: New Delhi, pp. 92–136. Sadgopal, A. (2006b) 'Privatisation of Education: An Agenda of the Global Market', *Combat Law*, 5(1), February-March, pp. 22–7.
8. Tilak, J.B.G. (1996) How free is ' Free' Primary Education in India?, *Economic & Political Weekly*, 31(4-5), pp. 275–85
9. Tilak, J.B.G. (2010) 'Neither Vision Nor Policy for Education', *Economic & Political Weekly*, 27 March 2010 Vol. xlv, No. 13, 60–4
10. Menon, R. (2008) 'The Bogey of Public Private Partnerships', Available for download *www.ieps.org.uk/papers1.php*. Another version Menon, R. (2008) 'Public Private Partnerships: Private Profiteers Peddling Education?', *Liberation*, July 2008
11. Kumar, K.M. Priyam and S. Saxena (2001) 'Looking beyond the Smokescreen', *Economic & Political Weekly*, 17 February 2001, Vol. xxxvi, No. 7
12. The ethnographic fieldwork draws upon my research for my doctoral thesis with Zakir Hussain Centre for Educational Studies, Jawaharlal Nehru University
13. Pseudonym used to maintain confidentiality of the respondents of the study
14. Mooij, J. and J. Jalal (2009) 'Primary Education in Delhi, Hyderabad and Kolkata: Governance by Resignation, Privatisation by Default', in Ruet, J., S. Tawa Lama-Rewal (eds.) *Governing India's Metropolises*, Routledge: New Delhi
15. *Social Jurist*, http://www.socialjurist.com/whats_new.php?id=5
16. *The Hindu* (2012) 'Toilets in Delhi Government Schools in a Mess, Reveals Survey', 30 March 2012
17. Mahapatra, D. (2011) 'SC spoils Delhi Government's pretty picture on education', *The Times of India*, 8 March 2011
18. Sadgopal, A. (2010) 'Right to Education vs. Right to Education Act', *Social Scientist*, Vol. 38, No. 9–12, September–December 2010
19. The fund sharing between Centre and State satnds at 65:35 from 2012–13. The other states not contributing includes prosperous ones like Karnataka, Maharastra, Punjab, Gujarat. Chopra, R. (2012), 'Kapil Sibal's Right to Education Act reeling under severe funds crunch', 5 May 2012, *Mail Online India*, http://www.dailymail.co.uk/indiahome/indianews/article-2140123/

Kapil-Sibals-Right-Education-Act-reeling-severe-funds-crunch.html (Accessed on 4 March 2013)
20. Directorate of Economics and Statistics, *Statistical Abstract of Delhi 2012*, Government of National Capital Territory of Delhi available for download *delhi.gov.in/DoIT/DES/Publication/abstract/SA2012.pdf* (Last accessed 7 January 2013)
21. Economic Survey of Delhi (2012–13) available for download http://delhi.gov.in/wps/wcm/connect/DoIT_Planning/planning/misc./economic+survey+of+delhi+2012-13 (Last accessed 30 May 2013)
22. Menon, R. (2009) Anatomy of a School Stampede, Liberation, October 2009, downloadable from http://www.cpiml.org/liberation/year_2009/oct_09/investigation_1.html (Last accessed 21 March 2013)
23. Balagopalan, S. (2005) 'An Ideal School and the Schooled Ideal: Educational Experiences at the Margins' in Chopra, R. and P. Jeffrey (eds.) *Educational Regimes in Contemporary India*, Sage: New Delhi
24. The neighbourhood low quality private school has been called the budget schools by the votaries of privatization. However, even these schools burn a hole in the budget of most parents in Morpur
25. Nawani, D. (2013) 'Reflections on Annual Status of Educational Research 2012', *Economic & Political Weekly*, 23 March 2013, pp. 19–22
26. Decision of the Delhi High Court, CM No. 5202/2012 in W.P.(C) No. 7796/2011), Social Jurist vs Government of NCT Delhi and ANR, 13 July 2012
27. Nambissan, G. (2012) Private Schools for the Poor: Business as Usual? *Economic & Political Weekly*, 13 October 2012, Vol. xlvii, No. 41, pp. 51–8
28. Vincent, C. and R. Menon (2011) 'The Educational Strategies of the Middle Classes in England and India', in Lall, M and G. Nambissan (eds.) *Education and Social Justice in the Era of Globalisation*, Abingdon, Routlegde: New Delhi, pp. 56-80
29. Anand, G. (2011) 'Class Struggle: India's Experiment in Schooling Tests Rich and Poor', *The Wall Street Journal*, 4 June 2011
30. 'A set of changes that are intended to make a person or place more attractive', defines the Macmillan Dictionary http://www.macmillandictionary.com/dictionary/british/makeover 'A changing of a person's appearance (as by the use of cosmetics or a different hairdo', defines the Merriam-Webster dictionary

(http://www.merriam-webster.com/dictionary/makeover)
31. http://www.navodaya.nic.in/welcome per cent20sbs.htm
32. Cabinet Note No. F.DE-15/Act/140/97 dated 27.03.1997 cited in 13 July 2012 Delhi Court Judgement GNCTD vs Social Jurist
33. Directorate of Education: Analysis class X and XII, 2010–11.
34. Saxena, S. (2012) 'Is Equality an Outdated Concern in Education?', *Economic & Political Weekly* , December 8, 2012, Vol. xlvii, No. 49, pp. 61–8
35. Miner, B. (2010) 'Looking Past the Spin: Teach for America', *Rethinking Schools,* available for download http://www.rethinkingschools.org/archive/24_03/24_03_TFA.shtml (Accessed 3 April 2011)
36. 'Idealism is not dead—Teach for India takes wing', *Education World,* 7 March 2013 http://www.teachforindia.org/media/media-archive, (Last accessed 4 April 2013)
37. http://www.teachforindia.org/fellow-ship/fellowship-faqs (Last accessed 22 March 2013)
38. Batra, P. (2005) 'Voice and Agency of Teachers', *Economic & Political Weekly,* 1 October 2005, pp. 4347–56
39. http://www.youtube.com/watch?v=Z5Hcy8u444Y, (Last accessed 3 January 2013)
40. http://acumen.org/
41. http://acumen.org/manifesto/
42. Gramsci, A. (1996) *Selections from the Prision Notebooks*, Orient Blackswan: Delhi

6

The Language Question: The Battle to Take Back the Imagination

Harjinder Singh 'Laltu'

Introduction

Most children in India drop out of school by the time they reach the stage of higher secondary education. There are a variety of reasons for this. Affordability, safety especially in case the child is a girl, lack of teachers, dependence of families on child labour, et cetera, are among the important material reasons. A very distinct and important reason is the stress education puts on a young mind. There is a psychological violence that a child experiences due to difficulties in the learning process and it often goes together with physical violence from the teacher. Much of this stress is due to the fact that most children in India are forced to learn, at the earliest stage of education, one or more languages that are alien to them. There is an increasing trend, where even the teaching of skills other than language is being done in either English, or in some cases, a language that is not the child's mother tongue. This is happening together with the large scale of privatization of education, with almost all the private schools claiming to teach in English medium. Other than high dropout rates, this has grave consequences in terms of unhealthy states of young minds, and possibly increasing physical violence even among those who reach the stage of college education.

That there are deep connections between language, linguistics, culture, and politics, is a well-known fact (Fabian

1986). European languages like English, Spanish, and French acquired near global status as the corresponding countries, that is, Britain, Spain, and France, respectively, colonized countries in different parts of the world. The languages came with the colonial masters as carriers of European modernity, establishing new politico-cultural orders of power. In all the colonies, in spite of Nationalist struggles for freedom resulting in the overthrow of colonial power, the sociocultural fabric remains severely fragmented. In many countries, where the freedom struggle was violent, a culture of violence has remained. And in others like India, where the struggle was relatively non-violent, new structures of violence have evolved. The sphere of education is one such arena where such structural violence is seen in issues like access to education, the medium, and the content of education, et cetera.

India is a country of enormous cultural and linguistic diversity. Nowhere is the issue of language as complex as in India, where there exist 3372 mother tongues, of which 1576 are listed in official records and the rest believed to be practiced without any official record. There are about 350 languages, of which 22 are officially recognized as National and state languages. A total of 87 languages have printed literature. At the time of Independence, while English was chosen as one of the official languages of administration, it was desired that it would be replaced completely by Indian languages eventually. The medium of instruction in school education was not a contention. Except for a very small number of private schools (some of them called 'public'), all schools run by the Government or by societies aided by Government support and even completely private schools used the mother tongue or a dominant regional language as the medium of instruction. The entire education machinery catered to less than a simple majority of the population, and it hardly appeared to be a problem. As democracy took roots, and as education became accessible and eventually became mandatory for every child, the issue of language became more and more relevant. However, the complexity of multinational and multicultural nation building allowed oppressive structures in education to persist.

Smaller countries like Bangladesh may have had an advantage in this regard. Noticeably, Bangladesh has surpassed India in many of the human development indices and it has an overall higher status. But even there, English has retained a hegemonic status and not much has been done to replace it with Bengali and other smaller languages in the higher education sector. It is interesting that Pakistan, where the major languages, English and Urdu, are both alien to most of the people, remains behind India in human development indices in spite of sustained aid from USA and NATO countries in the decades after Independence. It is worth exploring to what extent this backwardness is due to language policies.

Today, we have a variety of conflicting voices on language and education. Educationists over the world ask for the mother tongue to be the medium of instruction at the primary stage of education (Glanz et al 2011) and even for teaching foreign languages (Butzkamm 2003). The upper and middle classes, who have far greater control over politics than what their proportions in the population may indicate (and hence get their demands met), demand English to be made compulsory from the earliest stage of education. A similar demand comes from a section of Dalit intellectuals for very different reasons, emerging from millennia of oppression by institutions and upper castes, including in the arena of language.

In a world of conflicting political interests, it becomes a task for concerned citizens to identify those who are powerless and to voice their concerns. If language is a marker for privilege disparity, we need to understand it and take sides, keeping the marginalized at the center of our discourse. The negative effects of globalization are not just confined to matters of economy. The worst affected arena is the cultural one. Issues of language and education are tied to cultural politics intricately. The demand from some Dalit intellectuals for English, has to be seen with such intricacies in mind.

Language, Education, and Culture

The famous American critic Neil Postman once said, 'Almost all education is language education.' Even if we do not accept in entirety the determinism of the Sapir-Whorff hypothesis, there is overwhelming evidence of strong ties between culture and language. Linguists have deliberated on the intimate relationship between thoughts and language for a century. Vygotsky typifies the dominant trend in this debate: 'Thought is not merely expressed in words; it comes into existence through them' (Vygotsky 1986: p. 218)[1]. In Sapir's own words (Sapir 1958: p. 209):

> Human beings do not live in the objective world alone, nor alone in the world of social activity as ordinarily understood, but are very much at the mercy of the particular language which has become the medium of expression for their society [...] the 'real world' is to a large extent unconsciously built upon the language habits of the group. No two languages are ever sufficiently similar to be considered as representing the same social reality. The worlds in which different societies live are distinct worlds... We see and hear and otherwise experience very largely as we do because the language habits of our community predispose certain choices of interpretation.

Whorf extends this further: 'We dissect nature along lines laid down by our native languages. The categories and types that we isolate from the world of phenomena we do not find there because they stare every observer in the face; on the contrary, the world is presented in a kaleidoscopic flux of impressions which has to be organized by our minds–and this means largely by the linguistic systems in our minds (Whorf 1940)[2].'

Steven Pinker has stated that 'Language was the real innovation in our biological evolution; everything since has just made our words travel faster or last longer' (Pinker 1997). Like the air we breathe, language comes to us much before we are born. We are not consciously aware of the central function it has in human life. Irrespective of whether or not the listener is capable of seeing exactly what image in our mind we wish to transfer, we use language to describe things and to express our feelings. All our aspirations are formulated in a language. How good we are in persuading people depends on what language we speak. Our sense of humour is part of our language. All creative expressions like writing literature, and even metaphysical explorations like searching for the meaning of life, are materialized in terms of a language. The universe that we create, that is, the way we comprehend it, is represented in the language we use. Our notion of reality is highly dependent on the language we use.

One way we can see the intricacy of the relationship between language and culture is the difficulty experienced when translating a work of literature from one language to another. For languages that are far apart from each other, it is not an easy task at all to meaningfully translate from one to the other. Even when they are quite close, it is often an impossible task. It is remarkable how Rabindra *sangeet*, the musical compositions of poetry by Tagore, have survived for a century in Bengal as a distinguishing feature of Bengali culture, and yet, has practically no appeal to those who do not know the language. Translations and re-compositions in languages that are quite close to Bengali, have not had the desired effect. In spite of considerable integration of the Hindi and Urdu languages, rarely are the *ghazal*s written by Hindi poets as appealing as those written by Urdu poets. Interestingly, great poets like Firak Gorakhpuri or the contemporary Sheen Kaf Nizam, who grew up in traditional Hindu (Nizam a Brahmin) family environments, could not express their poetic constructs in the forms derived from the Sanskrit tradition; they chose to write in Urdu because they found it more convenient to express their feelings in Urdu. Language is, thus, more a mould and less a cloak of categories of thought. The linguistic relativity is a fact, and we cannot wish it away. This does not imply that thinking is entirely linguistic. All that is being said is that, language is probably the most important component of how thinking takes shape. Even when we speak one language, the choice of vocabulary, the phrases, the euphemisms, and the idioms used determine the character of a person. When the same person uses a language different from one that is most natural to them, often the content is devoid of the precision that is there in the natural language. We may think that we convey what we mean but the actual thought conveyed may not be the same. Several workers have pointed out recently that there are aspects of cognition that have complex relationship with the learning of language and intellectual growth, especially among disadvantaged groups, are strong functions of access to mother-tongue based education (Schroeder 2007).

If thought and language have an intimate relationship, then it naturally follows that culture, which is a compiled set of the characteristics of a particular group of people, defined by everything from language and a number of other features dependent on language like religion, social habits, music, and arts, must be very strongly bonded to language itself. Having said this, we need to recognize that the idea of culture is a contested one. There are serious conflicts based on global, local, and global sets of local cultures. Culture is a battle zone, where identities emerge and struggle to place themselves in a progressively hostile arena.

The role of education and schooling in culture reproduction can be seen by observing which cultural groups are being encouraged in formal education. It is in this sense that the issue of the medium of instruction gains relevance. With the replacement of Indian languages by English in the education of children from more privileged sections of society, have come the progressive marginalization of native cultures and the fast acceptance of the worst content of the Western cultures. This is disturbing even form a universalist perspective, since it is not the best of the West that is coming in, since that would require much more than merely making English a medium of instruction. We look into some more details of language, culture, and education in the following sections. We will often refer to the crisis as one between English and Indian languages. The reader is advised to read in it, as an extension, also a crisis between any non-mother-tongue alien language and the mother tongue.

Language and Culture Battles

The concerns for cultural crisis in relation to language are far deeper. There are some issues that are simpler. We discuss these first.

An argument can be developed that in an environment of

continuing hostilities, often it is forgotten that in spite of the Whorfian perspective that translation between one language and another is problematic, there remain universal elements of human experience. We take examples of four poems using the notion of a 'dream': 'Swapna Ghar' in Hindi by Kumar Vikal; 'Sootal Rahali Sapan Ek Dekhali' in Bhojpuri by Gorakh Pandey; 'Sabhto Khatarnak' in Punjabi by Paash and 'What Happens to a Dream Deferred' in English by Langston Hughes (Vikal 1993; Pandey 1983; Paash 1989; Hughes 1949). None of these poems is about the dream as a biological phenomenon, a neurological mystery that scientists endeavour to comprehend and analyse. While Kumar Vikal talks about the dream house of a woman whose life is destroyed forever by communal violence, Gorakh Pandey presents a woman dreaming of a life free of exploitation and with a place for love, that is yet to be. Paash tells us that we are defined by our dreams and nothing could be worse than when the dreams are gone. Finally, Hughes warns us that dreams that are deferred may not just sag away sugary sweet, they may explode. These four poems from different languages tell us that in spite of strong connections of language with cultural identity and the near impossibility of complete translations of thought processes from one language to another, there are fundamental human experiences that are cross-cultural. The instinct to survive, the struggle for a dignified existence, the resistance to forms of oppression based on inequality, the joy of love, are some such experiences which do not face the obstacles of translation and are often communicated fairly well in essence.

What is desired is a balance between the Whorfian perspective and the extreme universalism of those who believe that language is merely a cloak that we don while formulating our thoughts. Karl Popper has said, 'The fact is that even totally different languages are not untranslatable' (Popper 1970: pp. 56-7). Yet, it needs to be acknowledged that translation may on occasions involve a certain amount of circumlocution. For instance, if we attempt a translation of 'I wrote a hot poem' by the African American poet Nikki Giovanni in an Indian language, we will find that no tools are adequate for the task of explaining how 'one "goed" on red and stopped on green' after loving someone even though the idea that being in love leaves us lost 'somewhere in between' is translatable (Giovanni 1979). Quality works of literature from marginalized groups are, in general, highly intense and not translatable. Toni Morrison's *Beloved*, Alice Walker's *The Color Purple*, and similar works from African-American writing or Dalit writing in India illustrate the point. A good illustration is the quotation of four lines of *Abhanga* written by Tukaram that Dr Ambedkar used in the first piece of writing in the newspaper *Mookanayak*, which he started in 1920, or the *ulatbansi*s of Kabir and their contemporaries. Similarly, when we read the lines written by the Hindi poet Muktibodh, 'किसी काले डैश की घनी काली पट्टी ही आँखों में बँध गयी/किसी खड़ी पाई की सूली पर मैं टाँग दिया गया/किसी शून्य बिन्दु के अँधियारे खड्डे में/गिरा दिया गया मैं/अचेतन स्थिति में!' (Muktibodh 1985), we will be completely at a loss while searching for the translations of 'खड़ी पाई की सूली'. This issue will remain important forever in literary writing. The Nobel Prize winning Chilean poet, Pablo Neruda, said that the best translations of his own poems were Italian and that English and French 'do not correspond to Spanish—neither in vocalization, or in the placement, or the colour, or the weight of words.' He continued:

> It is not a question of interpretative equivalence: no, the sense can be right, but this correctness of translation, of meaning, can be the destruction of a poem. In many of the translations into French—I don't say in all of them—my poetry escapes, nothing remains; one cannot protest because it says the same thing that one has written. But it is obvious that if I had been a French poet, I would not have said what I did in that poem, because the value of the words is so different. I would have written something else (Plimpton 1981).

Thus, we need to recognize that, in the sphere of cognition, there exists a sub-space related to a linguistic creation of the mental universe that cannot be explained or elabourated using the usual tools of knowledge discourse. A balance leads us to limited or moderate Whorfianism (Chandler 1995), wherein we assume that the worldview may also be influenced rather than only determined by the kind of language we use. In other words, together with linguistic determinism to some extent, we must also look at the social context of language rather than only purely linguistic considerations. Similar arguments can be made about other forms of creative expression, like music and art, which define a culture.

The examples given above are modernist in nature, related to the existential angst of modern times. The deeper concerns are pervasive in temporal space. This is particularly visible in the context of the worldviews associated with languages in erstwhile colonized countries. We can go back to pre-modern times and examine the categories of social formations and engineering that existed before the encounter of the European colonial masters and the colonized countries. We find that there is a fast disappearing world of native cultures rich with aesthetics and wisdom that provide meaning to life. Sufi music and poetry is appreciated best in a native linguistic environ. Similarly, Bhakti literature and art can be appreciated best in Indian languages, but not in English. In fact, the reason for less of a divide between many Indian languages is the smooth and spontaneous integration across these languages that the Bhakti movement, including Sufism, carried out in the Middle Ages. The translation of works from non-European languages to European languages has undermined cultural worldviews in profoundly disturbing manners. For instance, an oft-quoted problem is the translation of '*dharma*' as 'religion' and '*Sanskriti*' as 'culture.' Some languages have specific words for concepts, and other languages use several words to represent a specific concept. For example, in certain forms of Rajasthani language, there are nearly 40 words for cloud, each meaning a distinct kind of cloud. The Arabic language includes many specific words for distinct varieties of horse or camel. In English, adjectives are used, such as quarter horse or dray horse. While there is no doubt that such 'categories' are deeply culturally rooted, one may argue that it is not clear whether the resolution of the crisis is culturally impossible. While it may be quite difficult (near impossible) to translate the aesthetic content of a work of art, it is certainly far easier, in a pragmatic sense, to translate an intellectual construct, albeit not on a word-by-word basis. In the case of abstract categories like *dharma*, the kind of un-verbalized thought embedded in it is different from what is meant by well-defined norms that go with categories of social behaviour. And if there is a wrong translation of such categories, the task is a simple one: correction of the error that was committed earlier. Thus, in a pragmatic context, paraphrases or translations tend to be less fundamentally problematic. However, in an absolute sense, particular words or phrases which have an important function in the original language may be acknowledged to present special problems in translation (Chandler 1995). In any case, whether we begin from a completely deterministic perspective or we choose the moderate alternative, we reach the conclusion in both cases that culture and language are intimately related. In the first case, it is a direct homogeneous relationship, and in the second, it has components that are originating in the social environment and are indirectly brought in. There is a two-way process—the sociocultural contexts shape the meaning of what we have to say, and the reverse holds equally—what we say determines our sociocultural existence.

There are two reasons why this 'deeper' crisis has drawn much attention recently. The first of these is a genuine issue, namely with more and more English language education, the ability to reconstruct a worldview associated with a verbal description or a 'category' in an Indian language is eroding fast. For example, almost all convent-educated young teenagers today will not be able to understand at all what the difference is between *dharma* and religion, while those educated via vernacular medium education will be able to make sense of it. The second reason is purely a reaction originating in the tendencies of cultural nationalism attempting to establish the hegemony of one or another sociopolitical worldview. The example of *dharma* and religion are often presented by both groups: those who are genuinely concerned about issues of language and culture, and others who are working with an agenda like Hindutva. A related issue is the notion of values and morals. Are there different moralities associated with different cultures? If yes, then does language in its association with a culture, foster a certain sense of morality and human values?

Globally, there are ideological confrontations emerging that range from humanist to reactionary values on issues of language and culture. While cultures that are dominant seek further respect and dominance, those that are marginalized are lost in mazes of multiple possibilities. It is interesting that a literature of questionable standing, namely that written in English, makes the most news in India, while even high quality writing in vernacular remains underexposed in terms of dissemination and citation. One of the justifications that are given by the neoliberal apologists of the English language is that, the language of the erstwhile colonial power is reclaimed as a language of resistance in the post-colonial era. The same explanation, when it is used by Dalits to 'claim' English, the language of power in India, is suspect in the eyes of intellectuals from the privileged upper caste minority. As Alok Mukherjee writes in his book *This Gift of English* (Mukherjee 2009: p. 312).

While English was initially sought by 'high' caste Hindus as an instrument of revival, and while in post-Independence India it was expected to serve the dominant group as a pipeline for communication within and a window without, now, groups that have been historically oppressed and disenfranchised, in particular, the Dalits, are looking to English as a means for emancipation and empowerment.

After all, the fact remains that the subaltern traditions of intellectual discourse have been marginalized in Indian languages. Why should it be a surprise if some Dalits try to claim English? If there is a point in reestablishing the deserving place for Indian languages, it must accompany reformulations that are reassuring to Dalits and marginalized groups in general. A rigid dispassionate outlook will keep the issue muddled forever; only with empathy for the deprived one can extend the debate beyond identity politics and hope for reaching a meaningful solution.

With the understanding that the arena of language is also, in many ways, one of culture, we can observe culture battles via the language divides. There are two major divisions:

a) The divide that has arisen because of major international languages that were tools of colonialism and imperialism; this divide is destroying the diversity that exists in world cultures, similar to how several other forms of diversity, for example, biodiversity, are destroyed by global capitalism. An example of this conflict is that between English and Indian languages. Skutnabb-Kangas has called English together with Spanish and French 'killer languages' (Skutnabb-Kangas 2000). Mohanty, et al., calls these languages, 'languages of social exclusion' that have destroyed the linguistic diversity, resulting in poverty and capability deprivation (Mohanty et al. 2009; Walker and Unterhalter 2007).

b) The divide that exists between languages that are hegemonic nationally and regionally—this is destroying local languages and cultures. An example of this conflict is the one between Hindi and regional languages and between a regional (state) language and smaller languages like the tribal languages in India.

Unfortunately, not all of the proponents of mother tongue as a medium of instruction in elementary education are mere pedagogues. Many of them are actually not interested in the mother tongue at all; they merely want to replace English with a language to establish new power equations. The most reactionary among these are those who want to replace English with Sanskrit. There is a sizable force of these revivalist tendencies and no amount of convincing restrains them. There are attempts to glorify pre-modern times and all existing social maladies are blamed on the colonial rulers. Such attempts may appear silly to a reasonable mind, but they are really originating either as negative consequences of the hurt that was caused by colonial oppression and subjugation of cultures, or as attempts by powerful groups to preserve existing social equations and relationships of dominance and subordination. The relation between the language used as a medium of instruction and culture is most clear when we understand these attempts better.

Education, Culture and Mother Tongue

In an absolute sense, the purpose of education is the enhancement of the knowledge acquisition process. If education is more than a utilitarian process and if it has any liberatory purpose at all, we need to ask what makes a mind capable of this. We will work within the paradigm that acquisition of knowledge (*vidya*) needs a formal process of education (*shiksha*). The goal is to help young people to develop their minds well, and become future citizens, who are productive not merely in the material sense, but also in the cultural sense (including aesthetics) and human sense (including ethos). Preserving the moral lives of children and providing them with certain human values is also a purpose of education. While recognizing that *vidya* may be acquired without an intervention of formal structures, we accept the vastness of organized information available today and the need to 'learn' as much of it as possible. Caution is needed here to distinguish the *shiksha* that is meant to destine the subjects (*praja*) as mere instruments of a 'system' (Singh 1987). We will assume that, the purpose of education is indeed to liberate a human mind from the confines of prejudiced growth, and to stretch their imagination to the limits of the horizons both spatially and temporally. It is in this context that culture becomes important. Culture is the resource upon which education is founded, especially at the earliest stage. At higher stages, education also contributes to the production of culture. As a learned person, each of us must be multicultural to some extent, but in the beginning of the learning process, we have only one culture, that of our parents and others close to the immediate environs. Cultural differences show up at every stage of education. Any epistemology has certain pragmatic aspects and this is where sharp differences may appear in the use of the language. In modern cultures, new skills are typically taught and learned through verbal instruction. In other cultures, especially in tribal societies, new skills are learned through nonverbal observation. There are cultures that encourage learning through language used, independent learning, and others that encourage cooperative learning. Noting such connections between culture and language, it then becomes imperative that the first few years of learning must be in a language that best facilitates the learning process. Educationists world over recognize that, a child comes to formal school carrying a vocabulary and a cultural worldview in their mother tongue, and any attempt to demand that they must learn an alien language at the earliest stage is deemed to be harmful. The pedagogical issues become redundant if the child experiences a crisis originating from their inability to accept a language that is not theirs, or is put into a situation stressful to them because of their inability to learn the alien language. Thus, many of the problems of inadequate education or learning abilities are related to the language crisis, experienced by those taught at the earliest stage of education. This is not to undermine the status of English as a global language or the status of Hindi as a predominant language in North India or the status of a regional language in a state in India. The general observation being restated here is that the failure in acquiring basic skills after years of formal education, or the large drop out rate before or after the completion of elementary education, is primarily due to the forced introduction of a language other than the mother tongue at the primary stage of education. This, then, also becomes the reason for the perpetuation of a world that is unequal, and hence, not secure.

We are witnessing in India, a race to replace vernacular medium education by English medium education purely from a utilitarian point of view. In terms of official sanction and power, English is better placed today than any other Indian language, including Hindi, and more than 17 states have already introduced English as a language from the beginning of primary education, namely Class I. When education becomes merely utilitarian, and that too in a world where a person does not find a role that is dignified and self-assuring, a crisis of multiple dimensions presents itself. First, there is the illusion that the language of power will naturally bring power sharing. As a result, poor masses are also attracted towards education in English for their children. When it becomes clear that this is not to be, then there is hostility towards self and others, with disastrous results. Among the range of problems that arise from education in a language that is not the mother tongue, the worst is the crisis ensuing from loss of imagination and original thinking. Mental slavery shows up at its worst form when, the enslavement is in linguistic terms. As a result of learning in an alien language that came to us with colonial masters and hence, with claims of superiority, our dreams are warped and our reality is more mystified than ever before. We can go back to the poem by Paash, where he so eloquently reminds us that of all the crises that we may encounter, the death of our dreams is the most grave in nature. Experiments conducted by a large number of groups have shown that when children are forced to go through elementary education in a non-mother-tongue language, they get depressed, they look visibly alienated, and are likely to dropout of education at the first opportunity. Mohanty et al., has shown that children from the Koya tribe in Orissa show signs of depression when, they are forced to learn in Oriya and there is a clear reversal, when the language of instruction is Koya. Such results abound from different parts of the world.

On the one hand, we face the reality that there is no real merit in English medium education (Rao 2013); the high quality often seen in convent educated students has to do with the investment of quality time and finances into quality teaching by the parents of the children. On the other hand, when addressing the issue of effective education in a friendly cultural environment, one has to resist the attempts by revivalists in redefining culture. In India, the brahmanical order has a strong political base and the efforts to establish the hegemony of Sanskrit happens through both systemic and informal means. This call for resistance, is not to undermine the importance that Sanskrit has in the canvas of Indian knowledge systems, and the etymological connections between the vocabularies of several Indian languages and Sanskrit. However, it needs to be recognized that the difficulties experienced by teachers and students alike, from the artificially constructed vocabulary for technical terms in Sanskrit, have enhanced the gradual replacement of Indian languages by English. Most often, these words in Sanskrit create no conceptual imagery in the mind of the taught; they merely carry a phonetic description that more than complicates simple observations and ideas, making the epistomy beyond the reach of most learners. It should also be noted, that many of these proponents of Brahminical order are actually brought up in highly Westernized circumstances, and their love for Sanskrit often happens at a later (adult) age development. Indeed, they are mental slaves of a feudal order that provided their ancestors positions of unchallenged and tyrannical power.

The forces that marginalize the holistic growth of a human being based on their own linguistic skills are many. Perceived gains in the market by engineered behaviourisms make our world culturally and socially regulated by free markets, and capital flow. This can be seen in how in the last three decades, the vocabulary of Hindi journalism has changed. Not only are brand names in English being used to name the vernacular product (for instance, consider a monthly paper titled *Public Agenda* or Hindi magazines carrying the names of their English counterparts like *India Today* or *Outlook*); even the words in the content are changed unnecessarily. Some of these changes are relevant and convenient, as for example, 'Supreme Court' for '*Ucchatam Nyayalya*' or 'Secretariat' for '*Sachivalaya*,' but numerous others are absolutely unnecessary, for example: 'exams' for '*Pareeksha*'/'*Imtehan*'; 'love' for '*prem*'/'*ishq*'; 'student' for '*chhatra*'/'*vidyarthi*'; 'games'/'sports' for '*khelkood*'; 'sportsman'/'player' for '*khiladi*'; 'court' for '*kachahari*'/'*adalat*'; 'Government ' for '*Sarkar*'; 'music' for '*sangeet*'; 'song' for '*geet*'; 'boys' for '*ladke*'; 'girls' for '*ladkiyan*'; 'city' for '*shahar*'; 'town' for '*kasba*'; 'newspaper' for '*akhbar*'; and so on. Often changes like these indicate an inferiority complex of the native language speaker. Using words like 'mother', 'sister', 'wife', and '*father*' for '*maan*', '*bahan*', '*patnee*', and '*pita*' respectively, is indicative of a cultural crisis. Using words like '*pakhana*' or '*tattee*' is regarded as uncivil, while using words like 'toilet' or 'shit' have become alright! In North India, the vernacular words for immediate relations have been replaced by the corresponding Western words, 'Mom', 'Papa', et cetera.

Such engineering is indeed annihilating the cultural world,

that many of the words that are rapidly becoming extinct carried with them. The situation is worsened by additional specificities, for instance in North India, major languages like Hindi remain extremely poor in areas like children's literature, or literature for the common person (romance novels, et cetera). Stubborn arrogance and showing off knowledge of sophisticated 'higher' ideas has made literary magazines intellectually inaccessible to ordinary people.

It is indeed amazing that in spite of repeated demands from leaders of National stature, it has not been possible to replace English by Indian languages as a medium of instruction in education and as the language of administration. Gandhi, Lohia, Tagore, and several other leaders of the Nationalist struggle expressed their views frequently on the subject, inevitably identifying English as the language of oppression. Gandhi called the imposition of English, a national crisis of the highest category. He thought that it was suicidal on the part of the learner, to use an alien language for learning. Tagore, perhaps the most prolific of them all, wrote eloquently in article after article on the need to make education joyful; the requisites for this including mother tongue as a major component. Unfortunately, these works of great thinkers remained matters of Nationalist discourse, and although they perhaps influenced education policies to some extent, no serious attention was paid to them while implementing policies. It is as if once the freedom struggle reached its political goal, such insights on the language issue were no longer relevant. As a result, in each state, we have lakhs of students failing in basic skills like mathematics. The failure frequencies in English language education are known to be very high; typically more than half of the student population appearing in final examinations fail in the subjects of mathematics and English language. Those who pass the examinations have spent more than half of their learning time in mastering these two subjects, ignoring all other subjects, especially creative ones like art and literature. Granted, much of the problem is the quality of pedagogical training for the teachers. But a large part of the problem is that the children have been made to suffer psychologically, throughout their schooling by the enforcement of alien languages on them. Innovative pedagogies fail to appear, since the alien language does not permit internalizing of conceptual elements, and students tend to memorize words with no insights. This is equally true for when artificial words in a 'National' language are imposed. Indeed, the language issue needs to be seen with a perspective beyond the paradigm of Nationalism, and more in the context of a holistic development of the human mind. Attempts to frame this within the national paradigm are bound to fail, or they may lead to undesired chauvinistic tendencies.

What to do

Is it possible to reverse the trend towards privatized English (or non mother-tongue) medium education? The many arguments given in favour of English medium education are all superficial. These typically invoke the international character of the English language, its role as a link language in the multinational and multicultural composition that India is, etcetera. It is known that learning an additional language comes easily, if one has mastery over their mother tongue. In a world with easy access to Internet, those who need to go across and beyond their geographical confines, can pick up languages easily. Indeed, illiterate migrant workers pick up languages functionally wherever they go without the help of any technology. There is some merit in the argument often put forward that, English is the language of science and technology. This only means that puritan attitudes in framing technical words must be shed, and commonly used English words for technical matters must be incorporated in Indian languages.

What has happened in the last two decades in the implementation of language aspects of education policies, is nothing less than cultural genocide. Learning English is one thing, but imposing it from the earliest stage of education, has produced two generations of citizens, mostly devoid of cultural strength and integrity, resulting in myriad social problems, a complete analysis of which may take years.

Given such a scenario, nothing less than a large-scale people's movement can be adequate to address the problems.

It will be a freedom struggle in its own right. Such a movement must not be spiteful towards the demand for English language education from marginalized groups, for understanding the roots of these demands is essential. They need to be cautioned with empathy that structural inequalities in access to knowledge and resources and the barriers experienced by students from such groups cannot be eliminated by falling for the illusion of 'claiming' the language of power. Instead, a renewed struggle must frontally attack the large-scale privatization, and simultaneous negligence of public funded education. People must be made aware that learning in an alien language destroys their meaningful existence. The affirmation of diversity, and the politics of representation for every voice cannot be done with education in a language that has the history of being used as a tool for large-scale oppression. It will not be an easy struggle, because the ruling classes have vested interests in depriving the majority of our people from opportunities to get meaningfully educated.

There is reason for hope. The number of people speaking one of the major Indian languages as a first language far exceeds those with English as a first language. This brings another question—that of participation of a sizable majority in the language and education discourse. At present, the idea that English is the only way to meet the current challenges is being sold to people, who are disabled by their social circumstances to participate in such a discourse. Thus, the entire enterprise of education in languages other than the mother tongue is reeking of inequality. If English comes with economic and political power, Indian languages have people's power with them. The lingua franca that English is claimed to be, represents a small English-speaking minority elite. In creative terms, they have very little to offer and it is no wonder that in all intellectual spheres, the contribution from the Indian elite to world knowledge production is far less, than what it should be, if we consider the proportion that it constitutes and the extent of national investment in education that they consume. Creative works in the English language from India, are generally of a quality much inferior to the works produced in the vernacular, however much it may be celebrated, because of the power that it carries. People across the country must work with commitment towards reversing the Government policy of forcing children at the earliest stage to learn English, or any language other than their mother tongue. All attempts must be made to enhance the quality and quantity of children's literature in native languages. A commitment towards becoming patrons of literature in Indian languages, in general, in all possible forms, must be developed.

Finally, an issue that we have left untouched here is the role of technology. Needless to say, it has a tremendous role in moulding culture. Hence, the use of technology in the context of language and education is something we need to look at very carefully. With the appearance of small portable gadgets that can translate from any one language to another, the debate acquires a completely new dimension. The least that we can say is that it becomes redundant how, national or international the character of a language is—and hence, education in the mother tongue and a stronger footing in one's own culture become more relevant. The technology of languages is an ideology in itself, that is likely to transform the world in ways that we are not able to fathom. We must look forward to it with an open mind.

REFERENCES

1. Butzkamm, W. (2003) 'We only learn language once. The role of the mother tongue in FL classrooms: death of a dogma', *Language Learning Journal*, 28: 29–39
2. Chandler, D. (1995) 'The Sapir-Whorf Hypothesis', http://www.aber.ac.uk/media/Documents/short/whorf.html
3. Fabian, J. (1986) *Language and Colonial Power*, University of California Press: Berkeley
4. Giovanni, N. (1983) *Those Who Ride the Night Winds*, 1st ed., William Morrow & Co.
5. Glanz, C., H. Pinnock, E. Gouleta, and F. Genesee (2011) 'Helpdesk Report: Mother Tongue Education and Girls and Poor Children' Human Development Resource Centre, UKAid (see also, http://www.heart-resources.org/2011/11/mother-

tongue-education-girls-and-poorvulnerable-children)
6. Hughes, L. (1990) *Selected Poems of Langston Hughes*, Random House
7. Mohanty, A., M. Panda, Phillipson Robert and Skutnabb-Kangas T. (eds) (2009) *Multilingual Education for Social Justice: Globalising the Local*, Orient Blackswan: Delhi
8. Mukherjee, A.K. (2009) *This Gift of English: English Education and the Formation of Alternative Hegemonies in India*, Orient Blackswan: Hyderabad
9. Muktibodh, G.M. (1985) *Muktibodh Rachnavali*, Rajakamal Prakashan: New Delhi
10. Paash, A.S. (1989) *Khilre Hoye Varke*, A. Chandan (ed.) Paash International Memorial Trust: Jalandhar
11. Pandey, G. (1983) *Jagte Raho Sone Walo*, Radhakrishna Prakashan: New Delhi
12. Pinker, Steven (1997) Organs Of Computation: A Talk With Steven Pinker, available at http://www.edge.org/3rd_culture/pinker/pinker_p1.html, accessed 11th February 2012
13. Plimpton, G. (1981) *Writers at Work: The 'Paris Review' Interviews*, Vol. 5, G. Plimpton (ed.), London
14. Popper, K. (1970) 'Normal Science and its Dangers', in I. Lakatos and A. Musgrave (eds.) *Criticism and the Growth of Knowledge*, Cambridge University Press: London
15. Rao, A.G. (2013) (Forthcoming) *The English–Only Myth: Multilingual Education in India, Language Problems and Language Planning*, Benjamin: New York
16. Rao, A.G. (2009) 'This Gift of English' (A review of Mukherjee, Alok K. (2009) *This Gift of English: English Education and the Formation of Alternative Hegemonies in India*, Orient Blackswan), *Muse India: The Literary Journal*, Issue 28, Hyderabad
17. Sapir, E. (1958) 'The Status of Linguistics as a Science', in D.G. Mandelbaum (ed.) *Culture, Language and Personality*, University of California Press: Berkeley, CA
18. Schroeder, L. (2007) 'Promoting cognitive development in children from minority language groups', *International Journal of Learning* 14(7). http://www.cgpublisher.com
19. Singh, H. (1993) 'Crisis in Higher Education in India', *Social Science Research Journal*, Panjab University, 2:33-45
20. Skutnabb-Kangas, T. (2008) (2000) *Linguistic Genocide in Education– or Worldwide Diversity and Human Rights?* Orient Blackswan: Delhi
21. Vikal, K. (1993) *Nirupama Dutt Main Vahut Udas Hoon*, Adhar

Prakashan: Panchkula
22. Vygotsky, L.S. (1986) *Thought and Language*, A. Kozulin (ed.), MIT Press: Baskerville
23. Walker, M. and E. Unterhalter (2007) *Amartya Sen's Capability Approach and Social Justice in Education*, Palgrave Macmillan
24. Whorf, B.L. (1940) 'Science and Linguistics', *Technology Review*, 42(6): 229; 42(6): 247
25. Whorf, B.L. (1956) *Language, Thought, and Reality: Selected Writings of Benjamin Lee Whorf*, J.B. Carroll (ed.), MIT Press: Cambridge, MA

NOTES

1. Also see Vygotsky, L.S. (1978) 'Mind in Society: The Development of Higher Psychological Processes', M. Cole et al. (ed.), Harvard University Press: Cambridge.
2. Also see Whorf, B.L. (1956) *Language, Thought, and Reality: Selected Writings of Benjamin Lee Whorf*, J.B. Carroll (ed.), MIT Press: Cambridge, MA

7

Constitution of Language: Neoliberal Practices in Multi-lingual India

Samir Karmakar

Language and linguality remain a contentious issue throughout the history of human civilization. The complexity of this contention increases with the systemic regimentation of the society—replicating hierarchical organizations of the capitalistic modes of beings. This article seeks to investigate the role of language in creating, distributing, reproducing, and legitimizing various modes of being and the tensions among them. This requires an understanding of the way language evolves in the history of recent past, as the embodiment of tensions among different modes of beings—permeating through the process of capital formation. Since historical development in itself is necessary, but not the sufficient condition to understand the issues of language and linguality, a discussion on contemporary linguistic practices with a special reference to India, will be brought into: we will discuss how linguality defines India in post-colonial period. This will, then, lead us into an investigation of Multilingual Education policy (henceforth, MLE) in India. Finally, we will conclude with a discussion on linguistic right to understand how conducive it is in nourishing the dream of multilingual world order—a world where no voice will be held back.

Language as Signifier of Consumer, Commodity, and Capital

To elaborate the above-mentioned outline of the discussion,

we need to start with the notion of 'language', which is not only the medium of expression but at the same time is the expression also. As expression, it contains a network of those narrations, which are crucial in appropriating 'long standing practices of cultural socialization often rooted in regional and national traditions' (Harvey 2005). What remains inherent in this narrative construction of 'regional and national traditions' is a process of alienation. You, me, and many like us—as individuals—stand in the center of this alienation. In a society, individual existence is relative to its connections with the existing systems of production and market. Dependence on the systems of production and market, needs to abstract away the individual from its reference, and reconstruct the multiple senses of it in the symbolic plane in terms of digits, tick marks, yes/no responses to gauge how and to what extent individual is subservient to the dominant alphabets of the time, namely capital, commodity, and consumer, to measure how useful individuals are to the system of production. Alienation dislocates meaning from signified-signifier relation to signifier only. It is not the signified rather the signifier, which earns utmost importance. As a signifier, individual existence earns meaning only from its relations with other signifiers. This network of relations constitutes a type of neoliberal symbolic space. In this symbolic space, individuals are being reproduced through the lenses of nation and state. True that creation of symbol and symbolic space is dependent on human actions; but once it comes into existence, it has its own life. It becomes as organic as we the humans are. For example, creation of money as medium of exchange is human dependent. However, its evolution into the monopoly capital, hardly leaves any opportunity to question its sovereignty. As a form of monopoly capital, it is so powerful that we can't even doubt it. In spite of being a symbol, its existence is much thicker than ours. Once what is supposed to be an immaterial abstract agreement of exchange, becomes the material basis for the neoliberal culture.

Individual choice of language cannot escape this vicious circle made up of capital, commodity, and consumer; because 'individuals' and 'choices' are historically formed through the process of alienation. If so, then how responsible and accountable an individual could be in making a choice of language. Skutnabb-Kangas *et al.* (2009) argued obliquely that 'the rhetoric of 'choice' is a pure spin in a world in which 'choice' is as free as the free market'. Literally, this means how implicit instructions are directing our choices. Reflection of this fact can be noticed in Shukla and Bordoloi's (2013) report from DISE education survey, which states that 'the share of private schools in total primary and elementary enrolment was 27 per cent and 37 per cent respectively' during 2010–11. Earlier, Mukherji (2012) reports from the same source that the number of children enrolled in English medium schools show 274 per cent rise since 2003–04. What can at most be shown from this discussion is, that a monolingual and monolithic ordering principle is already in place. We will identify this monolingual and monolithic ordering principle as English. The assertion of English in upper case, i.e. English, conceptualizes itself not much as a language of communication, but as a process/medium, which shapes our identity, our thought, and our aspiration through various means. As a process, it serves the purpose of internal reorganizations and new institutional arrangements to accommodate locals in the framework of competing global market forces. Stuart Hall's following argument, as is quoted by Canagarajah (2005), seems to be relevant here: 'global is the self-presentation of the dominant particular. It is a way in which the dominant particular localizes and naturalizes itself, and associates with it a variety of other minorities'. If so, then the 8th schedule of the Indian Constitution is actually a process to anglisize the vernaculars as the local associates of the Global English. Like English, all of them in one way or other construct the alphabets of consumer, commodity and capital. But, how does this construction works?

ANGLISIZED Bangla as Differential Positioning Mechanism: A Case Study

India, as a linguistic area, in the neoliberal regime is the projection of symbolic relations among the various language-speaking communities. The position of a speech community and the speech form it uses in a given point of space and time is historically determined. Consider the case of Bangla language. Projection of Bangla, as a signifier, is historically shaped by various principles of control, like the introduction of print media and school, along with the activities like translation of Bible, Law books, writing of grammars and text books for the vernaculars, preparing dictionaries et cetera, started towards the end of the eighteenth century. By that time, 19 law books were translated into Bengali (Shaw 1987). One can even find the name of School Book Society in the documents of Colonial Bengal. In between 1801 to 1832, Baptist Missionary of Shrirampore, with which William Carry's name is associated, published 2,12,000 books. In 1834, Baptist Mission of Shrirampore announced the publication of Bibles in 47 languages. In between 1818 to 1822, they received a print order of 47,946 books from the School Book Society of Kolkata (Shripantha 1977). This simply shows how crucial is the inception of print capital in fixing the status of Bangla as a signifier simply by opening several new horizons in market economy through its transmutation into commodity.

Neoliberal reality of Bangla—in synthesis with other signifiers in the linguistic space of 8th schedule—presupposes those connections, which it develops with other forms of non-linguistic signifiers during the colonial period. For example, proliferation of printed materials in colonial Bengal requires establishment of some other industries, like paper mill, foundry etc. In 1790, some Mr Brown established the Calcutta Paper Mill. This one was a failed effort. However, soon, with the patronage of the East India Company, a new mill was established in Bankipur followed by the birth of few other mills. This has a deep impact on the indigenous economical system in India at that time. With the introduction of newer technology, indigenous technique of producing paper at Patna lost its battleground. This indigenous technique fails to meet up the increasing demand of high quality paper in low price. On the other hand, both main and downstream industries introduced newer forms of labour divisions (or, in other words, significations) like moulding, composing, proof checking etc.

Emergence of Bangla in the symbolic space of India, as a signifier, embodies the complex network of various other developments, namely developments of market, labour, and industries: This formative period of Bangla envisaged a tremendous growth in the number of the people in the mills—the temples of Modern Industrialized Bangla. From 1879 to 1901, the numbers of people involved in cloth and jute mills as labour, increased by 295.5 per cent and 316 per cent respectively. Data shows, Kolkata had the highest numbers of mercantile houses (which is 62) till 1837, leaving behind Bombay (17), Singapore (15), Madras (10), Canton (11), and Penang (2) (Ghosh 1977). This indicates the awakening of a continent in the world geography—the inception of a growth, which continental history has never seen before.

The inception of this new era also demands new people. It needs to destroy those traditions, which stand against its development. It needs new forms of training, and newer versions of training manuals to introduce new values. This is the time when Madanmohan Tarkalankar (1850) wrote in his primer *'shishushikkhaa'*, those who write and read, can ride coach and horse.[1] The verse sets the norm in favour of the primacy of script, and individuals' mastery on it. It upholds the significance of literacy in achieving a prosperous life, as the moral of the modern times. This is not a rhyme, but a proposition, which states what could be the make up of an individual. It says how an individual should look like in future!

In spite of being the author of this historical truth, Madanmohan Tarkalankar's primer faced extinction, just like Mir Mosarraf Hosen's primer *'musolmaaner bangala shikkhaa'*, because of containing texts, which promote traditional values. Mosharraf's primer contains text like Allah is one, Allah is bigger than all, Allah has no fault and has no scandal.[2] Or, for example, Madanmohan Tarkalankar wrote in first part of *'shishushikkhaa'*, 'do enjoy, take dowry' (literal translation).[3] Neither the family prestige nor the lineage nor the caste identity, religious identity, and misappropriation of another's wealth but, the potential in terms of one's capacity to write and read becames the sole determinant of individual achievement.

In brief, the formation of industrial society, capital, and market gave Bangla a new lease of life—a life of signifier growing in the vicinity of other signifiers. Similar stories can also be found in other parts of India. All these stories might have some shuttle differences among themselves, but what they do share is the saga of commodity, consumer, and capital.

India as a Symbolic Space

Having an understanding of how language as a signifier emerges in the symbolic space, the discussion will concentrate now on how differential positioning of language is practiced within the framework of Nation and State, with a special reference to India. In spite of having its immense significance in the functioning of State, no definition of language is given in any official documents in India. Laitin (2000) argues that, 'theories of nationalism, democracy, regional assertiveness, and civil war have relied on vague and unspecified notions of linguistic heterogeneity, based upon estimates of the 'mother tongues' of a population'. In other words, the democratic instability of modern State is directly connected with the recognition as well as with the repudiation of regional assertions of different communities in the linguistic mosaic of Indian nationalism. This results into a series of questions: What would be the definition of mother tongue? Is it the language that a baby learn from her/his mother? Is it the language in which a baby converse in his/her childhood? What is the dialectics between language and mother tongue?

Though the puzzles are many, the answers revolve around the unpacking of one single concept—namely, language. What could be the definition of language is not the right question to start with; rather, we need to ask how language is produced through different processes. In other words, what is the legitimate language is not the issue at all; rather, one should ask how one particular language among many others is appropriated as a product—legitimized as 'the signifier' among the signifiers.

Linguistics: Litigating the Official Version of Language

Disciplinary rigour of Linguistics contributes a lot in this process of legitimizing language as 'the signifier' among the signifiers. The type of language, analysed and discussed in core linguistics, is objectified in a manner that it hardly recognizes it, as a consequence of a complex set of social, historical, and political conditions of formation, as Bourdieu (1991) indicated some time back. Linguistics hides the relations a language possesses with the other signifiers to bypass the contentious issues involved with formation of three C-s. Therefore, in academics, language with a plural marker '–s', is simply reduced into an absolute singularity in the name of scientific reductionism to make the problem tractable! Let's name this approach as 'official approach'. Instead of conceiving the meaning construing capacities of different languages differently, official approach explains languages with respect to a theoretical frame where chances are less to appreciate the otherness of the languages spoken by different groups of people. This frame dissects languages into parts, and compares similar and dissimilar parts within a language and also across the languages to organize them into a body of systemic knowledge. A form of linguistic knowledge abstracted away from its ground realities, then, is used as the basis of territorial and cultural autonomies—constituting the bases for the mega-systems, like market and nation.

Census: Officiating the Rituals

The theoretical frame and its way of dissection are generally not allowed to be questioned, since, they are considered as the most vital organs with the help of which government maintains the general health of the State by institutionalizing some languages out of many. By general health, I mean both economic growth and the provision of public goods. —It is believed linguistic diversity is negatively associated with both of them (Clingingsmith 2006). Scientific terms, like 'rationalization', 'classification' et cetera, are used to legitimize official rituals of including and/or excluding the other in a regular interval, to take control over the voices of dissents, which come into existence as the accidental by-products of the official policies. In terms of their importance, these processes can only be compared with the religious rituals. In spite of being empty in their content, they seem to be so rigid and so tightly knitted in the framework of nation and State, that no easy escape at least in near future is anticipated. They are being repeatedly used (as is noticed in the functioning of Office of Registrar General and Census Commissioner, while performing the rituals of census in the interval of every ten years) to come up with the newer versions of defensive mechanisms, by imposing newer versions of power equations among the equals to subdue a larger diffused mass of unequals. To minimize the threats of disintegration, mega-systems have discovered many tools and techniques to eradicate the chances of its own annihilation: language, map, currency are probably the most important among those tools and techniques.

Language, Map, Currency: Newer Forms of Spaces

If we open a linguistic map of India (fig. 1), we will notice how territory is distributed among those languages, which have passed the official tests of rationalization and classification in the name of 'mainstreaming'. With every ritual in the name of governance, democracy, and mainstreaming, it alters the existing make up of the nation and State by populating Eighth Schedule of Indian Constitution with the junior members. With every ritual Indian Territory and the associate virtual spaces get redistributed among the equals (though with the footnotes in the 8th Schedule mentioning who are the junior most!).[4]

As a ritual, official versions of rationality and classification are important in deciding who has the access to the territorial resources and who does not. This has a direct bearing not only on the survival of the languages but also, on the survival of the communities and the individuals. Extending this argument a bit then, we can say: just like the way, Natural Selection in the Darwinian model of biological evolution determines the appearance and disappearance of the genetic traits, official edition of mainstreaming decides appearance and disappearance of the languages in India. But, how?—To answer

Constitution of Language 169

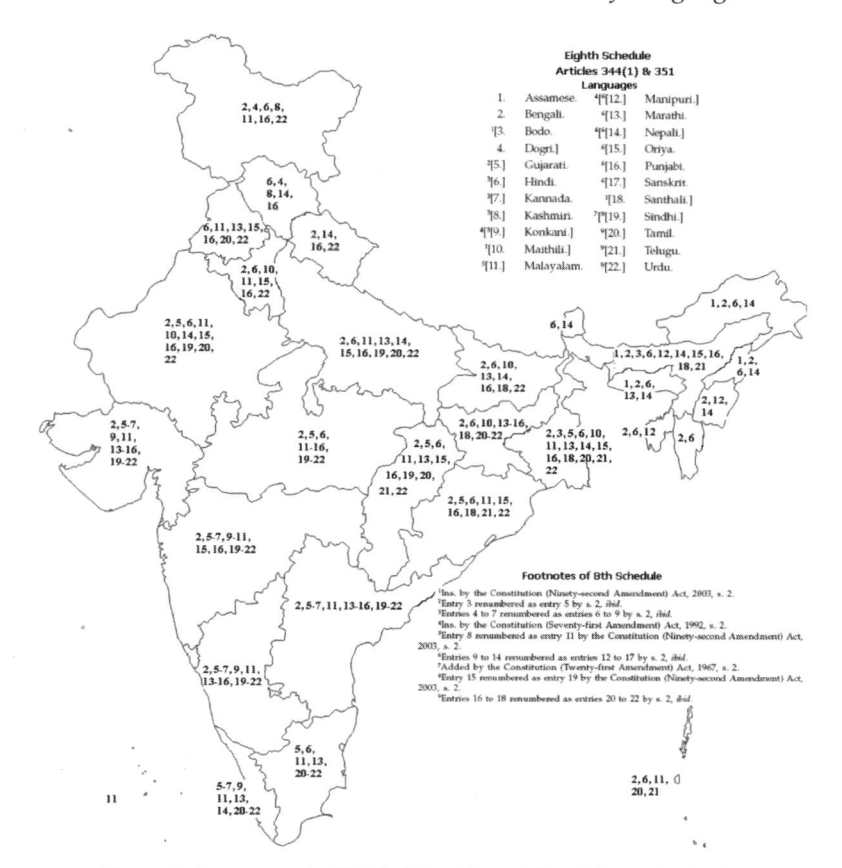

Figure 1: *Languages in Eighth Schedule and the claim on territories*

this question we will refer to two facts from the census. First one, is about the rule of excluding those speech forms having less than 10,000 claimants from the list of languages, that is 8th Schedule. In contradiction to this, speech forms like Bhojpuri (33,099,497), Chattisgarhi (13,260,186), Garhwali (2,267,314) are considered not as the languages of 8th Schedule but, as the mother tongues of Hindi in spite of having more than 10,000 claimants. This measure definitely results into the suppression of many voices. Second one, is about the inclusion of Maithili in the 8th Schedule in 2001 census elevating its status as mother tongue under Hindi to a Language containing no mother tongues under its head! This has a direct bearing on other issues also. One such issue we will discuss here: Before 2001, Maithili was not in bilingual relation with the mother tongues of Hindi. However, from 2001 onwards, because of being included in 8th Schedule, it stands in bilingual relation with all the mother tongues of Hindi. This simply shows, how insubstantial is the processes of rationalization and classification.[5] Insubstantiality of these processes unearths the hidden terrains of ambiguity, contradiction, and struggle beneath the symbolic space. What follows in, then, is that defining language and mother tongues is a neverending process, which in turn contributes in constructing tradition through which democratic nature of the State refracts and reflects the interplay of differences.

Script, Territoriality, and Business

In contrast to the linguistic map, if we consider the map of scripts (fig. 2), territorial divisions become less cumbersome because the number of scripts used in India is much lesser in comparison to the number of languages enlisted in the Eighth Schedule.

Though, official rituals of Registrar General and Census Commissioner redefine the power equations among the languages in every census by adding and deleting few languages, it will hardly dare to disturb the territorial distribution of the scripts. The reason no-doubt lies with the nexus holding between the script and the market. —After all, this nexus costs multi-million dollar business every year through publication houses and medias of various sorts. For example, in December 2012, Business Standard reports Bengal Print Media to lock in 48 per cent growth, which aggravates high-profile media war between ABP and Bennett Coleman and Co. Same war was witnessed some time back in Mumbai among Times of India, DNA, and Hindustan Times. Book bazaar is also not an exception: A recent report revealed how vibrant the book bazaar is in India (Sahai 2009): Harper Collins, a major foreign publisher, is growing in India at the speed of 30 per cent annually. Even though the size of English literate population (65 million) is much smaller in comparison to India's total population, it is much ahead of UK (60 million), and Australia

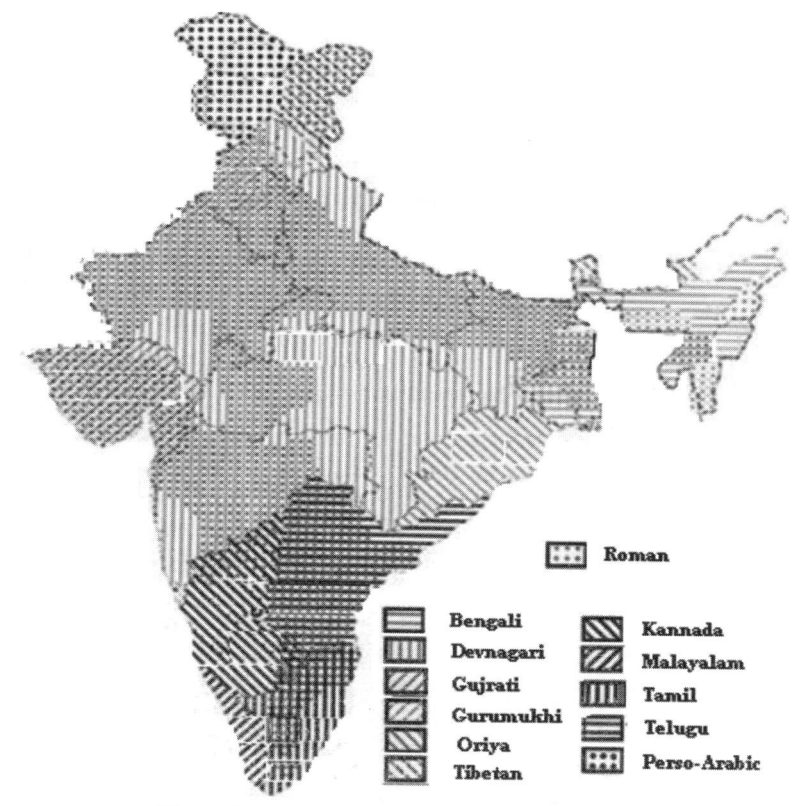

Figure 2: *Territorial distribution of the Indian Scripts*

(20 million). India has a growing market for English language preceded only by US (215 million). Vernaculars are also not lagging behind. As per the report of Federation of Indian Publishers, the number of titles published in India in 2004 is 82,537. Even if we exclude the titles having no ISBN number, the shares of the vernaculars in the market are huge. Figure 3 is representing the symbolic space of the book bazaar construed by the vernaculars. The topography of the space represents, vernaculars' holds on the process of capital formation and the relative hierarchy among themselves.

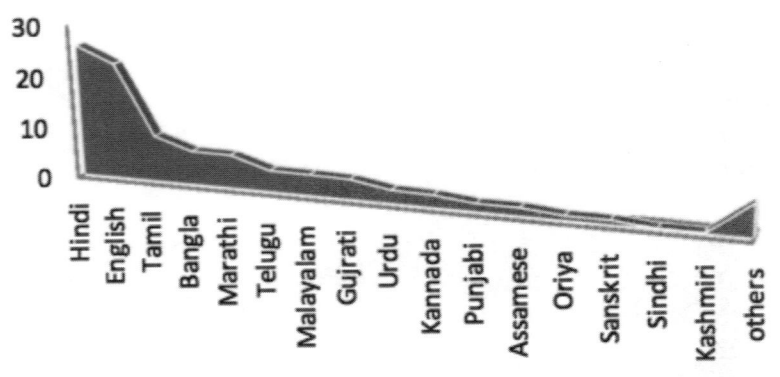

Figure 3: *Landscape representing vernaculars hold on the market*

The acclivity/declivity of the symbolic space, representing hierarchy among the vernaculars, depends on from which perspective one is looking at it also. For example, with the inclusion of criterion like 'per capita number of titles published per 100,000 persons', the landscape projects a different type of order among the vernaculars (ref. fig. 4):

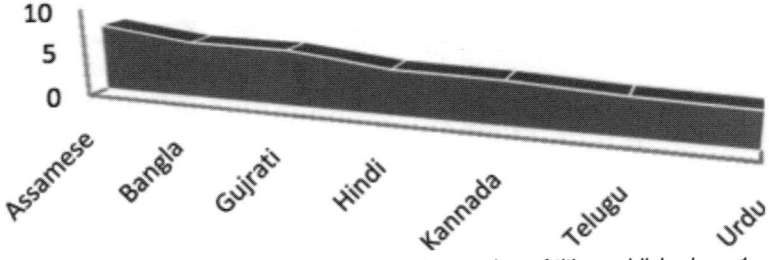

Figure 4: *Landscape representing 'per capita number of titles published per 1 million persons'*

Another reason, for not disturbing the territorial distribution of the scripts is their significance in imposing permanence on relations among the mega-systems—like *panchayat*s, states, political parties, multinational companies, courts, and democracies. At the International level, when Roman script is being used for documentation, in national level Devnagari script along with its regional allies are used as the local associates of the global Masters. The distribution of the scripts and their scope in documenting the national tradition in the milieu of the global economy ultimately create a hierarchy through which megasystems are intervening in the life of the individuals.

As one another tool and technique, we will bring currency notes in our discussion from two distinct phases of Indian Nationalism: one from the pre independent era, and, another from post independent period (fig. 5).

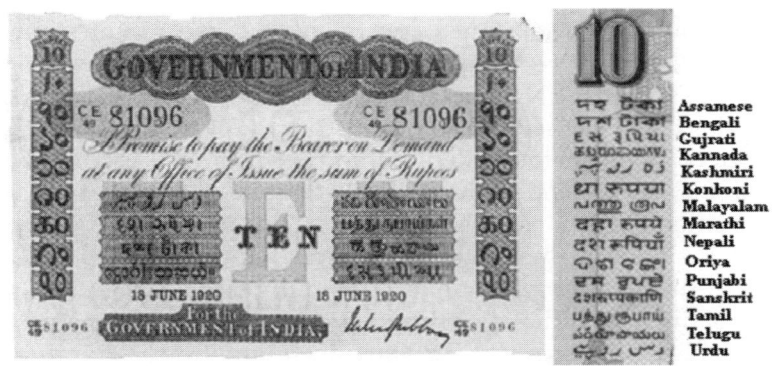

Figure 5: *Languages in the symbolic space of currency*

The number of linguistic scripts on these two notes will tell us how the State perceives the sub-national territorial autonomies in pre and post-Independence eras; what amount of individual freedom in terms of individual access to the territorial and national resources are licensed to whom and how. Concentrating on the note of 1920 will also reveal, how colonial masters had perceived the relative significance of the recognized linguistic nationalities in those days. One can easily notice a distinct break between English numeral 10 and the numerals from the vernaculars. Rulers of independent India didn't recognize this colonial break between English and the vernacular, but has still failed to come out of colonial hegemony whose reflection can be easily noticed in the alphabetical ordering of the languages both in currency, and in the Eighth Schedule. In current Indian currency, Indian scripts are sequenced following the order of Roman alphabets! This instantiates Macaulay's dream, articulated in 1836, containing a colonial intention of creating 'a class of persons, Indian in blood and color, but English in taste, in opinion, in morals and in intellect'; we are still bearing Macaulay's dream with us as an invisible coronet symbolically represented at the top with the depiction of a much bolder and pronounced English number **10**, followed by an enlightened fraternity of Indian scripts. Such instances show how the order of the political and economical alphabets are continuously dividing as well as suppressing us into smaller pieces, to strengthen the hold of the global market by weakening the State's control over those innumerable nations, which live within the Nation. The trend of inventing nations within the Nation, can only be compared with the cancer in the body of the State—a cancerous growth, which splits society in an uncontrolled fashion, affirming a permanent fragility to the Indian State. The immune systems of these innumerable nations within the Nation, are determined by their relative holds on the territorial resources, which again, are useful in defining the regional tone of the global capital. As a consequence, India, as a linguistic area, always remains a fearsome battleground for warring linguistic communities whose shadows can even be seen in the rituals of reorganizing Indian states again and again, even in the post-Independence period. Under this situation, linguistic right in the context of multilingualism needs a deeper look, to understand the problems of Education and formation of Nation from a holistic viewpoint.

Linguistic Space at the Level of the Individual and Education as Space Engineering in India

The language that the children learn in their home environment differs from the languages valued by the institutions and organizations. This difference is recognized as the universal problem in the educational systems across the countries. The problem is worst in the developing country like ours, due to different intervening layers of various issues, pertinent to economical growth and increasing population size.

In India, the problem becomes acute mainly because of the number of different languages people speak in their day to-day's conversation. As per the Census Report 2001, the number of languages specified in the Eighth Schedule is 22. The report has identified 122 languages and 234 mother tongues. Even if we overlook the politics of defining the status of language, and the criterion census has fixed to exclude a good number of languages under the category of 'others', the situation seems challenging since, we clearly lack resources to deal with the problems of multilingual education at this larger scale.

Under this situation, when National Curriculum Framework 2006 (henceforth NCF 2006) position paper advocates the necessity for teaching of Indian Languages, we need to know how many languages: Are we talking of teaching 1635 odd languages? Are we talking about the teaching of 122 languages and 234 mother tongues? Or, should we narrow down our focus to the teaching of 22 scheduled languages? Interestingly, policymakers, academicians, and politicians prefer to keep themselves silent on this account. Therefore, the entire burden of implementing the suggestions made in NCF 2006 position paper actually goes to them, who want to translate the suggested objectives into real practices.

Though, position papers and policies are explicitly arguing for linguistic rights, mother tongue instruction, and inclusion of the home language, one thing we need to understand, as has been already pointed out by researchers, is that policies and positions papers are generally designed to minimize the complexities of social multilingualism, which are considered to be inconvenient for the functioning of the State and Nation. This can be traced not in the explicit suggestions but, in the implicit assumptions. These implicit aspects of a policy also reflect the perception of the common mass, which is constructed as we have argued earlier. Failing to judge the common perception and its evolution will definitely lead to the adverse situation not expected before. For example, in past few years, the number of English medium students is grown by 150 per cent in spite of the government policy of promoting MLE (Nagarajan 2010).

One way of capturing the aspiration of people on the issue of language education, is to consult the census report. The census report of 2001, projects a rather horrifying situation: most of the languages, except Hindi, are showing negative growth. It is even more distressing when we contrast it with the growth of English in India as mentioned above. A recent study by NUEPA, referred in the *Times of India*, shows that the number of English-opting students from Class I to Class VIII has grown by 150 per cent in last decade, while the number of students opting Hindi grew by just 32 per cent (Nagarajan 2010). No doubt a comparative growth analysis of Hindi with a special reference to English, will show only a retarded growth. Under this situation, we think 22 is the magic number to start with. But, then, we need to make it specific what phrases like 'Indian Languages' or 'home languages' mean in different policy documents. After all, their meanings are subject to some political choices, which we are left with. To make it clear, let's consider the example of Hindi. As per the census report 2001, it is an umbrella term containing at least 49 different varieties, which are used in marketplaces as well as in home environments to communicate with each other. Are we talking about bridging the gap between these 49 languages and the language of instructions, which is definitely supposed to be the standard Hindi? If yes, how? While discussing the textbook designing, we always emphasize on incorporating local cultures. So, the question is how reasonable is it to produce culturally rich textbooks for these many varieties of Hindi, even if we overlook the other 122 languages and 234 mother tongues and 1635 different languages spoken across the country. If we go beyond the production of texts, then the most pressing questions will be the following one: do we have enough number of teachers trained in these many languages to demolish the barrier between the school culture and the home culture?

While talking about MLE, policy documents and researches assume that lacking equal access to the education results into the unequal development and growth, and finally, ends by adding up the problem of cultural intolerance and separatist movements. As a consequence, while defining the goals of MLE these policies and researches keep the following four agendas in their back: the right to mother tongue education to all linguistic communities, national integrity and cultural tolerance, the promotion of the cultural pluralism in future, and the production of better learners equipped with better adaptive capacities. However, these suggestions always remain in the documents. Implementation of true MLE, which is not a threat to the integrity, presupposes the simultaneous development of other signifiers, since language as a signifier survives and grows in the vicinity of other signifiers, which have already been argued before. Failing to satisfy this presupposition will always lead to a disastrous situation. One such situation, Mallikarjun (2003) refers to in figure 6 from the reports of All India Education Survey conducted by NCERT: The digits in the figure shows a steady decrease in the numbers of Indian languages as medium of instruction as one moves from the primary to higher secondary level.

Fifth Survey	Sixth Survey	
Primary	43	33
Upper Primary	31	25
Secondary	22	21
Higher Secondary	20	18

Figure 6: *Shrinking Spaces*

If 'progress', as Harvey (1990) argues, 'entails the conquest of space', then the data represented in figure 6 indicating Indian Languages are losing their ground as medium of instruction. It is not tough to imagine the fate of MLE in graduate and postgraduate levels.

Focusing on the point of national integrity and cultural intolerance, again, shows the extreme insensitivity of the policymakers and researchers: Consider the bilingual transfer model developed by Central Institute of Indian Languages, Mysore. This model proposes a specially designed successive dual language medium of instruction program, for tribal groups in India. As per this bilingual transfer model, as the name itself suggests, tribal languages are used in the initial days of education along with the dominant regional languages. As the learner moves towards higher education with the gradual improvement in his/her expertise in the nearest regional language, the tribal language structurally gets replaced with the regional language as the medium of instruction. The same thing can also be noticed in NCF 2006 position paper on teaching English in India. In most of our State-run primary and secondary schools, mother tongue instructions are given in the classroom along with English and Hindi medium of instructions. After a certain level, students are generally encouraged to switch to the system where, English is the medium of instruction. This approach of gradual replacement of the non-dominant forms of linguistic communication by the dominant ones, will only widen the linguistic divide in India and will leave India as fertile ground for intolerance, defeating the agenda of promoting cultural pluralism.

One way to address the failure of MLE policy is, definitely to construct an academic explanation simply bypassing the issues that are economically pertinent. One such academic explanation is provided by Schiffman (1996). According to him, understanding the true nature of language related policy documents is relative to the implicit, unofficial, unwritten, *de facto* aspects of people's perceptions along with the explicit, official, written, *de jure* aspects of the position papers. Very often the success and failure of a policy depends on the implicit, unofficial, unwritten, *de facto* aspects, which include an in-depth investigation into the ideas, values, beliefs, attitudes, prejudices, myths, religious strictures, and all the cultural baggage that we bring to our dealings with language from our culture. Schiffman's assertion to understand the linguistic culture of the population to achieve the stated goals of the policy documents is commendable, but at the same time, his assertion is problematic, because it excludes economical factors. Public opinion/choice is not something that is given, but constructed. In Eagleton's (1976) language, 'men are not free to choose their social relations; they are constrained into by the material necessity—by the nature and stage of development of their mode of economic production'.

Multilinguality in India is a historically proven fact. The reality of multilingualism in India hardly requires any recognition from the Government; rather we should be aware of what type of multilingualism State wants to promote. Is it subtractive? The answer to this question will explain how through multilingual education policy, the Indian State wants to promote a specific type of lingual composition, whose background is structured by the tension between 'Industrial India' and 'Agricultural India'. Discussing multilingual practices without associating it with its background, will lead us to some fallacies. The significance of the background as the tension between industrial and agricultural India in language shift is emphasized by Clingingsmith (2006). According to him, 'both manufacturing employment and urbanization provide incentives to learn new languages'. This explains why, the numbers of institutes teaching languages are increasing steadily; it also explains why India witnessed a rise in number of bilingual speakers in recent times, however, with a fall in the number of speakers of Indian Vernaculars (ref. fig. 7) resulting into a puzzle. Following Clingingmith, at least two criteria for increasing bilinguality in the context of subtractive multilingual policy can be identified: one, smaller the size of the speech community greater is the chance of becoming bilingual; and, two, bilinguality will increase with the increasing gap between the manufacturing industry and the agricultural sector.

On adding one more criteria with the above-mentioned two, we will get a solution of why the size of vernacular speakers is decreasing. One needs to consider the functional interrelationships between the languages participating in a bilingual relation in particular, and multilingual relation in general. In most of the cases, it is claimed, even today, that vernaculars are not fit for activities required for the production houses and progress, just like the way long time back, Macaulay told in 1835 that 'the dialects commonly spoken among the natives of this part of India contain neither literary nor scientific information, and are, moreover, so poor and rude that, until they are enriched from some other quarter, it will not be easy to translate any valuable work into them. It seems to be admitted on all sides that the intellectual improvement of those classes of the people who, have the means of pursuing higher studies can at present be effected only by means of some language not vernacular among them'. If so, then it is not hard to imagine how transitional bilingualism, as an instance of subtractive multilingualism, leads to the marginalization, neglect, and dispossessions of languages in India.

Spacing in the Disguise of Linguistic Right

Talking about linguistic right is not something trendy. People have been talking about it for decades across the globe, and India becomes the breeding ground for language activists. In spite of all these, graphical representation of the census data on decadal growth of the scheduled languages of India (2001), it is still showing the negative trend:

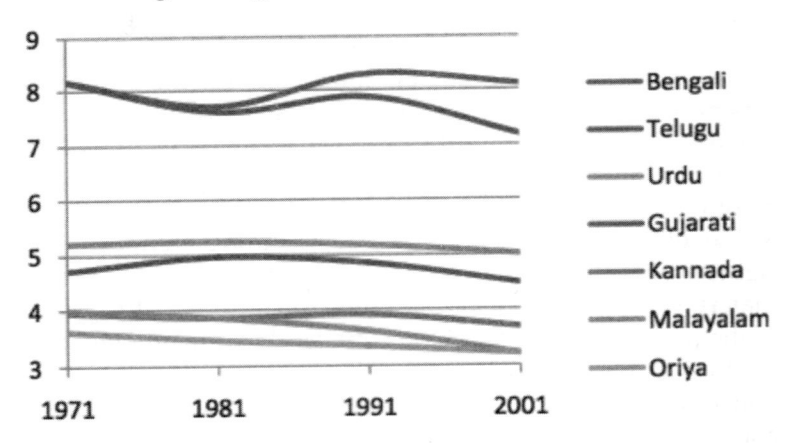

Figure 7: *Decadal growth (or, decay?!) of Indian Languages*

Between the translation of digits into graphs and the celebrations of language day prevails a form of contradiction: on the one hand we are celebrating the language days and on the other hand we are witnessing increasing number of languages on the death row. Failure in maintaining the multilingual norm will definitely hold back majority's access to the resources, and the prosperities in India. Since, the situation is worsening every day, one needs to rethink, if human rights perspective to the linguistic empowerment is defunct.

'All human beings are born free and equal in dignity and rights. They are endowed with reason and conscience and should act towards one another in a spirit of brotherhood.' This is the way the Universal Declaration of Human Rights (1948) proclaimed, born in the last century anticipating a massive economical set back ahead. An embryonic form of the Universal Declaration can be traced back in US president Franklin D. Roosevelt's address delivered on 6 January 1941 enunciating four freedoms for the human beings: freedom of speech, freedom of worship, freedom from want, and freedom from fear. These four freedoms are proposed to ensure integrity, safety, and stability of American world against the perceived threats lying beyond its border. But what constitutes these threats? The fear about the fall of democratic States beyond the American continent.

To prevent the fall of democracy beyond the boundary of American continent, a system of all-inclusive national defense was proposed. This defensive mechanism, as Roosevelt argues in the same lecture, would require 'a swift and driving increase in... armament production' by achieving 'full support of all those resolute people, everywhere, who are resisting aggression'. Roosevelt has further set the tone for freedom as 'supremacy of rights everywhere'. The aspiration of four freedoms, finally, is materialized in the proposal on human right in the beginning of the second half of the last century. What remains imperative in this entire discourse is to push the border beyond their continental boundaries to attenuate *beyond-the-boundary* contenders. Restoration of linguistic rights in India, needs to be evaluated through the lens of this history also. But even before that, the makeup of the lens has to be revealed.

Right-based articulation of linguistic empowerment is one among many measures to expand the boundary of nation and State, —a benevolent version of including the others. Right to education in mother tongue in multilingual societies, is an effort to hide extremely hegemonic form of monopoly capital. Recent policy documents on education in general and language in particular, are the strategic implementations to establish the hegemony.

Introduction of mother tongue in elementary education is not enough to empower the people linguistically, until and unless it's presence in the entry point to the market is assured. What is required to assure the latter one is the political and economical empowerment of all.

The introduction of the mother tongue in elementary education, as is proposed by different agencies, is mainly from the angle of cognitive development. In order to facilitate young learners' cognitive development, their mother tongues are proposed to include in the language curriculum in elementary level under the assumption that, as has been pointed out by the World Bank in 'Priorities and Strategies for Education (1995)', this approach will 'promote the cognitive development needed for learning a second language'. As the learner moves to the higher education, mother tongue will be gradually replaced by English only.[6]

Eminent linguist Krishnamurti (1990) once declared that most of the prominent universities and institutes in India use English as their medium of instruction. The situation has deterioratedeven have much with the rise of global economy. If things keep on going in this direction, we will end up with a monolingual world order with its handful of local associates across the globe. The most obvious consequence of this is a nasty conspiracy to keep non-English mother tongues subservient to either English or ENGLISIZED vernaculars. It is not simply an issue of beeing subservient to anyone; it is a way to produce armaments beyond the boundary, to ensure greater stability and peace in global centers. Only those will be allowed to be part of the global fraternity, who speak, think, and act alike, as Theodore Roosevelt announced on 5 January 1919:

> There can be no divided allegiance here...we have no room for but one language here and that is the English language, for we intend to see that the crucible terms our people out as Americans, of American nationality, and not as dwellers in a polyglot boarding-house; and we have room for but one soul loyalty, and that is loyalty to the American people.

The position paper by the National Focus Group on Teaching of Indian Languages (2006) puts emphasis on mother tongue education at the elementary level, with the provision of introducing English 'woven into the texture of developing strategies of teaching in a multilingual classroom', just like the way monopoly economy has its flow hidden in the texture of national economies! The position paper by National Focus Group on Teaching of English (2006) also argues in favour of introducing 'English at the initial level'. Later on, the National Knowledge Commission (2007) recommended the same. While doing so, all these reports do not forget to show their concern for the multilingual, echoing the concern of the benevolent compassionate saviour. All of them have prescribed the model of transitional bilingualism aiming at language shift.

The World Bank, as yet another avatar of benevolent saviour along with others, shed crocodile tears for MLE to hide the face of the monopoly capital with a subaltern version of national capital. In the name of strengthening the local linguistic capital, which is a form of national capital, monopoly will eliminate *beyond-the-boundary* threats by identifying and including the local allies.

In such a situation, the slogan of 'Mother Tongue and Multilingual Education' is, as absurd as the myth of unicorn. Advocating multilingualism and mother tongue education within the frameworks of Nation-State and Human Right will only strengthen Franklin D. Roosevelt's effort to imbue humanity with the most deceptive concepts of freedom ever been introduced in the history of civilization 'under guidance of God' as rights. Further Franklin D. Roosevelt warns 'it is immature—and incidentally, untrue—for anybody to brag that an unprepared America, single-handed, and with one hand tied behind its back, can hold off the whole world'. In fact, language as capital is that hand which has been untied to ensure 'the star-spangled banner shall wave' forever.

A true multilingual approach should unleash the scope to all at every level of the tertiary educational system in India; and this can be achieved only through the political and economical empowerment of all. If this demand sounds too much to achieve the stated goal of multilingualism, we need to recognize linguistic liberty is still a distant dream, even after half a decade of political independence of India.

NOTES

1. লেখো পড়া করে লেই / গাড়ড় লঘাড়া চরড় লেই (ড়শুড়কিষা ১: ২৭)
2. আল্লা এক। আল্লা কেরেে বরড়া। আল্লাে লকারাে ল াষ লেই।
   লকারাে ব াম লেই (মুেমােরে বাঙ্গাো ড়কিষা) Quoted from Bandopadhyay (2005)
3. লকোঁতুক করাে। লোঁতুক ধরাে। (ড়শুড়কিষা)
4. Symbolic ordering of space and time provides a framework through which the inhabitants of a land learn who they are and in what relations they are in with the others. Individual as a scheme represents a space where State practices its forces of repression and socialization. New meanings are invented for the older materialization/embodiment of space by imagining radical differences
5. Laitin (2000) seems to be relevant here: 'lack of consensus on how to measure either the degree of ethnic heterogeneity within a polity or the degree of difference between any two ethnic groups in that polity'
6. How innocent could be the ambush to clear the blockage in the name of 'God', 'an impressive expression of the public will and without regard to partisanship'!

REFERENCES

A World Bank Review (1995) *Priorities and Strategies for Education*, The World Bank: Washington, D.C.

Bandyopadhyay, S. (2005) *Abar Shishushiksha* (Again Child Education), Anustup: Kolkata

Bourdieu, P. (1991) *Language and Symbolic Power*, Polity Press: Cambridge

Canagarajah, S.A. (2005) 'Reconstructing Local Knowledge, Reconfiguring Language Studies', in S.A. Canagarajah (ed.) *Reclaiming the Local in Language Policy and Practice*, LEA: London

Clingingsmith, D. (2006) Industrialization and Bilingualism in India, *Journal of Human Resources*

Eagleton, T. (1976[2002]) *Marxism and Literary Criticism*, Routledge: London

Ghosh, B. (1979) *Banglar Nabajagriti* (Bengal's Renaissance), Orient Longman Ltd.: Kolkata

Harvey, D. (1990) *The Condition of Postmodernity: An Enquiry into the Origins of Cultural Change*, Blackwell: Cambridge

Harvey, D. (2005) *A Brief History of Neoliberalism*, Oxford University Press: New York

Krishnamurti, B.H. (1990) 'The Regional Language Vis-à-vis English as the medium of instruction in higher Education: The Indian Dilemma', in Pattanayak, D.P. (ed.) *Multilingualism in India*, Multilingual Matters Ltd.: Clevedon

Laitin, D.D. (2000) 'What is a Language Community?' *American Journal of Political Science*, 44(1), pp. 142–55

Mallikarjun, B. (2003) 'Globalization and Indian Languages', *Language in India*, Vol. 3, No. 2, http://www.languageinindia.com/feb2003/globalization.html (Last accessed on 30 April 2013)

Mukherji, A. (2012) 2 crore Indian children study in English-medium schools. *The Times of India*, 02 Mar 2012. articles.timesofindia.indiatimes.com/2012-03-02/india/3116237_1_english-medium-enrolment-district-information-system (Last accessed on 18 March 2013)

Nagarajan, R. (2010) English, Language of the Future, *The Times of India*, 27 November 2010. http://articles.timesofindia.indiatimes.com/2010-11-27/parenting/28234237_1_english-medium-schools-english-medium-unrecognized-schools (Last accessed on 30 April 2013)

National Focus Group on Teaching of Indian Languages (2006) National Council of Educational Research and Training: New Delhi

Sahai, S.N. (2009) Publishing industry on a roll, *Business Standard*, 17 May 2009. http://www.business-standard.com/india/printpage.php?autono=358315&tp=, (Last accessed on 2 April 2013)

Schiffman, H.F. (1996) *Linguistic Culture and Language Policy*, Routledge: London

Shaw, G. (1987) The South Asia and Burma Retrospective Bibliography (SABREB) Stage I: 1556–1800. Reported in *Jakhan Chaapaakhaanaa Elo* by Shripantha, Poshchimbongo Bangla Academy: Kolkata

Shripantha (1977) *Jakhan Chaapaakhaanaa Elo* (When press came). Kolkata: Poshchimbongo Bangla Academy.

Shukla, R. and M. Bordoloi (2013) Why large section of Indian households today prefer private education over government's? *The Economic Times*, 3 January, last retrieved on 18 March 2013. articles.economictimes.indiatimes.com/2013-01-03/news/36130452_1_nsso-consumption-expenditure-national-survey-office (Last accessed on 3 March 2013).

Skutnabb-Kangas, T., R. Phillipson, A.K. Mohanty and M. Panda (2009) Multilingual Education Concepts, Goals, Needs and Expense: English for all or Achieving Justice? *Social Justice Through Multilingual Education*, Multilingual Matters: Bristol

Tarkalankar, M.M. (1850) *Shishushikhaa* (The Infant Teacher), 2nd edition, Sanskrit Press: Kolkata

8

A Relevant Economics for India: Dark Past, Bleak Future

Rajesh Bhattacharya

Section I: Introduction

The economic performance of India in the last three decades has been discussed and debated extensively. In general, the high growth rate of India in the last three decades has been hailed as proof of the success of neoliberal reforms (Rodrik and Subramanian 2005; Panagariya 2008; Bhagwati and Panagariya 2012). The critics of this view point to the increasing immiserization of agriculture, the informalization of the labour force, and the rising inequality during the same period as proof of failure of neoliberal policies (Chandrashekhar and Ghosh 2002; Patnaik 2004; Vakulabharanam 2005). Without going into this debate, we may note that over time, politics and policymaking in India have been forced to grapple with the twin problems of managing growth and managing economic exclusion accompanying growth. It is clear that political parties favouring either one to the detriment of the other have faced and will continue to face the problem of legitimacy in the Indian context. It is this political economy of Indian growth that has spawned the policy discourse on inclusive growth, which reflects the sharpening of social contradictions during the period of growth and the deepening of a crisis of governance unprecedented in independent India's history.

This essay is not about India's economic performance or inclusive growth. It is about the discipline of economics as it has evolved in Indian academia. I argue in this essay that contemporary practices of teaching and research in economics in India don't prepare students, teachers, and researchers to engage with the Indian political economy in a sophisticated and socially relevant way. This acquires immense significance as, in recent times, a whole range of policy initiatives in the field of higher education—massive expansion of private institutions, entry of foreign universities, the government's thrust on improving research output in higher educations, and establishing international and world-class universities—is poised to radically alter the scenario of higher education in India in the coming decades. However, among these wide-ranging policy initiatives, there is hardly any emphasis on encouraging socially relevant knowledge to tackle the particular economic problems in India. In this essay, we will argue that this has partly to do with the way the discipline of economics has evolved over time and partly to do with the way Indian academia is intellectually dominated by the Anglo-American academic tradition to which it is inextricably connected through flows of people, funds, and honour. The neoliberal policies have exacerbated this problem to the highest degree by not only imposing a uniform set of economic policies worldwide, but a unique set of economic ideas—most prominently, the idea that free markets and institutions protecting property rights with minimal government intervention maximize economic performance—through curriculum, research methodologies, and public policies.

Under the hegemonic sway of these ideas, economists in India have little to contribute to an understanding of the growing crisis of governance in India, as evident in the lack of insightful work on major issues like farmer suicides and agrarian distress, industrialization and land acquisition controversy, mining and displacement of tribal population, et cetera. Yet, governments are routinely brought into and thrown out of power over these issues. More than at any other point of time in independent India's history, we require economic theories that address these issues in a way that is relevant to understanding capitalism as it is developing India. Simplistic comparison with recent success stories of East Asian, Chinese, or Japanese capitalisms or the historical cases of the rise of British, American, or German capitalisms will not help us in this endeavour as even a cursory glance at the histories of these countries makes abundantly clear their difference with the Indian case.

As the Indian State plans to reform the higher education system to transform India into a 'knowledge society', there is a danger of the Indian higher education system permanently falling victim to what Rudolph (2005) referred to as the 'imperialism of categories'—a mode of analysing based on universalization of categories of thought derived from specific histories of other societies and thus ignoring the uniqueness of a society's own history. Currently, the Indian higher education sector is at the crossroads. Even though the private higher education institutions have become numerically dominant in the last decade, public institutions still dominate the 'top ten' lists in all branches of higher education. But this might change as domestic private and foreign universities expand faster in the future as compared to public institutions. Unless the State-run higher education institutions recognize the need for radically reorienting the curricula and encouraging research to produce independent and contextually relevant knowledge tradition in a vast, pluralistic society like India, the expansion of domestic private universities and the entry of foreign universities, selling globally uniform academic commodities, will make it extremely difficult to do so in future. Moreover, knowledge has increasingly acquired the character of capital and is valued for its return on investment. Further, accumulation of knowledge has become the chief means of global competition among firms and countries. This purely instrumental approach to knowledge introduces the risk of harnessing the entire higher education sector to the needs of capitalist accumulation and undermines the primary goal of education as a means to understand society.

This essay is organized as follows. In Section II, I argue that

A Relevant Economics for India: Dark Past, Bleak Future 189

the dominant history of capitalism in independent India is coloured by the debate on the relative merits of State-regulated and free-market capitalisms in the Western economic tradition of the twentieth century. Arguing for a fresh perspective, this essay foregrounds the contradiction between capitalism and democracy—rooted in the contradiction between accumulation and need in a dual economy—as the central feature of the social history of capital in India. In Section III, I argue that a certain *scientism* pervades the economics discipline and resists 'embedding' the economy in the society. As a consequence, economics valorizes general principles over contextualized knowledge. This has a crippling effect on society's ability to manage powerful economic processes at work that often plunge the society in crises of governance. In Section IV, I present intellectual precedents of the central concern of this essay in selected writings by Indian economists throughout the history of independent India. In Section V, I look at contemporary reforms of the higher education sector of India in the context of the global political economy of knowledge production and argue that these reforms will undermine the possibility of the emergence of a socially relevant tradition of economic thought in India. In Section VI, I conclude by summing up the arguments of this essay in a connected manner.

Section II: Beyond State vs. Market: The Uniqueness of Indian Capitalism

According to the dominant account of Indian capitalism, India exemplifies the stylized economic history of many Third World countries. According to this story, Third World countries embarked on a rapid process of industrialization after the World War II in an effort to 'catch up' with the advanced industrial economies of the West. In the initial decades of development—roughly till the end of the 1960s—the development-oriented nation-states of these countries followed an autarkic development policy based on import-substitution in a more or less 'planned' economy with regulated markets and significant State ownership of the means of production in the economy. This *dirigiste* regime ran out of steam and encountered serious crises in the 1970s, which led to its abandonment, for good or for bad. Industrialization henceforth proceeded under a different and competing policy regime characterized by reliance on free international and domestic trade, non-interventionist State and unregulated private capitalist enterprises—the regime popularly referred to as the neoliberal regime. If we leave aside the first two decades of independent India—when there was broadly a political consensus on the role of the State in India's development—the major debate since the 1970s has been the relative merits of the State and the market in fostering growth and poverty reduction. Government policies aimed at regulating the private sector and managing poverty since late 1960s have been severely criticized for its failure in both eradicating poverty and enabling growth. On the other hand, pro-business and pro-market reforms since 1980s have been criticized for intensifying exclusion and widening social cleavages, calling into question the sustainability of the higher growth regime achieved in the post-reforms phase.

In this whole debate, Indian capitalism has been looked through the Western lens. Ever since the two World Wars and the Great Depression rocked the Western economies in the first half of the last century, there has been an intense debate on the best way to manage capitalism—that is, whether to have minimal or substantial government involvement in the economy. Thus, two distinct ideas of the State vied for supremacy in the West—the liberal State and the welfare State (Esping-Andersen 1990). The liberal State is premised on the idea that class contradictions in capitalism are automatically ameliorated through economic growth and economic growth is maximized in a free-market economy that encourages competition and innovation. The liberal view envisages a minimal role of the State committed only to protection of property rights, enforcement of contracts and minimal social safety net for the poor. The welfare State is premised on the idea that class-contradictions in capitalism need to be stabilized by the State through some sort of capital-labour accord. The State would ensure productivity growth and competitiveness as well as redistribution to the working class of resulting economic gains, thus facilitating rising profits for capitalists and rising well-being of workers.

The success of East Asian capitalisms has given birth to a new idea of the State—the 'developmental' State (Onis 1991). The 'developmental' State is different from the liberal State in that economic growth is actively engineered by the State through purposive, selective and clinical interventions in all kinds of markets coupled with a harsh reward-punish system for domestic capitalists to facilitate rapid capital accumulation and innovation. The 'developmental' State is different from the welfare State in that it is authoritarian; it represses democracy and working class mobilization, in particular, and insulates the State from popular demands. On the other hand, the 'developmental' State in East Asian countries like Japan, South Korea, and Taiwan had undertaken radical land reform programmes at the outset to ensure a certain egalitarian distribution of income during the process of capital accumulation. However, the idea of the 'developmental' State is firmly anchored in the traditional discourse on the relative merits of State and market in enabling capitalism. The 'development' State exemplifies the opportunities for late industrializing countries to use State power to manipulate market forces to engineer rapid industrialization.

The Indian State, by comparison, is arguably far more complex. Unlike the Western liberal and welfare States, democracy had taken root and consolidated itself in India at very low levels of per capita income (Nayyar 1998). Substantial reorganization of property in favour of the emergent indigenous capitalist class—'primitive accumulation', in Marx's words—was and still is constrained, to a large degree, by the political compulsions of democracy in India (Sanyal 2007; Chatterjee 1995). Moreover, compared to other Western liberal democracies, poor and marginalized people have, over time, come to vote more and more in elections compared to the richer sections of the society (Nayyar 1998; Palshikar and Kumar 2004; Suri 2004). This has resulted in unprecedented popular demands on the State and the State remains central to the life of the overwhelming majority of the Indian population.

Unlike the East Asian developmental States, the Indian State could not subordinate politics to the problem of capital accumulation; the brief Emergency period of 1975–7 amply illustrated the impossibility of the triumph of bureaucratic governance over political democracy. But, even before that, clinical interventions in the economy by the Indian State through five-year plans to facilitate industrialization through rapid capital accumulation had to be abandoned by the mid-1960s in response to emergencies, both external and internal. The political consensus that supported the Planning exercise had started to fray as early as mid-1960s. By the early 1970s, the Indian State had decisively taken a populist turn, as much in response to the political crisis of the 1960s as in response to rising poverty that accompanied early industrialization drives (Dandekar and Rath 1971).

While pro-business and pro-market reforms since mid-1980s have transformed Indian capitalism, the resulting social contradictions of free-market capitalism have once again brought the State back with vengeance through a series of public policies of unprecedented scale and significance—for example, the NREGA, the Food Security Bill, the new Land Acquisition Bill and the Forest Rights Act, et cetera, each of which can potentially be a game-changer not only for poverty-alleviation programmes, but development of capitalism in general. Just like the economic crisis engendered in the early five-year plans precipitated the remarkable acts of State intervention by the Indian State (nationalization of bank, insurance, and coal sectors, MRTP and FERA Acts, reservation for small-scale sector, et cetera) in the late 1960s and early 1970s, the crisis of post-reforms Indian capitalism have precipitated the recent spate of policies.

The main contradiction in India is the contradiction between capitalism and democracy, more specifically, the contradiction inherent in the *co-evolution* of capitalism and democracy. Both capitalism and democracy are processes in society, with their relative autonomy and mutually constitutive effects on each other such that they support and undermine each other at the same time. None can be reduced to the other in a causal framework. The Indian experience is an exemplar of this *co-*

evolution of capitalism and democracy and thus defies categories drawn from histories of Western and Eastern capitalisms. First, the institutionalization of democracy in early stages of industrialization in India effectively ruled out the emergence of the 'developmental' State, which is based on a State-capital accord through suppression of democratic politics. Second, the low level of industrialization and consequently, the low level of capitalist surplus in the economy, ruled out the emergence of any welfare State based on a capital-labour accord supported by the State through tax-transfer policies. Finally, at the time of Independence, the Indian capitalist class either lacked the political legitimacy or economic strength to embark on the path of rapid capital accumulation by itself and thus actively sought or otherwise necessitated the commanding presence of the Indian State in the economy to jump-start industrialization. Subsequent attacks against the interventionist State by the business groups failed to dislodge the State from its prominent position in Indian society, because by then, democracy had consolidated itself around State, rather than capital. The continued enchantment with the Indian State ruled out the emergence of the liberal State.

The co-evolution of capitalism and democracy in India has evolved against a persistent dualism in the economic structure—characterized by the coexistence of a capitalist economy (composed of large capitalist agricultural farms, the public sector and the formal corporate sector) and a (predominantly non-capitalist) petty business economy (peasant farms, small retail and unorganized manufacturing enterprises) (Sanyal and Bhattacharya 2009). In dominant academic and policy discourses, the distinction between the formal and the informal sector captures this dualism. A more nuanced distinction from the political economy perspective has been offered by Sanyal (2007) in terms of a distinction between the 'accumulation-economy' and the 'need-economy'—by which he referred to two different spaces of production, one organized around accumulation of capital and the other organized around satisfaction of 'needs' (that is, subsistence). The accumulation-economy expands by breaking down the 'need-economy', usurping the latter's resources but excluding the labour released from therein. Democracy requires that the excluded labour is rehabilitated again, through State interventions, in an economic space that supplies their 'needs'. This becomes a necessary condition for the political legitimacy of capital, that is, for political conditions of reproduction of capital. Thus, the twin processes of capitalism and democracy keep reproducing this dualism in this economy. The political economy of Indian capitalism is characterized by the contradiction between short-term urgency of needs and the long-term requirements of economic growth. This contradiction is manifested in the political space in the dual politics of ostensible pro-poor policies (Bardhan 2008) and pro-business 'reforms by stealth' (Jenkins 1999). The State is thus called upon to perform a heroic balancing act mobilizing immense political skills and economic calculation. The discourse on inclusive growth is a consolidation of a unique stance by the Indian State vis-à-vis the Indian society—a commitment to democracy (hence, inclusion) and capitalism (hence, growth).

It is this twin problem of accumulation and subsistence/needs—as it is shaped by the complex interaction between capitalism and democracy—that needs to be recognized and theorized in order to meaningfully engage with the Indian society. Yet, Indian economic discourse is dominated by sterile debates on the merits of State versus market in economic development or growth vs. welfare objectives in public policy. We need to go beyond the terms of these traditional debates and recognize the deep contradictions between democracy and capitalism which makes resolution of any of these conflicts in any one direction almost impossible.

Section III: Economics: Scientism Against Society

The emergence of economics as a discipline is contemporaneous with the birth of capitalism. In two and a half centuries of its life, the discipline of economics has transformed itself into a social science with a claim to scientific status akin to that enjoyed by natural science disciplines. This claim to scientificity is based on the economists' claim to 'knowledge' of 'objective' laws

A Relevant Economics for India: Dark Past, Bleak Future 195

governing economic processes. Since the Second World War, Western capitalist economies have oscillated between more and less State-regulation of capitalism. The kind of Keynesian policy regime that was adopted in the Western countries after the Second World relied on the techno-bureaucratic efficiency of a rational, benevolent State in containing the instability of free-market capitalism. Conversely, the neoliberal policy regime initiated since the 1980s was premised on the belief that socially desirable goals like full employment and economic growth are automatic outcomes of a free-market economy and that government interventions are futile and unnecessary. In both cases, economics as a discipline has been called upon to provide the objective rationale for and against State intervention respectively. The laws of the market as theorized in economics resemble 'natural laws' in physics while policy interventions by the regulatory State resemble surgical interventions in the medical sciences. This *scientism* inherent in economic thought effectively banishes from thought the role of the society in actively shaping the economy.

This *scientism* has an intellectual history in Western thought. Bruno Latour (2007) argued that the Western quest for truth was premised on the view that social or public life does not lead us to 'eternal' truth. But eternal truth always empowers the knower to intervene in social or public life:

> The Philosopher, and later the Scientist, has to free themselves of the tyranny of social dimension, public life, politics, subjective feelings, popular agitation... the Scientist, once equipped with laws not made by human hands that he has just contemplated because he has succeeded in freeing himself from the prison of the social world, can go back ...so as to bring order to it with incontestable findings that will silence the endless chatter of the ignorant mob. ...The Scientist can go *back and forth* from one world to the other no matter what: the passageway closed to all others is open to him alone (Latour 2007: pp. 10–11).

Thus, the possibility of society's (complex and contradictory) reaction to economic outcomes is lost to economists who are all too eager to ignore such considerations as fit only for the 'ignorant mob'. To economists, economics is all about perfection of methods agreed upon by the majority among economists. Thus, in the heydays of Keynesianism, no one paid attention to Michal Kalecki's warning that the very success of Keynesian policy in achieving economic prosperity would lead to an assertive working class and invite backlash from the business elite who would then undermine the Keynesian policy regime (Kalecki 1943). Similarly, at the height of neoliberalism, no one cared to read Karl Polanyi's history of industrial capitalism, in which he argued that industrial societies of the nineteenth and twentieth centuries displayed a pendulum-like 'double movement'. One side of that movement was toward free and flexible markets that enabled the material and technological gains associated with the Industrial Revolution. The other side was a reaction to the disruption that these markets imposed on people's lives, threatening nature and society on a large scale and prompting the society to take steps towards self-preservation by erecting social barriers to the operation of the markets (Polanyi 1944). Of course, any reference to class-contradictions within capitalism a la Marx were brushed aside as politically motivated.

But *scientism* also serves as a shield for economists who must legitimize the role of economics in society, as pointed out by Davis (2008). Davis argues that economics as a discipline must justify its value to the non-specialist public when it comes to public policy. Because of the sheer dominance of the economic sphere in the modern society, economic policies advised by economists have immense consequences for the public—one need only think of the debates on austerity in EU in the wake of recession, the controversies around labour market regulations and capital flows in developing countries, the conflict around WTO negotiations and so on. On the other hand, economists' forecasts, whether at the micro or macro level, are often unreliable and there is very low consensus on values underlying these policies. As a result, economists are often called upon as professionals to engage in high stakes, high uncertainty policies. Faced with the possibility of public criticism, the economics discipline tries to mobilize the general esteem in which science is held in our society to shield itself from public criticism of failed policy.

The following quote from Nobel Laureate Robert Lucas' defense of economics in the wake of the current economic crisis amply illustrates the point.

> What can the public reasonably expect of specialists in these areas, and how well has it been served by them in the current crisis? One thing we are not going to have, now or ever, is a set of models that forecasts sudden falls in the value of financial assets, like the declines that followed the failure of Lehman Brothers in September. The main lesson we should take away from the EMH for policymaking purposes is the futility of trying to deal with crises and recessions by finding central bankers and regulators who can identify and puncture bubbles... [R]ecommending pre-emptive monetary policies on the scale of the policies that were applied later on would have been like turning abruptly off the road because of the potential for someone suddenly to swerve head-on into your lane. The best and only realistic thing you can do in this context is to keep your eyes open and hope for the best. ...They [the economists] have forecasted what can be forecast and formulated contingency plans ready for use when unforeseeable shocks occurred. They and their colleagues have drawn on recently developed theoretical models when they judged them to have something to contribute (Lucas 2009).

Lucas is doing two things here—emphasizing the sophistication of the discipline and pointing to the limits to which the public can expect the economists to perform in averting a crisis. What is striking in this quote is that the financial crisis is almost treated as a natural disaster before which economists, even with their increasingly sophisticated tools, are helpless. Thus, what is essentially a socially created institution—the financial system—is represented as a natural system and the one indisputable scientific truth, uncovered by economists, is that in this 'natural system' sudden falls in the value of assets is unpredictable. Any interference with the natural laws of the markets is considered 'political'; any social regulation of the economy a tool for political manipulation. This distrust of society and of politics is a hallmark of Science as it is usually understood in the modern society. But what is termed 'politics' in the economists' perception is essentially a struggle to 're-embed' the runaway economy in the society. Democracy, the favourite pasture of the political animal, is a nightmare.

The consequences of this scientism are writ large over the entire third world. Thus, since the Second World War, third world countries have oscillated between models of State-directed and market-driven development paradigms, much in synch with the oscillation of the Western capitalist countries between Keneysian and neoliberal policies. The developing countries are expected to adopt the best practices of economics as progressively discovered by economists in the advanced capitalist countries 'who have been there and done all of that' and hence discovered the truth the hard way. Since economics is about immutable, objective laws, unqualifiable by social differences, the developing countries need not 'reinvent the wheel' and thus, can draw upon the latest knowledge produced by the Western economists who have pondered about the economics of capitalism longer due to their early start. The problem with such an approach was poignantly pointed out by Albert O. Hirschman, one of the profoundest development economists, who arrived at the following evaluation of early development interventions in the poorer world, of which he himself was one of the most illustrious architects.

> The Western economists who looked at them [the underdeveloped countries] at the end of World War II were convinced that these countries were not all that complicated; their major problems would be solved if only their national income per capita could be raised adequately. At an earlier time, contempt for the countries designated as 'rude and barbarious' in the eighteenth century, as 'backward' in the nineteenth and as 'underdeveloped' in the twentieth had taken the form of relegating them to permanent lowly status, in terms of economic and other prospects, on account of unchangeable factors such as hostile climate, poor resources, or inferior race. With the new doctrine of economic growth, contempt took a more sophisticated form: suddenly it was taken for granted that progress of these countries would be smoothly linear if only they adopted the right kind of integrated development program! Given what was seen as their overwhelming problem of poverty, the underdeveloped countries were expected to perform like wind-up toys and to 'lumber

through' the various stages of development singlemindedly ...[T]hese countries were perceived to have only interests and no passions (Hirschman 1981 in Kanth 1994: p. 260).

This attitude is not peculiar to Western economists; this attitude reflects the so-called scientific attitude. During the run-up to the Planning period in independent India, the discussion of economic future of independent India drew passionate responses from different political groups; the conflict between the business groups, the Gandhians and the socialists was resolved outside the political sphere—in the sanitized and sane world of the Planning Commission, where experts devoted themselves to crafting a future for India unimpaired by the 'squabbles and conflicts of politics' (Chatterjee 1995: p. 202). Whenevre the State gave in to political compulsions, it was criticized for letting politics interfere with good economics.

But if politics is about re-embedding the economy in society, the denial of politics forecloses the possibility of socially specific traditions of economic thought. While there are regularities in the experience of capitalism across societies—specifically in the nature of markets and the logic of capital—the global history of capitalism shows incredible diversity. The histories of the rise of capitalism in England, USA, Germany, Japan, South Korea, and China, for example, illustrate very different paths of capitalist development. Each path has its own associated social history. By denying the specificity of social history of capital in each country and by focusing exclusively on general features of capitalism—markets, property rights and accumulation—we can't go far in understanding capitalism and responding to the contradictions and crises engendered by developing capitalism. The *scientism* of economics is an obstacle to writing the social history of capital. Since development of capitalism is nothing but the political rise of the capitalist class, denying politics is akin to denying the social history of capital. As we pointed out briefly in the last section, the interaction between democracy and capitalism is at the heart of the social history of capital in India and this arguably places India in a very special position in the global history of capitalism. Unfortunately, the tradition of economics in India is blind to this incredible history.

Section IV: The tradition of economic thought in India

While economics, like all other academic disciplines in India, have always been heavily under the influence of the Anglo-American tradition, debates on economic planning for the future of India, at the time of and in the early decades of independence had elicited much creative thinking among Indian economists. In many instances, they asserted the specificity of the Indian economic context in their theoretical works and in their comments on practical aspects of planning. In his presidential address to Indian economic conference in 1949, V.K.R.V. Rao made the following comment.

> Economic development of an under-developed economy cannot be brought about by a blind application of Keynesian techniques. These are, after all, really intended for an industrialized economy with unemployed resources and constitute a contra-cyclical rather than a developmental apparatus (quoted in Rao 1952: p. 8).

This was echoed in the Draft Outline of the First Five-year Plan by the Planning Commission in 1951 where it recognized structural deficiencies as the main characteristic of underdeveloped economies and the real danger of inflationary impact if Keynesian full-employment policies were adopted. This recognition by Indian economists came before Arthur Lewis's celebrated 1954 paper titled 'Economic development with unlimited supplies of labour' where he argued that for the analysis of underdeveloped countries, both neoclassical and Keynesian theories—the two dominant and competing economic theories—were to be abandoned and a return to classical political economy of the nineteenth century is necessary. Similarly, writing in 1966, P.R. Brahmananda argued that a 'wide spread agreement prevails on the realism and relevance of the classical method under economic conditions obtaining in countries like India' (Brahmananda 1966: p. 428). It must be remembered that these views were expressed when Western economics was absorbed in the debate between Keynesian and neoclassical theories; a return to classical political economics of the nineteenth century was thus a radical break from the dominant Western economic discourse.

Among Western economists working on development issues in the third world, there were voices warning against blind adherence to economic theories developed in the West.

> It is inherently implausible that a 'general theory' or even propositions of any generality, can be derived from the experience of a few [Western] countries with highly unusual, not to say peculiar, characteristics. Teaching which concentrates on this type of economy is somewhat distorted, and the distortion is dangerous if those teaching fail to stress continually that they are dealing with what is a highly special case (Seers 1963: p. 80).

Commenting on the reigning undergraduate textbook of the time, Paul Samuelson's *Economics*, Seers suggested that '[t]he title of Samuelson's text should not be 'Economics' but 'The Economics of the United States in the Twentieth century'. What comes through from these selected quotes is the recognition of dangers of adopting one economics for all societies at all times. Yet this is what happened during the intellectual revival of *monoeconomics* (a term used by Hirschman 1981 in Kanth 1994) in the 1970s. The failure of early development policies—based on the presumption that underdeveloped countries were structurally dissimilar from the advanced countries and thus needed special theoretical frameworks—contributed in no small measure to the downfall of this paradigm. In his Nobel Prize lecture, T.W. Schultz remarked noted that '[i]ncreasing numbers of economists have come to realize that standard economic theory is just as applicable to the scarcity problems that confront low income countries as to the corresponding problems of high income countries.' (Schultz 1980: p. 640)

Subsequent teaching and research in India has almost universally coincided with the Anglo-American tradition in theory and methods. Economics departments have become back-offices for academic output in the Anglo-American universities. The faculty shies away from unconventional thinking for fear of losing global recognition and even local prestige. For students of economics, the Indian universities and colleges have become launching pads for their entry into graduate programmes abroad. Thus, any syllabus with significant local content or deviating much from the established economics curricula in Anglo-American world, is bound to reduce the marketability of students in international academia. In his preface to the 1990 revised edition of his book, *Macroeconomics: Dynamics of Commodity Production*, Amit Bhaduri pointed out the problems in teaching unconventional approaches to economics:

> [T]he international system of academic reward and recognition makes students from the Third World especially vulnerable to the changing intellectual fashions of the United States. Each generation of bright students gets into the fashionable mode of theorizing of the day, without even being convinced of the intellectual merit of that fashion. Because, for the young, aspiring student this is the safest way to gain recognition for his academic ability. It is difficult to stop this trend when academic acceptability requires conforming to the fashion (Bhaduri 1990: p. viii).

The first step to open up the space for a relevant economics for India would be to pluralize the space of economics syllabi in the economics departments of Indian universities. This is what Chakravarty argued for in his observations on the teaching of economics in India when he urged us to 'recognize the diversity of epistemological perspectives and in the process prepare our students much better for the study of Indian society.' (Chakravarty 1988: p. 1168). However, this is a long step and both the inherent *scientism* of economics and the dominant intellectual currents among Indian economists discourage any effort in this direction.

Section V: Knowledge as capital and reforms of the higher education sector in India

The higher education sector in India is already undergoing significant transformations and is set to undergo further drastic reforms in the coming years. The widely held belief is that the public higher education sector in India, in general, has grievously suffered due to defective and indifferent government policies in independent India. This sordid state of affairs becomes obvious not only when compared with international institutions, but is also reflected in the public image of the higher education institutions. The universities and colleges of India, barring a handful, are hardly the institutions society owns as its precious possessions. In public perception, they are like any certificate-issuing government office. Private institutions, except a very few, are held in even lower esteem as they are considered essentially placement offices, where jobs can be bought for money, rather than centers of education. As far as India's contribution to knowledge is concerned, it is often argued that we were much closer to the global research frontier under the colonial rule than now.

On the other hand, the higher education space has seen a social revolution of some sort, aided to a great extent by the reservation policies. Students from different social groups—peasant families, urban slum households, lower castes, tribal groups, minorities and of course, women—now sit side by side with elites in classrooms at institutions of higher learning, participating in the same lofty academic discourse with the elites. This has radically transformed the public institutions of education in India, which earlier used to be dominated by elite classes in colonial India and in the early decades of Independence. Nothing short of a revolution in academic and popular discourses should have followed from the entry of these hitherto-marginalized groups. However, unfortunately, the democratization of the education space has been accompanied by the secular decline in the quality of these institutions since independence. As a result, Indian academic institutions missed out on the tremendous dividends from this democratic transformation.

In this context and in the context of the arguments in the preceding sections, the current set of proposed and ongoing reforms of the higher education sector—potentially a game-changer—assume immense importance. In a nutshell, the ongoing reforms—implemented by stealth and/or by policy announcements—belong roughly to what has been called the neoliberal package of reforms already implemented/proposed in other social and economic sectors. Several trends are well-recognized. First, public funding of higher education institutions is increasingly supplemented by and often substituted by other models of revenue-generation by institutions—revenue-generation from government and industry projects, self-financed courses, distance-learning programmes, and escalation of student fees in various obvious and not-so-obvious forms. This has increasingly imposed a 'business model' on institutions of higher learning channelizing initiatives and efforts away from quality towards marketability. While, the increasing cost of running higher education institutions does make it necessary to think about sustainable models of funding higher education, any reforms aimed at diluting the essence of education—free pursuit of knowledge—is bound to have a disastrous impact on society in the long-run. Each society is unique and must rely on its own collective genius to solve its problems.

Second, even though public academic institutions officially still retain a policy of permanent employment contracts for faculty members and arguably an easy tenure and promotion system, glaring faculty vacancy figures in universities and colleges point to the overwhelming presence of part-time, contractual and guest lecturers among the teaching community. Thus, there is increased contractualization of university and college faculty. This has serious implications for members of faculty pursuing unorthodox areas of research or teaching unconventional ideas in class. This development will constrict the space for pluralism of thought and democratic dialogue, both of which are absolutely essential for any inclusive approach to understanding an incredibly diverse society like India.

Third, the higher education sector is poised to undergo a massive expansion in the coming years, most of which is expected to take place in the private sector, within or outside the public-private partnership model. Moreover, it is being envisaged that foreign universities will enter the Indian higher education sector, and together with private universities, would make up for the supply shortfall in higher education which, it is argued, is financially unfeasible for the government to do alone, even with the best of intentions. But, more significantly, the entry of domestic private and international universities is also expected to create competition for the public sector to upgrade its infrastructure and enhance its academic performance to meet global standards. But competition in the sphere of knowledge has the unfortunate effect of encouraging conformism in ideas. Governance through competition has the effect of homogenizing processes of production of ideas through a harsh reward-punish market mechanism. The marketability of academic products (students and ideas) will be the sole criterion for evaluating the processes of production of knowledge. Moreover, all traditions melt away in the market place; only those of immediate value survive. Yet, in the realm of ideas, no tradition is ever superseded. The collective wisdom of humanity is not just the latest theories or latest data, but the entire wealth of accumulated, preserved knowledge.

In official discourse, the thrust behind education policy reforms comes from the recognition that today's economy is a knowledge-driven economy or in short, the 'knowledge economy'. Just as in the past, accumulation of physical capital was the means to remain competitive in the world economy—and, for developing countries, to catch up with the advanced countries—competition in the contemporary global economy is driven by accumulation of knowledge/intellectual/intangible capital. As production gets globally dispersed, what matters is not the dominance of material production and physical capital, but dominance of immaterial production (Hardt and Negri 2001) and knowledge capital (Burton-Jones 1999). Immaterial production based on knowledge capital dominates the global value-chains. In the past, countries specializing in industrial products dominated those producing primary products; today, countries specializing in immaterial production dominate countries specializing in material production. But what is knowledge/intellectual/intangible capital and immaterial production? In *Empire*, Hardt and Negri distinguishes between material and immaterial production in the following manner.

> Material production—the production, for example, or cars, televisions, clothing, and food—creates the means of social life. ... Immaterial production, by contrast, including the production of ideas, knowledges, communication, cooperation, and affective relations, tends to create not the means of social life but social life itself (Hardt and Negri 2001: p. 146).

In the business literature, intellectual/intangible capital

comprise of three components—human capital, structural capital, and relational capital. Human capital is the sum total of skills, know-how and expertise of the labour force of an organization and represents the collective human capabilities of an organization in dealing with problems faced by the organization. Structural capital is often decomposed further into organization capital, process capital, and innovation capital. Organization capital includes elements like culture, structure, organizational learning (Martín-de-Castro et al 2006). Process capital includes organizational routines, techniques, procedures, and programmes that implement and enhance the production and delivery of goods and services. Innovation capital includes intellectual properties such as patents, trademarks, and copyrights—a product of the organization's ability to create new knowledge, most ostensibly through R&D. Finally, relational capital includes customer relationships, supplier relationships, trademarks, and trade names, licences, and franchises (Bontis 1998; Joia 2000).

The elements constituting these new forms of capital clearly belong to the domain of culture, knowledge, and communications; hence, the importance of education to contemporary business. The normal outcomes of education are now special forms of capital for business and the source of its competitive strength. The importance of intellectual capital can hardly be overstated. Investment in intellectual capital now outstrips that in physical capital in several advanced countries. According to an OECD report (OECD 2013), in Sweden, the United Kingdom and the United States, investment in knowledge-based capital matches or exceeds investment in physical capital. The report emphasizes that this importance of knowledge capital is going to increase in future as countries compete over the upper segments of the value-chains.

> Usually, the value created in a GVC is unevenly distributed among its participants. The allocation of value depends on the ability of participants to supply sophisticated, hard-to-imitate products or services. Increasingly, the supply of such products or services stems from forms of KBC [knowledge-based capital] such as brands, basic R&D and design, and the complex integration of

A Relevant Economics for India: Dark Past, Bleak Future 207

software with organisational structures...KBC can determine the geographical pattern of value creation in a global value chain as the much studied iPhone shows. The largest share of the value created by the iPhone accrues to providers of distribution and retail services in the United States and to Apple, mainly to its innovations in design, marketing and supply-chain management. For each iPhone4 sold, at a retail price of USD 600, Apple earns around USD 270, while Korean firms supplying core components earn USD 80, and Chinese enterprises that undertake the assembly earn USD 6.5, a mere 1% of the total value (OECD 2013: p. 23).

In contemporary global economy, knowledge occupies a peculiar role in production. As the domain of private property rights extends over knowledge products and knowledge products themselves become commodities, the economic return to commoditized and property-rights-protected knowledge has become the most significant component of corporate valuation. Knowledge is the new 'land' in contemporary political economy securing high 'ground rent' for the owner; the business firm as the owner of knowledge capital is the contemporary analogue of the classical landlord (Teixeira and Rotta 2012; Basu 2008).

Higher education reforms plan to enhance the competitiveness of domestic business through accumulation of knowledge capital. The global political economy and not individual social contexts is the driver of these reforms. This instrumentalist view of knowledge is very far from the idea of knowledge as the means to make sense of life around us. As India joins this competitive race along with all other countries, through higher education reforms, the need to develop critical indigenous traditions of economic thought in understanding its unique, complex and traumatic process of capitalist transformation and the periodic crises of governance is likely to be swamped by the capitalist logic of competition.

Section VI: Conclusion

This essay presents a set of distinct but connected arguments regarding the necessity and the possibility of a relevant economics for India. The argument for contextualized knowledge follows from an epistemological position that, while not denying the usefulness and the necessity of universal categories in construction of theory, nevertheless resists totalitarian impulses in constructing theory based on general, abstract categories.

A study of the development of capitalism in different societies reveals diverse social histories of capital. Each society's experience of development of capitalism is unique. By denying the authenticity of specific social histories, *scientism*, in effect, upholds a *natural*, as opposed to social, history of capital. Thus, development of capitalism is a presented by economists as the history of natural coming-together of certain institutions like free markets, a minimal State and the institutions governing property rights and contracts. This essentially well-behaved history is disturbed only by the society itself when it interferes to alter the course of history for or against capitalism. Thus, *scientism* works against society, by denying the society its right to write its own history.

I have argued that, in the case of India, her unique history of co-evolution of democracy and capitalism remains largely unwritten in the absence of a tradition of economic thought that could definitively break away from the standard historical model presented in the orthodox theory of the period. There is an intensifying social crisis in contemporary India as society struggles to find a way to make sense of itself in the face of growing contradictions of capitalism. But the hegemony of *monoeconomics*, supported by an infrastructure of globally integrated markets for academic products that makes exit costly, holds society captive to irrelevant ideas and passive before its own contradictions.

The contemporary discourse on reforms of the higher education sector in India makes it extremely unlikely that this hegemony of *monoeconomics* would be broken. As knowledge becomes accumulable capital and the chief means of international competition, contextual demands on knowledge would be trumped by the global struggle for dominance.

REFERENCES

Bardhan, P. (2008) 'Democracy and Distributive Politics in India,' in Shapiro, I., P.A. Swenson and D. Donno (eds.) *Divide and Deal:*

A Relevant Economics for India: Dark Past, Bleak Future   209

The Politics of Distribution in Democracies, New York University Press: New York and London
Basu, P.K. (2008) *Globalisation: An Anti-text: A Local View*, Aakar Books: Delhi
Bhaduri, A. (1990) *Dynamics of Commodity Production*, Macmillan: New Delhi
Bhagwati, J. and A. Panagariya (eds.) (2012) *India's Reforms: How They Produced Inclusive Growth*, Oxford University Press: New York, USA
Brahmananda, P.R. (1966) 'Capitals Proportions, Mechanisation and Employment,' *Indian Journal of Industrial Relations*, 1(4): pp. 427–1
Bontis, N. (1998) 'Intellectual capital: an exploratory study that develops measures and models,' *Management Decision*, 36.2: 63–76
Burton-Jones, A. (1999) *Knowledge Capitalism: Business, Work and Learning in the New Economy*, Oxford University Press: Oxford
Chakravarty, S. (1986) 'The Teaching of Economics in India', *Economic and Political Weekly*, 21(27): pp. 1165–8
Chandrasekhar, C.P. and J. Ghosh (2002) *The Market that Failed: A Decade of Neoliberal Economic Reforms in India*, Leftword: New Delhi
Chatterjee, P. (1995) *Nation and its Fragments*, Oxford University Press: New Delhi
Dandekar, V.M. and N. Rath (1971) *Poverty in India*, Sameeksha Trust: Bombay
Davis, J.B. (2008) 'The turn in recent economics and return of orthodoxy,' *Cambridge Journal of Economics*, 32.3: pp. 349–66
Esping-Andersen, Gøsta (1990) *The Three Worlds of Welfare Capitalism*, Polity Press: Cambridge
Hardt, Michael, and Antonio Negri. (2001) *Empire*, Harvard University Press: Harvard
Hirschman, A.O. (1981) 'The Rise and Decline of Development Economics,' in *Essays in Trespassing: Economics to Politics and Beyond*, Cambridge University Press: New York. Reprinted in Kanth (1994)
Jenkins, R. (1999) *Democratic Politics and Economic Reform in India*, Cambridge University Press: Cambridge
Joia, L.A. (2000) 'Measuring intangible corporate assets: linking business strategy with intellectual capital,' *Journal of Intellectual Capital* 1.1: pp. 68–84
Kalecki, M. (1943) 'Political Aspects of Full Employment,' *The Political Quarterly* 14.4: pp. 322–30

Kanth, R. (ed.) (1994) *Paradigms in Economic Development: Classic Perspectives, Critiques, and Reflections*, M.E. Sharpe: New York

Latour, B. (2007) *Politics of Nature*, Orient Longman: New Delhi

Lewis, W.A. (1954) 'Economic Development with Unlimited Supplies of Labour', *The Manchester School*, 22 (2): pp. 139–91

Lucas, Robert (2009) 'In defence of the dismal science,' *The Economist* 6

Martín-de-Castro, G., J.E. Navas-López, P. López-Sáez and E. Alama-Salazar (2006) 'Organizational capital as competitive advantage of the firm,' *Journal of Intellectual Capital* 7.3: pp. 324–37

Öns, Z. (1991) 'The Logic of the Developmental State', *Comparative Politics*, 24(1): pp. 109–26

Organization for Economic Cooperation and Development (OECD) (2013) *New Sources of Growth: Knowledge-Based Capital: Key Analyses and Policy Conclusions - Synthesis report*. Available at http://www.oecd.org/sti/inno/knowledge-based-capital-synthesis.pdf (last accessed on 26.09.2013)

Palshikar, S. and S. Kumar (2004) 'Participatory Norm: How Broad-Based Is It?' *Economic and Political Weekly*, 39(51): pp. 5412–17

Panagariya, A. (2008) *India: The Emerging Giant*, Oxford University Press: New York

Patnaik, U. (2004) 'The Republic of Hunger', *Social Scientist*, 32 (9/10): pp. 9–35

Polyani, K. (1944) *The Great Transformation*, Rinehart: New York

Rao, V.K.R.V. (1952) 'India's First Five-Year Plan: A Descriptive Analysis,' *Pacific Affairs*, 25(1): pp. 3–23

Rodrik, D. and A. Subramanian (2005) 'From' Hindu growth to productivity surge: The mystery of the Indian growth transition,' *IMF Staff Papers* 52(2): pp. 193–228

Rudolph, S.H. (2005) 'The imperialism of categories: Situating knowledge in a globalizing world,' *Perspectives on politics* 3.1: pp. 5–14

Sanyal, K.K. (2007) *Rethinking Capitalist Development: Primitive Accumulation, Governmentality and the Post-colonial Capitalism*, Routledge: New Delhi and UK

Sanyal, K.K. and R. Bhattacharya (2009) 'Beyond the Factory: Globalisation, Informalisation of Production and the New Locations of Labour', *Economic and Political Weekly*, 44(22): pp. 35–44

Schultz, T.W. (1980) 'Nobel lecture: The economics of being poor.' *The Journal of Political Economy*, 88(4): pp. 639–51

Seers, D. (1963) 'The Limitations of the Special Case', *Bulletin of the*

Oxford University Institute of Economics & Statistics, 25.2: pp. 77–98

Suri, K.C. (2004) 'Democracy, Economic Reforms and Election Results in India', *Economic and Political Weekly*, 39(51): pp. 5404–11

Teixeira, R.A. and T.N. Rotta (2012) 'Valueless Knowledge-Commodities and Financialization Productive and Financial Dimensions of Capital Autonomization,' *Review of Radical Political Economics*, 44.4: pp. 448–67

Vakulabharanam, V. (2005) 'Growth and distress in a South Indian peasant economy during the era of economic liberalisation,' *Journal of Development Studies*, 41.6: pp. 971–97

9

Mapping the Changes in Legal Education in India

Srinivas Burra

Changes in legal education in India have taken place in a significant way in the last 25 years and these developments are largely seen as having positive effects. There has been a general consensus among the large section of the legal academia and legal community that these developments need to be taken forward for the purpose of bringing in qualitative changes. This chapter attempts to critically evaluate the efforts made in the post independent India to bring changes in the legal education and particularly focuses on the developments in the last 25 years. While doing so, it identifies some conspicuous drawbacks of the dominant model of legal education that is, national law school pattern. Part One deals with the current situation of legal education followed by discussion on the regulatory mechanism of the legal education in India in Part Two. Part Three deals with the post-independence India efforts towards bringing in changes in legal education. Part Four elaborates on the national law school model adopted in the last 25 years. part five critically evaluates the changes that took place in the form of national law school model. Part Six concludes with certain observations underlining that there are certain aspects which are essential for even meeting the constitutional goals of making available rights framework of the Constitution and statutes to every citizen of India.

1. Legal Education in India: Contemporary Scenario

Primarily, though not exclusively, legal education is expected to provide necessary expertise to a person to represent before a court of law and to be a judicial officer. Legal training is also necessary for several categories of people involved in the adjudicatory process. In addition to this, advanced level of legal education is also required to be a legal researcher and an academic to impart legal education in colleges and universities. Therefore, the existing legal education is expected to meet these requirements.The legal profession is in the form of the adjudicatory system started during the early years of British rule (Schmitthener 1968–9). During that time, the attorneys who practiced before the courts did not have formal training in legal education. A few privileged used to go to Great Britain to receive legal education during the British era. However, that changed over a period of time and 'faculties of law were among the first established in the early modern universities at Calcutta, Bombay and Madras' (Report 1962: p. 224). In post-Independence India, in most of the university systems, law faculties have become an important discipline of learning. Growing demand for legal professionals have led to the establishment of law colleges outside the university system but affiliated to particular universities.

Thus presently, legal education in India is imparted at the departments of law in the traditional university set up and through the colleges affiliated to the traditional university system. In addition to these, the changes that took place in the last 25 years have led to the establishment of national law schools, which started with a National Law School in Bangalore in 1987. Altogether there are more than 1100 law schools today producing more than 50000 law graduates every year (*The Explosion* 2009). The duration of the bachelors degree in law and the curriculum has also undergone changes over a period of time in post-Independence India. Initially, the Bachelor's law degree used to be two years' duration after the bachelors degree. Later on, it was made into the three year's degree after the bachelor's degree in other streams. In the 1980s, mainly with the establishment of national law schools, the duration of the

Bachelor's degree in law has become five years after the 10 plus two schooling. Now, both five years' course after the 10 plus two and the three years' course after the Bachelor's degree are offered. However, the national law schools offer only the five years' law course. The LLB course is offered as a full time course with a few exceptions of evening classes.

2. Regulation of Legal Education

Presently, the legal education, mainly the Bachelor's level legal education is regulated by the Bar Council of India (BCI). This takes place by way of prescribing standards of professional conduct and etiquette and exercising disciplinary jurisdiction over the bar and setting standards for legal education and granting recognition to universities whose degrees in law will serve as necessary qualification for enrolment as an advocate (Advocates Act 1961). BCI was established by an act of parliament that is, the Advocates Act of 1961. Article 7 of the Act deals with the functions of the BCI. Specifically, in accordance with Article 7(I)(h)[1] of the Act, the BCI performs the task of promoting legal education in India and lays down the standards of such education in terms of curriculum, duration of the course and other related aspects. Further in accordance with Article 7(I))(i)[2] of the Act, the BCI also inspects and accredits the institutions that offer essential degrees in law to enroll a person as an advocate. Thus, the essence of the Act in this regard is seen as overseeing the legal profession and the related aspects. In accordance with that mandated task, the BCI also assumed the power of regulating the legal education in terms of curriculum and other aspects. The further, logically linked function is to monitor the institutions that offer basic law degree. These tasks as mandated in the Advocates Act and as they are executed by the BCI seem to have premised on the understanding that the primary purpose of legal education is to produce the persons who are qualified to be as advocates and opt the profession of litigation. However, the regulation of higher education in India in general is entrusted to the University Grants Commission (UGC), which was established under the University Grants Commission Act of 1956. Therefore, as part of the regulation of higher education, the UGC also has authority over legal education in universities. Thus, it is argued that the BCI is not the only body that regulates legal education and other bodies such as the UGC and the concerned universities play significant roles. It is also pointed out that in the absence of clear division of tasks between various bodies and because of overlapping functions and regulation of legal education is seen as in constant state of confusion.

Thus, it is observed that

> 'The regulatory structure for legal education in India is currently seriously flawed and needs careful reconsideration. A typical law college has four mastersat a minimum; the University to which it is affiliated; the state Government; the University Grants Commission; and the Bar Council of India. These four agencies have varying mandates, interests and constituencies and do not provide coherent guidance for the improvement of legal education in the country'.[3]

Despite such observation, it is found that BCI exercises overarching jurisdiction in the regulation of legal education without consulting other bodies. This is not seen as a positive aspect and it is said that

> In the light of the concept behind theAdvocates Act, 1961...very limited powers were conferred on the BCI. But, during the last few decades, in as much as there was no other regulator to take care of emerging needs and trends, the BCI has been dealing with all aspects of legal education under Resolutions, Rules and Regulations instead of limiting itself to the maintenance of minimum standards of legal education for the purpose of entry into the bar (Report 2007: p. 13).

The BCI is argued as having a limited role, as it is compared with the UGC and the Medical Council of India (MCI). It is pointed out that constitutive statutes of the UGC and the MCI talk about the maintenance of standards of education, which are absent in the Advocates Act, which only mentions the minimum standards of legal education and that too in the context of practice before the courts (Report 2007: p. 14).

Therefore, it is underlined that the role being played by the BCI in the regulation of legal education is beyond its mandate, and therefore, it is suggested that a new regulatory mechanism is needed with all the powers to deal with all aspects of legal education (Report 2007: p. 21). The need for such new mechanisms is being felt because the present BCI regulatory system is a deficient one for reasons that, inter alia, the BCI, consisting of elected practicing lawyers is ill equipped to decide on the needs of legal education beyond the court room requirements and the defects in the present system of inspection and accreditation are leading to poor quality of law schools. The demand for revamping the regulatory mechanism of the legal education has certain valid reasons which are much bigger than the technical reasons of the BCI going beyond its mandated power and the above mentioned are some of the valid grounds warranting immediate attention of the policymakers.

However, what needs to be explored is whether by restructuring the regulatory mechanisms alone would it be possible to address all those problems besetting the legal education in India? As will be argued below, the answer would be negative as the focus on the institutional restructuring alone seems to leave important issues aside which are essential for bringing in significant changes that are necessary to make the legal education more comprehensive and inclusive. It is important to look beyond the regulatory and institutional restructuring as the changes in the legal education, albeit with certain specificities, are taking place as part of the larger changes in the field of education in general. Further, to understand and analyse the issues involved in the structure of the legal education it is imperative to look at some of the developments from the early period of the post-Independence India as there have been efforts for long towards bringing in changes in the legal education.

3. Reforms in Legal Education

Taking into consideration the major changes that took place in the field of legal education at different times, they are divided into different stages. It is argued that the first generation of reforms in legal education started with the establishment of the national law schools in 1987 which are 17 such law schools established so far (Vision Statement 2010). There is another view which classifies the changes in legal education so far, as first generation and second generation reforms (Menon 2012). According to this, the first generation legal reforms started after Parliament enacted the Indian Advocates Act of 1961 aiming at integrating the legal profession throughout the country. Through this process the Bar Council India was empowered to promote legal education and regulate its standards. During this time, the major changes that took place were that the LLB became a postgraduate programme of three years, there was a rapid expansion of law teaching institutions, mainly in the private sector, a core curriculum was developed, and a one year compulsory post LLB apprenticeship was established (Menon 2012).

According to this view, the second generation legal reforms started with the establishment of national law school in Bangalore. It led to the establishment of more such law schools now admitting nearly 2000 students every year (Menon 2012). Those who look at these developments positively argue that the national law school experiment was a turning point in Indian legal education particularly in respect of academic excellence, social relevance, and professional competence. Therefore, it is argued that the third or next generation reforms should expand the national law school model across India so that there would be overall qualitative increase in the legal education in India. Thus, this model is evidently emulated by almost every private law school established in the recent past. Except in governing structures, the national law schools and the private law schools are similar in fees structure, curriculum, social composition of students and teachers, and the overall focus of the academic pursuit. However, the national law school, as a successful model, is questionable on several grounds.

Before venturing into the criticalevaluation of the national law school model, it is of contextual significance to look at some of the efforts undertaken in post-independence India, which in many respects laid foundation for the national school model. The legal education in independent India was considered qualitatively low. It was found that in the majority of the universities there was a need for improvement in legal education (Report 1962: p. 225). Accordingly, as far back as in 1948–9, recommendations were made for a thorough reorganization of the law school system that included staff recruitment, duration of the law courses, and conditions to be created for research (Report 1962: pp. 228–9). Though deficiencies were found and recommendations were made, there were not much effort needed to undertake the task of revamping the legal education system. This was very much evident from the Law Commission of India Fourteenth Report on the 'Reform of Judicial Administration' of 1958 (Law Commission 1958). This report, while pointing out the deficiencies of the Indian legal education, cited another report which identified the role the lawyers should play and the role of legal education towards that end. The reports quoted as follows:

> If society is to be adopted to the profound changes in the basis of social and economic life, resulting from changes in world conditions after the war, and in India, particularly after 1947, we feel that is mainly the lawyers that India must look to. The legal profession is called upon to take stock of this situation and to contribute to wide socialadjustments. If it fails do it, it will ultimately be eliminated from the revolutionary scene... We feel that lawyers cannot remain aloof from these processes of evolution and legal education cannot wait until all other problems of the nation are solved. On the contrary lawyers will be called upon to play an important part in these evolutionary processes. Their education, therefore, is of vital importance. This, therefore, is the right time for setting legal education on a sound basis.[4]

Though this view seems to give excessive role to the legal profession and legal institutions in the social processes, it largely sums up the need for reform of legal education and more importantly the purpose, which the reforms should serve. Similar concerns on the state of legal education were expressed by others also, that is, primarily from the point of view of strengthening the quality of legal education.[5] Such views continued to dominate various later studies also. However, the University Grants Commission workshop on Legal Education looked at the issue in a more comprehensive manner. As part of the workshop, Prof. Upendra Baxi in his working paper addressed the need for making the legal education socially relevant, and at the same time, focusing on the quality of legal education (towards 1975–7). Prof. Baxi aptly contextualized the social orientation of the legal education which was identified, though with a different purpose, by the Bombay Legal Education Committee in 1949. However, what is ironical is that none of these reports and recommendations could lead to major changes in the quality of legal education in India till 1980s when it all started with the establishment of a national law school. None of the government bodies paid any serious attention to improve the legal education system. However, prior to the establishment of the first national law school in Bangalore in 1987, a serious attempt was made to bring in changes. This was, however, not by any governmental or statutory body, but by the Ford Foundation.

As stated above, several committees and reports since Independence were pointing out the sorry state of legal education in India, however, without much efforts being initiated from the relevant bodies towards legal education reform. Interestingly, the field of legal education attracted the attention of an external agency that is, the Ford Foundation. The Ford Foundation was established in India in 1952 and it was Ford Foundation's first programme outside the United States. Legal education is one of those fields in which Ford concentrated in its initial days in India. Ford Foundation engaged some of the prominent professors in the US Universities to study the status of legal education in India. In accordance with its unstated larger goals of promoting 'democracy' and free market systems and the 'rule of law', Ford's efforts must have been that to promote rule of law. It is essential to promote necessary legal education towards those objectives, which in the economic and political realm were already adopted in India. Ford's effort was to encourage an American law school model in India (Krishnan 2004: p. 448). Accordingly, the Ford engaged prominent professors from American law schools to travel to India to study the Indian legal education system in Indian universities and make recommendations.[6]

As a result of the assessment of the Ford engaged professors and based on their recommendations, financial support was first given to establish the Indian Law Institute in New Delhi in December 1956, which was intended to be modeled on the American Law Institute[7]. As there was no prominent institute focusing on research in the field of law, the purpose of the establishment of an institute of this nature must have been to promote legal research with its immediate practical relevance to the existing legal system. Further based on the recommendations of these US professors, Ford Foundation made its financial support to the Faculty of Law of the Benares Hindu University in 1964. This was followed by the similar support to the Faculty of Law, Delhi University. Along with the financial support to these institutions, several Indian professors, with the support of the Ford Foundation, travelled to the US to study the American law school system. As mere financial support does not help to bring in the necessary changes, the Ford Foundation's idea must have been to expose Indian law professors to the US law school system, in order to implement the absorbed planning and execution of the curriculum and the pedagogy. This effort from the Ford Foundation in certain respects delivered the results they wanted as some of the professors who went on such missions to the US later went on to be in the forefront of reforms in legal education, which took place in the form of the national law schools. However, this support did not continue for long. Based on further reports of the US professors, the Ford Foundation withdrew from engaging itself in the field of legal education, as the task of reforming it was found to be gigantic. Some of the professors engaged by the Ford Foundation were of the view that changes should come from within and with the help of the Indian academicians. What needs to be emphasized is that its initiatives by way of engaging in providing financial assistance to the Indian Law Institute and the law faculties of the BHU and DU and by way of interacting with some of the prominent faculty members of these institutions, Ford's idea of introducing the American law school model in India received serious consideration in India. Though this did not result in immediate changes but significantly similar to what was discussed was realized to a large extent through the establishment of national law school in 1987.

4. National Law Schools

In the history of Indian legal education, the establishment of the National Law School at Bangalore in 1987 is considered as a turning point towards bringing in significant changes.[8] With the active involvement of Prof. N.R. Madhava Menon, the founder Director of the Bangalore Law School, the Bar Council of India involved itself with the Karnataka State Government and established this law school (Krishnan 2004: p. 472). This law school is considered as a trendsetter as several other states followed this model and established similar institutions. The major changes that these law schools adopted were that the duration of the course was made five years after the 10 plus two, similar to medicine and engineering courses in India. Clinical legal education has become an important component of the curriculum. Teaching methods have undergone changes with active participation of students in the classroom interactions. As these law schools are being seen as models to be emulated, several private universities are following the similar pattern. It is also being seen as the model to be replicated by all the institutions that impart legal education (Report of the Working Group on Legal Education 2007: pp. 16–17). More importantly, though argued as having started before the economic liberalization in India, the establishment of law schools, in fact, coincided with economic liberalization and their 'success' in many respects is due to the larger changes that were brought in by the Indian State in the neoliberal framework of the withdrawal of the state.

5. National Law Schools and Legal Education: Critical Evaluation

Since Independence, every committee or commission that worked on legal education invariably referred to the poor quality of legal education in India and the need for bringing in changes. Ford Foundation attempted to mould Indian law schools on the model of the American law schools. These efforts were not taken forward, as the Ford Foundation withdrew its support and active involvement. Thus, the primary effort of the National Law School, Bangalore was to address the problem of quality. The experience of the founder director Prof. Madhava Menon in the US law school model legal education became handy for him when he started working on it. The legal aid clinics model being adopted by some of the American law schools impressed Prof. Menon. Though Ford Foundation stopped funding legal education in India, it supported the legal aid clinics in American law schools (Krishnan 2004: p. 484). In that sense, though Ford Foundation discontinued its funding, its initial ideas of changing legal education in India came to be implemented later on through the national law school models. Therefore, it is not a surprise that, despite withdrawing from legal education, the Foundation supported the National Law School, Bangalore financially at its inception (Krishnan 2004: p. 492). The emphasis of the curriculum at the law schools was different from what was being followed in other traditional law schools. The conspicuous contribution of this model was to redefine the relation between the teacher and students in terms of intellectual interactions which gave rise to confidence building of students, at the same time posing an intellectual challenge to teachers, forcing them constantly meet the expectations of the students.

It is said that one of the major objectives which led to the establishment of this law school was to develop socially relevant public interest oriented legal education with quality. As the National Law School of India Act (1986) says, the objectives of the law school are, inter alia,

> to develop in the student and research scholar a sense of responsibility to serve society in the field of law by developing skills in regard to advocacy, legal services, legislation, law reforms and the like...to promote legal knowledge and to make law and the legal processes efficient instruments of social development...

Purportedly to meet its larger objectives, the National Law School, Bangalore (later on followed by others) brought in sea changes in what is taught and how it is taught. However, what

Mapping the Changes in Legal Education in India 223

needs to be underlined, based on the experience of the graduates of these law schools, is that what is taught and how it is taught do not seem to have gone to serve the purpose of creating socially relevant lawyers and legal researchers. It is evident from the fact of where the law school places itself in the larger Indian reality. The website of the National Law School Bangalore states:

> The challenge for the Law School is to stay ahead especially in the context of globalisation. The Law School has the social responsibility of continuing to be a Centre of Excellence in the field of legal education, a position which it came to occupy within the first ten years itself due mainly to the dedicated efforts of the Faculty and students during those initial and formative years. Globalisation has thrown up new challenges, and the professional legal education has to cater to the growing demands for skilled legal professionals who can effectively function in the emerging legal order. The present challenge is to measure up to internationally acceptable levels of excellence.

Further, the website says that the General Council of the Law school in its resolution dated 26 August 2006 states that

> [T]his Law School was established with a view to cater to the requirements of the legal profession, law teaching and research, and judiciary and it is expected that the students who study in this School will eventually become legal practitioners, law teachers or engage in legal research or enter the judiciary in due course.

It is clear from the above that the purpose of the law school is cater to the demands of globalization rather than to make critical intervention in the process through learning methods and curriculum and find possible solutions to the problems posed by globalization. Thus, as stated above, its social responsibility lies only to the extent of remaining a centre of excellence in a particular sense that is, meeting the demands of globalization. However, this is very much at odds with the objective, assuming that its objective was to be socially relevant in achieving the minimum constitutional goals.

It is pertinent to mention here that globalization which the National Law School intends to serve, is unleashing a devastating effect on certain sections of the Indian society. The role of the judiciary in achieving the constitutional goals is being questioned. Ironically, this is pointed out by one of the former Directors of the National Law School, Bangalore. While discussing the role of the Indian judiciary, he observes that

> The 22 years since 1991 have seen a radical change in the approach of the court. It did not go back to the first phase of resisting social change. Instead, it seems to have shifted (as a general trend) to a different approach to social change—through market-based economic growth rather than through redistribution of wealth or breaking down social oligopolies as envisaged in the Constitution.
>
> This is not an isolated view. Social change through market-based economic growth enjoys the support of a strong political consensus (across the political spectrum). It is the aspiration of a new and powerful middle class. However, this approach is not in line with many aspects of the specific provisions of the constitutional vision of social justice. It does not give primacy to the working class—whether in the unorganized sector or in the organised sector. It has little room for either redistribution of assets (even through protection of minimum wages, progressive taxation and other labour rights) or for breaking down social injustice through, for example, affirmative action. It favours the use of coercive measures to put down the struggle of the poor to retain access to land, water and food. It demands better and stronger top-down executive governance and a whittling down of democracy where needed in the interests of growth (Gopal 2013: pp. 10–11).

This is what the present model of economic policies and globalization means to the constitutional ideals. Therefore, any socially sensitive legal education should essentially be challenging this model of development and seek to creatively intervene in the larger scenario. The curriculum and the pedagogy adopted by these law schools, while producing excellence in a particular way, largely served the needs of the market. It is found that many students who joined these law schools had the vision of placing themselves in social change when they entered. However, it was found that this idealism did not get translated into practice when they passed out (Ballakrishnen 2009: p. 147)). It is observed based on a study of the 2010 graduates from the three prominent law schools, that is, Bangalore, Hyderabad, and Kolkata that 44.2 per cent of the graduates chose a career in Indian and international corporate law firms, 20.9 per cent chose legal and business positions in large companies, less than five per cent joined the Indian Civil Services, and less than one per cent joined NGOs or public interest organizations (Papa and Wilkins 2011: p. 189). It is observed that this pattern looks 'similar to what one might see in a top US law school is further evidence that the India legal profession, like its US counterpart, may be divided into two separate and self replicating hemispheres, in which one of the primary functions of elite law schools is to feed students into the expanding corporate arena' (Papa and Wilkins 2011: p. 189). This phenomenon is recognized by the founder Director of the National Law school, Bangalore himself who underlined that the curriculum at the national law schools be geared to the private sector (Menon 2012: p. 8). What needs to be pointed out is that the national law schools run on the financial support largely from the student fees. As a result, the fee structure is high. Those who join these law schools by paying high tuition fees are attracted to toward the private sector where they start their career with better pay packages, and therefore, are less inclined to go into litigation in general, and into the lower judiciary and litigation at the lower courts in particular.

5.a. Exclusionist in Nature

An important dimension of legal education in India that does not get necessary attention is the exclusion of certain sections of Indian society from access to legal education. As stated earlier, several committees worked on the status of legal education and some of them wanted it to be turned into socially relevant legal education. However, there was hardly any emphasis on socially inclusionist legal education in India. This mirrors the political and ideological positions and the privileged social background of those who have been in the forefront of reforming legal education and their reluctance to make legal education socially inclusionist and egalitarian. As a result, of this overly exclusivist nature of legal education, there has been only a miniscule presence of people coming from socially disadvantaged sections of India in the higher judicial positions. It has not been considered as a serious issue by the policymakers and educationists. This is not merely a reflection of the apathy of policymakers towards the selection process of the judges and others. It is equally a reflection of the reality of Indian legal education, which does not encourage students from these sections to pursue legal education. Making the legal education socially representative does not merely empower the socially disadvantaged which in itself isan essential component of a democratic society, it also brings myriad life experiences into the judicial process and legal scholarship. This would make the adjudicatory process and judicial outcomes representative of social reality and inclusionist. If not in substantive and comprehensive sense, even the rhetoric of formal equality cannot ignore the need for social inclusionist judiciary. The need for a socially representative judiciary is very much felt by other countries also. The UK advisory panel on Judicial Diversity said in February 2010 that

> In a democratic society the judiciary should reflect the diversity of society and the legal profession as a whole. Judges drawn from a wide range of backgrounds and life experiences will bring varying perspectives to bear on critical legal issues. A judiciary which is visibly more reflective of society will enhance public confidence (cited by Gopal 2013: p. 12).

The Indian situation is such that the Indian judiciary does not reflect the Indian social reality in terms of representation. A study conducted for the period between 1950 and 1989 shows that in the Indian Supreme Court, Brahmins who constituted 5.3 per cent of the total population occupied 42.9 per cent of the judge positions and other forward castes who constituted 29.7 of the total population, occupied 49.4 per cent judge positions. On the other hand, Scheduled Castes who constituted 14.6 per cent of the total population occupied 2.6 per cent judge positions, Scheduled Tribes who constituted 6.9 per cent of the total population not represented at all and other backward classes (OBCs) who constituted 26.1 per cent of the total population occupied 5.2 per cent of the judge positions (Gadbois 2012: p. 344). Though this situation seems to have improved later on slightly. A critical aspect in this context is to make the legal education socially inclusionist so that it would lead to socially inclusionist legal profession leading ultimately to socially inclusionist Indian judiciary. Surprisingly, none of the important committees and reports on legal education seem to have given adequate emphasis on the social and economic hierarchies that plague the India society and the need for any reform in the education to address it as an essential component. However, this was found to be an important obstacle towards reforming legal education in India by American professors engaged by the Ford Foundation to study legal education in India (cited by Krishnan 2004: p. 459). Mr Arthur von Mehran in his report to the Ford Foundation in 1963 said that the resource poor, caste conscious society glued to non-egalitarian customs are preventing the serious social progress and a dynamic, rational legal system based on equality and individual liberty and governed by fair rules and procedures simply could not thrive in that environment (cited by Krishnan 2004: p. 460). This observation is a significant one but was not taken into consideration seriously by any of the committees and reports prior to or after it was pointed out by American professors. The non-egalitarian and hierarchized social structures did not allow the socially and economically deprived sections to access education in general and legal education has been far from the reach of many from those sections. This is also very much reflected in scholarship in the field of law. Legal scholarship in India is predominantly confined to the formalistic analysis of texts, rules, and interpretations. The theoretical formulations and analysis of law with alternative standpoints did not emerge in the India legal academia. Subjecting law and legal processes to critical interrogation, took place elsewhere in the form of critical legal studies and critical race theory, and did not take place in India. This seems to be mainly, but not exclusively, because the quality of legal education has been far from the reach of the subaltern social groups in India like Dalits, Adivasis, OBCs, and minorities whose living experiences would have brought critical perspectives into legal scholarship. The living experiences of Dalits and other deprived sections are never seriously considered as subjects of legal analysis. A similar situation exists with regard to the feminist analysis of discipline of law. In fact, in India, rarely does one come across social analysis of law and law's role in perpetuating and essentializing hierarchies. There could have been, for example, a Dalit or subaltern legal theory critiquing the Indian law and the legal system, which is happening vibrantly in the case of other social sciences. Such intellectual movements are not new to the field of law in other contexts like in the United States. Critical Race Theory[9] and LatCrit Theory[10] have put in robust critique of the field of law in the United States from the view point of blacks and Latinas/os. However, scholarly legal writing in India primarily remains a formalistic analysis without having much to do with social reality at large, with a few exceptions.[11]

Therefore, any effort towards bringing in changes in legal education cannot afford to exclude the social dimension of scholarship in and of law in India. However, none of the reform efforts seem to focus on this issue. More importantly, the law schools that are being seen as the models to be emulated are further perpetuating the exclusionist nature of legal education in India. Admission into these law schools is based on the merit in the common law admission test conducted at the all-India level. They seem to implement the Scheduled Castes and Scheduled Tribes reservation in the admission into the LLB programme. However, as pointed out earlier, the fee structure of these law schools is high and therefore it is difficult for students coming from socially and economically deprived sections to get into these law schools by paying the exorbitant fees and living expenditure in these institutions. The most socially exclusionist policy adopted by the law schools is that none of them seem to follow the reservation policy for recruitment of teachers and non-teaching staff. Though there does not seem to be any empirically established statistics on this aspect, a random enquiry into some of the law schools suggests that reservation policy is not followed in recruitments. As pointed out in the previous section, this is another form of excluding the myriad experiences in the imparting of legal education and scholarship. While promoting excellence of a particular kind, which is mainly to suit the globalizing market, the law school model completely overlooks the constitutionally established inclusionist measures. This policy effectively reinforces the standard anti-reservation strand, that is, it denies the constitutionally enshrined right to equal opportunity, and secondly, it sends across the narrow understating of the knowledge system that promoting excellence and equal opportunity are mutually exclusive. However, what needs to be underlined is that this view of excellence is not comprehensive as it does not reflect the living experiences of the different classes and thus remains narrow and also does not promote the larger societal goals of equality and justice.

5.b. More Market Friendly than Being Socially Relevant

The success story of the Bachelor's degree in these law schools has certain problematic consequences. Firstly, the success of the bachelors programme is being primarily measured in terms of their placement with legal firms and the corporate sector. Therefore, the argument for emulating this model essentially involves producing law graduates to serve primarily the market and the corporate sector. The success is not measured taking into consideration the legal field in its totality but to confine it to its limited success in the corporate sector. The second consequence is largely related to the first one. By way of measuring the success of law schools in terms of placement of students in the corporate sector, the core element of legal education, which is to lead law graduates to the legal profession on the litigation side with a social responsibility of serving the needy is neglected. If legal education and the profession have to serve, the purpose of being instrumental in delivering justice to the needy, the quality of legal education of the law school model should be primarily serving the poor and the needy in realizing their constitutionally given rights to justice. Various other factors also contribute to this situation. Because of the non-inclusionist nature of the law schools in terms of student composition, teachers' social background, and many others with respect to curriculum, the graduates are primarily moving towards market driven jobs than into socially relevant litigation. This was rightly pointed out by the National Knowledge

Commission working group on legal education, which stated that 'in the last fifteen years, ever since the NLSUs have been established, meritorious students both from NLSUs and some other law schools are joining law firms and corporate houses in greater numbers than those who opt for the bar and the subordinate judiciary. One of the objectives of establishing the NLSUs was to improve the quality of the barf and the subordinate judiciary' (Report 2007: p. 17).

5.c. Neglecting the Postgraduate Programmes

One of the success stories that is often emphasized is the LLB. The Bangalore law school started with their five-year LLB programme. Their Master's programmes started later. A largely similar pattern was followed by other law schools. The emphasis of the national law schools has been primarily on the bachelor's degree programme that is, the LLB. Though most of these law schools have Master's programmes, it is generally argued that they is not as successful as the Bachelor's degree. Thus, the law schools project their success by showing how many of their Bachelor's degree holders got into prominent law firms and multinational companies and rarely does one comes across their projection of the Master's and research programmes.

The consequence of this is the absence of focus on postgraduate studies and research in national law schools. As a result, there is a paucity of teachers and researchers in the field of law, which is being felt by the law schools themselves. With all their infirmities, the law faculties in the traditional university system maintained a fair balance between the graduate programmes and postgraduate and research studies. Thus, the task of producing postgraduate researchers and teachers is still primarily left to the traditional university system where the legal education is being neglected in most places because the focus is solely directed towards the law school model. Historically, there has not been much emphasis on research in legal education. As a result, one does not find scholarly recognized journals of repute being published from India, with the notable exception of the *Indian Journal of International Law* (IJIL) published by the Indian Society of International Law (ISIL) and the *Journal of*

Indian Law Institute (JILI) published by the Indian Law Institute (ILI). So far, the law schools, despite their presence for the last two decades, have failed to fill this gap.

6. Conclusion

Several committees and experts who analysed the status of legal education in post-Independence India found major shortcomings in it. The Ford Foundation focused on reforming legal education with its larger purpose of promoting market friendly legal system and formalistic understating of rule of law. Though the Ford Foundation withdrew from promoting legal education in India, the conceptual framework with which it entered legal education continued to influence later similar efforts. Ford's larger objective of moulding Indian law schools on the model of American law schools was realized later in the form of the national law schools. The situation was ripe for national law schools to succeed in India as their establishment coincided with economic liberalization, which created a particular set of jobs for the law graduates from these law schools. The placement of law graduates from these law schools is being celebrated as a success and there have been suggestions to emulate this model by other law schools. However, one cannot but be skeptical of this model if one is to take into consideration the field of law in its totality. The law school model has further reinforced the exclusionist nature of legal education as its admission system, recruitment policy, and in many respects, even the curriculum do not accommodate the socially disadvantaged sections. Law graduates from these law schools are also attracted to the corporate sector and are not inclined to the litigation side. This situation ignores the fundamental requirement of delivering justice to the needy. It is rightly observed that the

> main challenge facing India's legal and judicial systems is delivering justice to poor people. For the most part, people deprived of constitutional or legislative rights have little access to courts...Increasing number of the best law graduates are moving to corporate law practice and civil and criminal litigation at the local level is suffering from a serious dearth of adequately qualified

legal professionals (Report of the Working Group on Legal Education 2007: p. 18–19).

Further, there is a negligence of the postgraduate and research studies leading to the dearth of qualified teachers and researchers. From post-Independence days, legal education in India is considered as qualitatively low. It has been socially exclusionist in nature because of certain structural inequalities in Indian society. The national law school model, which is seen as a significant development, has further aggravated the situation. Legal education in the traditional university system has been neglected in the last two decades because of the withdrawal of the State from the field of legal education. The national law school system, which emerged in the last decades, largely runs on high student fees, and as a result, has distanced itself from large section of the Indian society. The overall orientation of these law schools is, therefore, socially exclusionary, economically inaccessible to the deprived, and primarily serves the corporate sector. Thus, any effort towards reforms should be focused on emphasizing the need for State financing of legal education with equal access to all sections of the society. There is a dire need to revamp the curriculum to make it socially relevant towards achieving, at the very minimum, the constitutional goals of equality and justice for all.

NOTES

1. Article 7(1)(h) reads as follows: 'to promote legal education and to lay down standards of such education in consultation with the Universities in India imparting such education and the State Bar Councils'
2. Article 7(1)(i)reads as follows: 'to recognize universities whose degree in law shall be a qualification for enrolment as an advocate and for that purpose to visit and inspect universities...'
3. First National Consultation Conference of Heads of Legal Educational Institutions (2002). cited by (Basheer and Mukherjee 2010)
4. *Report of the Bombay Legal Education Committee*, (1949) p. 5, quoted in the Report of the Law Commission of India, pp. 523–4

5. The Gajendragadkar Committee was established by the University of Delhi in 1963 to improve the quality of legal education in Delhi University
6. Prof. Carl B. Spaeth of the Stanford Law School visited India in 1956 along with Herbert Merillat, a lawyer. Prof. Arthur von Mehren of Harvard Law School in 1962–3; Kenneth Pye of the Georgetown University Law Centre in 1966–7 and a few others. For details see (Krishnan 2014)
7. The American Institute of Law was founded in 1923. The Institute drafts, discusses, revises, and publishes Restatements of the Law, model statutes, and principles of law that are enormously influential in the courts and legislatures, as well as in legal scholarship and education. For details, see, http://www.ali.org
8. The National Law School of India University came into existence through a notification under the National Law School of India University Act (Karnataka Act 22 of 1986). The first batch of students was selected throughnational entrance test, and regular academic activities began on 1 July 1988
9. Critical race theory began as a movement in the field of law which 'questions the very foundations of the liberal order, including equality theory, legal reasoning, enlightenment rationalism, and neutral principles of constitutional law' (Delgado and Stefancic 2001: p. 3)
10. 'LatCrit theory is an infant discourse that responds primarily to the long historical presence and general sociolegal invisibility of Latinas/os in the lands now known as the United States . As with other traditionally subordinated communities within this country, the combination of longstanding occupancy and persistent marginality fueled an increasing sense of frustration among contemporary Latina/o legal scholars, some of whom already identified with Critical Race Theory (CRT) and participated in its gatherings. Like other genres of critical legal scholarship, LatCrit literature tends to reflect the conditions of its production as well as the conditioning of its early and vocal adherents' (Valdés)
11. Prominent exceptions are scholars like Upendra Baxi, mainly but not exclusively in the field of domestic law, and B.S. Chimni in the field of international law. However, one comes across a few voices in the feminist analysis of legal field in India which include but not limited to Flavia Agnes, Ratna Kapoor, Nivedita Menon and Kalpana Kannabiran. A welcome initiative in this regard is the Law and Social Sciences Research Network

(LASNET), started at the Centre for the Study of Law and Governance at Jawaharlal Nehru University, New Delhi

REFERENCES

Advocates Act of India (1961)
Basheer, Shamnad and Sroyon Mukherjee (2010) 'Regulating Indian Legal Education: Some Thoughts for Reform', http://papers.ssrn.com/sol3/papers.cfm?abstract_id=1584037 (Last accessed on 17 September 2013)
Ballakrishnen, Swethaa (2009) 'Where did we come from? Where do we go? An Enquiry into the Students and Systems of Legal Education in India' *Journal of Commonwealth Law and Legal Education*, Vol. 7 (2): 133-154
Dasgupta, Lovely (2009-2010) 'Reforming Indian Legal Education: Linking Research and Teaching' *Journal of Legal Education*, Vol. 59(): 433-449
Delgado, Richard and Jean Stefancic (2001)*Critical Race Theory: An Introduction*, New York University Press: New York
Gadbois, JR George H. (2012) *Judges of the Supreme Court of India: 1950-1989*, Oxford University Press: New Delhi
Galanter, Marc & Jayanth K. Krishnan (2003-2004) '"Bread for the Poor": Access to Justice and the Rights of the Needy in India' *Hastings Law Journal*, Vol. 55 (), 789-834
Gopal, Mohan (2013) 'Supreme Court and the Aam Admi' *Frontline*, May 3: 10-13
Krishnan, Jayanth K. (2004) 'Professor Kingfield goes to Delhi: American Academics, the Ford Foundation, and the Development of Legal Education in India' *American Journal of Legal History*, Vol. 46 (): 447-499
Krishnan, Jayanth K. (2005) 'From the ALI to ILI: The Efforts to Export an American Legal Institution' *Vanderbilt Journal of Transnational Law*, Vol. 38 (5): 1255-1293
Law Commission of India (1958) Fourteenth Report (Reform of Judicial Administration), http://lawcommissionofindia.nic.in/1-50/Report14Vol1.pdf (Last accessed on 17 September 2013)
Menon, N.R. Madhava (2012) 'The Transformation of Indian Legal Education: A Blue Paper' *Harvard Law School Program on the Legal Education*, http://www.law.harvard.edu/programs/plp/pdf/Menon_Blue_Paper.pdf (Last accessed on 17 September 2013)
National Law School of India University Act (Karnataka Act 22 of 1986)

Papa, Mihaela & David B. Wilkins (2001) 'Globalization, Lawyers and India: Toward a Theoretical Synthesis of Globalization Studies and the Sociology of the Legal Profession' *International Journal of the Legal Profession*, Vol. 18(3): 175-209.
Report of the Expert Panel on the National Law School of India University. 1987-1996.
Report of the University Education Commission (December 1948-August 1949), vol. I, Ministry of Education, Government of India, 1962, http://www.teindia.nic.in/Files/Reports/CCR/Report%20of%20the%20University%20Education%20Commission.pdf ((Last accessed on 17 September 2013)
Report of the Working Group on Legal Education (2007) National Knowledge Commission, http://knowledgecommission.gov.in/downloads/documents/wg_legal.pdf (Last accessed on 17 September 2013)
Schmitthener, Samuel (1968-69) 'A Sketch of the Development of the Legal Profession in India', *Law and Society Review*, Vol. 3 (): 337-382.
Towards a Socially Relevant Legal Education: A Consolidated Report of the University Grant Commission's Workshop on Modernization of Legal Education (1975-77), http://www.ugc.ac.in/oldpdf/pub/report/1.pdf (Last accessed on 17 September 2013)
The Explosion in the Number of Law Colleges in India-Few Thoughts, http://theunwillinglawyer.blogspot.in/2009/07/explosion-in-number-of-law-colleges-in.html (Last accessed on 17 September 2013)
Valdés, Francisco. Lat Crit: A Conceptual Overview. http://www.latcrit.org/content/about/conceptual-overview/ (Last accessed on 17 September 2013)
Vision statement delivered by the law minister, Veerappa Moily during the course of the second day at the conference of National Consultation for Second Generation Reforms in Legal Education, held at the Vigyan Bhawan in New Delhi on 1and 2 May, 2010. http://www.barcouncilofindia.org/law-ministers-vision-statement-for-second-generation-reforms-in-legal-education/ (Last accessed on 17 September 2013)

10

Countering Neoliberal Conception of Knowledge, Building Emancipatory Discourse: A Historical Overview of Phule-Ambedkar's Critique and Gandhian Nai Taleem[1]

Anil Sadgopal

What is the compelling reason that prompted the writing of this paper? Is there any historical necessity today to examine the educational discourse that evolved for more than a century during India's anti-colonial struggle? What might have been the ideological context(s) of this discourse and its linkage with the intense debates on socioeconomic goals and the development model that India must pursue after Independence? A possible answer to such questions may be found in the following profound statement on the implications of prevailing neoliberalism and its impact on our minds, values, and society, apart from moulding the direction of development.

Neoliberalism attempts to eliminate an engaged critique about its most basic principles and social consequences by embracing the 'market as the arbiter of social destiny'. Not only does neoliberalism bankrupt public funds, hollow out public services, limit the vocabulary and imagery available to recognize anti-democratic forms of power, and produce narrow models of individual agency, but it also undermines the critical functions of any viable democracy by undercutting the ability of individuals to engage in the continuous translation between public considerations and private interests by collapsing the public into the realm of the private. (Giroux 2004)

Giroux's reference to 'market as the arbiter of social destiny', 'narrow models of individual agency', and 'collapsing the public into the realm of the private' as hallmarks of neoliberalism also happen to be reminders, though distant ones, of what may have been the factors in facilitating the advance of colonial power in the Indian subcontinent in the nineteenth century. It would be no one's claim that the present crisis of capitalism that has led to neoliberalism has any parallels with the phase of capitalism in the nineteenth century and its inevitable engagement with the feudal conditions then characterizing India. Yet, the ruthless pursuit of market and natural resources by the East India Company and its successful strategy of co-opting the then ruling Indian elite (for example, the *bhadralok* of Bengal), in its project of colonization, do persuade us to dwell upon how these neoliberal imperatives may have then also operated, albeit in their rudimentary forms. The educational discourse and the contextual ideological debates during the anti-colonial struggle that this paper proposes to examine could not have but engaged with and responded to these dominant historical processes of colonization. This then is the rationale for taking a historical overview of the educational discourse during the anti-colonial struggle and drawing lessons therefrom for the on-going struggle against the comprehensive neoliberal assault on India's education, apart from a similar assault on the people's resources of *jal-jangal-zameen-jeevika* (Nater-forest-land-livelihood).

1.0 Lord Macaulay's Minutes and Seeding of a Colonial Education System

We begin with Lord Macaulay's Minutes of February, 1835 which he penned in his dual capacity as Member of the Council of India and Chairperson of the Committee of Public Instruction of the British *Raj*. The following excerpts from the minutes should reveal how the colonial rulers planned to make education an instrumentality for advancing the interests of the East India Company, thereby reinforcing the British Empire.

... the dialects commonly spoken among the natives of this part of India [i.e. Bengal] contain neither literary nor scientific information, and *are moreover so poor and rude that, until they are enriched from some other quarter, it will not be easy to translate any valuable work into them.* ... the intellectual improvement of those classes of the people *who have the means of pursuing higher studies* can at present be affected only by means of some language not vernacular amongst them. [emphasis mine] (Para 8)

... a single shelf of a good European library was worth the whole native literature of India and Arabia. The *intrinsic superiority* of the Western literature is indeed fully admitted ... [emphasis mine] (Para 10)

... We have to educate a people *who cannot at present be educated by means of their mother-tongue*. We must teach them some foreign language. ... In India, *English is the language spoken by the ruling class. It is spoken by the higher class of natives at the seats of Government.* [emphasis mine] (Para 12)

... *it is impossible for us, with our limited means, to attempt to educate the body of the people*. We must at present do our best to form a class who may be interpreters between us and the millions whom we govern - *a class of persons Indian in blood and colour, but English in tastes, in opinions, in morals and in intellect.* ... [emphasis mine] (Para 34)

(Lord Macaulay's Minutes, 2 February 1835)

This document, 'farsighted' as it was for advancing the interests of British trade and commerce, presented the central thesis of the education policy that was to be pursued by the colonial rulers for more than a century. We can today identify the following policy elements that were seeded and promoted by Lord Macaulay's Minutes, explicitly or implicitly:

- All knowledge in various disciplines—literature, philosophy, social science, or science—in languages used in the Indian subcontinent, including Arabic and Sanskrit, is inferior to knowledge available in European languages, among which English surpasses the rest. There is no aspect of knowledge in any Indian language, including literature, which is worthy of being encouraged among the 'learned natives of India'.

- The Indian languages stood reduced to merely being dialects 'commonly spoken among the natives' and further dubbed as being 'so poor and rude that, until they are enriched from some other quarter', were not even good enough for translating the Western literature of 'intrinsic superiority'.
- In its own vested interest, the British rulers must 'educate' the ruling class of India, which can't be 'educated by means of their mother-tongue'. The medium of *'instruction'* (mark, not *education*) has to be English since it was already being spoken 'by the higher class of natives at the seats of Government'.
- The goal of English 'instruction' will be to co-opt the upper classes and upper castes, irrespective of their religious background, to think, speak, and act in the interest of the colonial empire and be its ally in making the Indian masses subservient.

Thus, the colonial educational policy was designed to facilitate the British capital in its project of loot, exploitation, and hegemony in India. Yet, 'limited means' (recall the 'resource crunch' rhetoric of the present Indian ruling class) would be claimed whenever the colonial rulers would be confronted with the question of educating the masses. It should surprise no one that basically the same colonial framework, with due adjustments, has guided the education policy of the post-Independence Indian State till to date, serving the interests of primarily the Indian corporate capital (the so-called 'national bourgeoisie' to which we will return later) during the first four decades and those of the neoliberal economic order in the next two decades.

2.0 Emergence of Phule as an 'Organic Intellectual'

In 1848, Savitribai and Jotirao Phule established a Marathi medium girls' school in Pune. A fair proportion of students were drawn from Dalit and other backwards sections of society. This was arguably one of the earliest 'national' schools of 'modern' India that departed from the British policy of using English education to co-opt 'the higher class of natives' as an ally. Phule went ahead to build an anti-caste discourse as documented in his *Gulamgiri (Slavery* 1873) and *Shetkaryacha Asud (Cultivator's Whipcord* 1883), both written originally in Marathi (Deshpande 2002: pp. 23–99 and 113–89). In these two seminal works, Phule emerges as an organic intellectual who uses historiography to reveal the history of the subaltern castes namely, *shudra-atishudras* (Bagade 2012, Unpublished Paper). He infers that knowledge of the true history of the *shudra-atishudra* castes would lead to anti-caste revolution to liberate the entire people from the shackles of caste system or *Varnashram*.

In 1882, Jotirao Phule (by then reverently called Mahatma Phule) presented his historic 'Memorandum to the Indian Education Commission' that is, 'Hunter Commission' (Phule 1882), wherein he dwelt upon how the British government's funding of education tended to benefit 'Brahmins and the higher classes' while leaving 'the masses wallowing in ignorance and poverty'. He drew attention to the irony that this happens when 'the portion of the revenues of the Indian Empire are derived from the greater ryot's [that is, peasantry's] labour—from the sweat of his brow.' Things have not fundamentally changed since then.

Phule's empirical study of almost half a century of the practice of Macaulayian policy in the Bombay Presidency had convinced him to question the socio-political character of knowledge in education imparted by the government—*from primary school onwards to higher education*. As probably the earliest recorded statement of resistance to colonial framework, Phule's Memorandum asserts: 'The system [of primary education] is imperfect in so far as it does not prove practical and useful in the future career of the pupils... Both the teaching machinery employed and the course of instruction now followed, require a thorough remodeling.'

The Memorandum expresses Phule's deep concern that almost all the teachers employed in the primary schools were Brahmins not used to productive manual labour, '...and the boys who learn under them generally *imbibe inactive habits* and try to obtain *[government] service*...' He proposed that the primary school teachers should be those 'who will not feel *ashamed to hold the handle of a plough or the carpenter's adze* when required, and who will be able to *mix themselves readily with the lower orders of society.*' [emphasis mine] The Memorandum demanded that the mother tongue should be the medium of education in school education. Further, 'knowledge of *agriculture* and a few lessons on *moral duties and sanitation*' along with practical experience and '*some useful arts*' should be included in the curriculum which will require 'revision and recasting' of the textbooks. Evidently, the alienation of the peasantry from the knowledge and pedagogic content of the colonial schools and colleges became the focus of Phule's critique. Regarding higher education as well, Phule argued in favour of providing equal access to all and ensuring that its curriculum is relevant to the aspirations and needs of the young people. His alternative educational vision constituted his resistance to the colonial policies.

3.0 Gandhian Civilizational Debate

There is no known link, ideological or otherwise, between Phule and Gandhi, except for a broadly common experience of Indian socio-cultural milieu under the colonial impact. Yet, Phule's critique of the Macaulayian framework uncannily appears to be a trailblazer of the civilizational debate that Gandhi's Hind Swaraj (1909) initiated a quarter century later, questioning the ideology of colonial hegemony and exploitation. Gandhi interpreted the British education policy in India in terms of his intuitive understanding, rather than a coherent theory, of the imperialistic design of the British *Raj*. He countered the basic proposition of the colonial rulers with the following assertions:

> ... The foundation that Macaulay laid of education has enslaved us... Is it not a sad commentary that we should have to speak of *Swarajya* [Self-Rule] in a foreign tongue?
>
> ...by receiving English education, we have enslaved the nation. Hypocrisy, tyranny, etc. have increased; English-knowing Indians have not hesitated to cheat and strike terror into the people.
>
> ... It is we, the English-knowing men, that have enslaved India. The curse of the nation will rest not upon English but upon us.
>
> (*Hind Swaraj* or *HS* (1909), Chapter XVIII)

Gandhi raises the level of this debate when he writes:

> The curriculum and pedagogic ideas which form the fabric of modern education were imported from Oxford and Cambridge, Edinburgh and London. But they are essentially foreign, and *till they are repudiated, there never can be national education*... The question then is this: The choice must be clearly and finally made between national and foreign education, the choice of type and archetype, of meaning and purpose, of ends and means.' [emphasis mine]
> (*Young India*, 20 March 1924)

Making a case for what he called 'national education', Gandhi invariably questioned the socio-political character of education imparted in British *Raj*. For instance, here he contrasts the character of students from Gujarat Vidyapeeth, a 'national university' created in 1920 as part of the freedom movement, with those from the Government colleges or universities:

> One of our students has gone to jail in Bardoli [farmers' movement] and many more will go. They are the pride of the Vidyapith. Much as they may desire to do likewise, can students of Government [i.e. British institutions] dare to do so? It is not open to them to go to Bardoli and help Vallabhbhai [Patel], as it is to you. They can only give secret sympathy. What is literary training worth if it cramps and confines us at a critical moment in national life? ...
> (*Young India*, 21 June 1928)

Like Phule, Gandhi, too, was deeply concerned about the outcome of colonial education:

> Is the goal of the education that you are receiving that of mere employment, whether in the Government departments or other departments? If that be the goal of your education, if that is the goal you have set before yourself, I feel and I fear that the vision which the Poet [Rabindranath Tagore] pictured for himself is far from being realized.
> (Cited from an 'Address to Students', 27 April 1915)

> I have never been able to make a fetish of literary training... literary training by itself adds not an inch to one's moral height and that character building is independent of literary training... the Government schools have unmanned us, rendered us helpless and godless. They have filled us with discontent, and providing no remedy for the discontent, have made us despondent. They have

made us what we were intended to become, clerks and interpreters. (*Young India*, 01 June 1921)

...There is no doubt that the young people [children of agriculturists] when they come back knew not a thing about agriculture, were indeed deeply contemptuous of the calling of their fathers ...The fact that the tragedy of this destructive breach was limited by the need of the Government for only a specified number of clerks and deputies, should not really mask the reality of the transaction[2]. ... The system must be scrapped; enquiry must be made promptly as to what constituted the elements of education before Indian Universities [under British *Raj*] were constituted, before Lord Macaulay wrote his fatal Minutes...
(*Young India*, 20 March 1924)

4.0 Pursuit of an Alternative Vision

Gandhi's conceptualization of education organically emerges from his critique of the exploitative and violent character of 'modern Western civilisation'. His struggle for *swaraj* was to be founded on moral and spiritual awakening of the Indian people. This enlightenment of the masses, therefore, was the purpose of education.

For Gandhi, education posed *critical civilizational, philosophical,* and *moral* issues. It is in this essential perspective, and definitely not in isolation thereof, that we need to comprehend and interpret Gandhi's thoughts that lay at the foundation of his alternative vision of education:

What is the meaning of education? If it simply means a knowledge of letters, it is merely an instrument, and an instrument may be well used or abused...

Now let us take higher education. I have learned Geography, Astronomy, Algebra, Geometry etc. What of that? ...I have never been able to use [this knowledge] for controlling my senses... It does not enable us to do our duty.

Moreover, I have not run down a knowledge of letters under all circumstances. All I have shown is that we must not make of it a fetish. It is not our *Kamdhenu*.[3] In its place it can be of use, and it has its place when we have brought our senses under subjection, and put our ethics on a firm foundation...
(*Hind Swaraj* (1909), Chapter XVIII)

Given the insight gained from his educational experiments in South Africa—first at the Phoenix School at the Phoenix Settlement before writing *Hind Swaraj* (1909) and later at the Tolstoy Farm (1911–13)—combined with his study of the Indian conditions, Gandhi was in a position to offer a constructive alternative to the nation to replace colonial education. Here are some glimpses of his alternative vision:

> I would develop in the child his hands, his brain and his soul. The hands have almost atrophied. The soul has been altogether ignored. (*Young India*, 12 March 1925)

> When our children are admitted to schools, they need, not slate and pencil and books, but simple village tools ... This means a revolution in educational methods. But nothing short of a revolution can put education within reach of every child of school-going age. (*Young India*, 11 July 1929)

> ... The utterly false idea that intelligence can be developed only through book reading should give place to the truth that the quickest development of the mind can be achieved by the artisan's work being learnt in a scientific manner...
> (*Harijan*, 09 January 1937)

On the contested question of language and education, Gandhi offers the following thought-provoking ideas (*HS*, Chapter XVIII), his critique of 'English Education' notwithstanding:

> ... In our dealings with the English people ... for the purpose of knowing how much disgusted they [the English] have themselves become with their civilization, we may use or learn English ... Those who have studied English will have to teach *morality to their progeny through their mother tongue,** and to teach them another Indian language; but when they have grown up, they may learn English, the ultimate aim being that we should not need it. ... . A little thought should show you that immediately *we cease to care for English degrees, the rulers will prick up their ears.* [emphasis mine]

> [***Note** on 'Those who have studied English ... *through their mother-tongue*': 'Gandhi makes a noteworthy distinction here between using English for the acquisition of *secular* knowledge and using the mother-tongue for the acquisition of *ethical* knowledge.' (Cited in *Parel*, 1997: p. 104, Footnote 207.)

5.0 What is *Nai Taleem*?

The ideas of *Nai Taleem* were successively articulated by Gandhi in *Harijan* during 1930s. This was also the period when the intellectual exchange on several profound philosophical and political issues between Gandhi and Tagore peaked, though it had started in 1914–15 (Bhattacharya 1997). Gandhi presented his vision of *Nai Taleem* at the All India Educational Conference held at Wardha in 1937. In his inaugural address, Gandhi unfolded his plan to liberate India from Macaulay's education and establish in its place what he called Basic Education Scheme (*Buniyadi Shiksha*), later incorporated in the broader canvass of *Nai Taleem*. We cite below from this address:

> What I am going to place before you today is *not about a vocation that is going to be imparted alongside education*... whatever is taught to children, *all of it should be taught necessarily through the medium of a trade or a handicraft* ... We aim at *developing the intellect also with the aid of a trade or a handicraft* ... instead of merely teaching a trade or a handicraft, we may as well educate the children entirely through them. Look at *takli* [spindle] itself, for instance. The lesson of this *takli* will be the first lesson of our students through which they would be able *to learn a substantial part of the history of cotton, Lancashire and the British empire*... How does this *takli* work? What is its utility? And what are the strengths that lie within it? Thus the child learns all this in the midst of play. Through this he also acquires some knowledge of mathematics. When he is asked to count the number of cotton threads on *takli* and he is asked to report how many did he spin, it becomes possible to acquaint him step by step with good deal of mathematical knowledge through this process. And the beauty is that none of this becomes even a slight burden on his mind... While playing around and singing, he keeps on turning his *takli* and from this itself he learns a great deal. [emphasis mine]
> (Mahatma Gandhi's address at the Wardha Education Conference, 22 October 1937)[4]

Gandhi further elabourates upon his pedagogy:

> Our education has got to be revolutionized. The *brain must be educated through the hand*. If I were a poet, I could write poetry on the possibilities of the five fingers. Why should you think that the mind is everything and the hands and feet nothing? Those who

do not train their hands, who go through the ordinary rut of education, lack 'music' in their life ... Mere book knowledge does not interest the child ... The brain gets weary of mere words, and the child's mind begins to wander. The hand does the things it ought not to do, the eye sees the things it ought not to see, the ear hears the things it ought not to hear, and they do not do, see or hear, respectively what they ought to... An *education which does not teach us to discriminate between good and bad, to assimilate the one and eschew the other* is a misnomer. [emphasis mine]

(Discussion with Teacher Trainees, *Harijan*, 18 February 1939)

5.1 The Spear-head of a Silent Social Revolution

As noted earlier, the Gandhian pedagogy cannot be viewed in isolation of the civilizational, philosophical and moral context of the struggle for *swaraj* in which it took shape. The Gandhian proposal of Basic Education presented at the Wardha Conference attempted to *place productive manual work at the centre of the school curriculum* from which would organically emerge knowledge, values and skills.

The term 'pedagogy', as used in this paper, is not synonymous with either the 'methods of teaching' or the 'teaching-learning process' or their other convenient utilitarian, technical or marketable versions. We have consciously used 'pedagogy' to denote education that emerges dialectically from its materialistic reality—economic, socio-cultural and political —and, in the process, questions, critiques and ultimately transforms the reality itself. Gandhi's conception of *Nai Taleem* was shaped, though only intuitively, by this philosophical framework. It is precisely because of this framework that *Nai Taleem* defies all reductionalist attempts to dilute or distort and thus trivialize its vision to a mere 'scheme' or a 'technique'. Uncompromisingly, it stands out for its civilizational, philosophical and moral implications along with its transformative potential. Such a conception of 'pedagogy' was further elaborated and enriched with theory, evidently independently of Gandhi, by Paulo Freire in his *Pedagogy of the Oppressed* (1970).

Indeed, *Nai Taleem* was an anti-imperialist philosophical construct that called for building a civilizational critique of colonial education. Gandhi, therefore, envisions that *Nai Taleem* would prepare 'organic intellectuals' in the Gramscian sense:

> ... if the person who has received *Nai Taleem*, is enthroned, he would not feel vanity of power, on the other hand, if he is given a broom, he will not feel ashamed... There would be no place to vain rejoicing in his life ... My *Nai Taleem* and the village industries are mutually complementary. When they both will be a success, we will attain *swaraj*.
>
> (*Bapuni Chhayaman*: pp. 157–8
> [Translated from Gujarati; Source: NCERT, 1998: pp. 86–7])

Since *Nai Taleem* was expected to make a major impact on the rural economy, it had to ensure that the villages did not become 'a mere appendage to the cities' and were not exploited by the latter. Gandhi believed that *Nai Taleem* will 'check the progressive decay of our villages and lay the foundation of a juster social order...' (*Harijan* 09 October 1937). This is why Gandhi elabourates upon his conception of Basic Education '*as the spear-head of a silent social revolution fraught with the most far-reaching consequences*' (*emphasis mine, ibid.*).

5.2 The Defining Elements

The central thesis as it emerged from the Wardha Conference address, along with the elabourations and clarifications offered by Gandhi elsewhere, allow us to present the four defining elements of *Nai Taleem*.

A. Holistic Approach: Integration of Head, Heart, and Hand[5]

In Gandhi's conception, child development is holistic, that is, constitutive of integration of head, heart and hand. He advances his principal thesis: 'Man is neither mere intellect, nor the gross animal body, nor the heart or soul alone... A proper and harmonious combination of all the three is required for the making of the whole man and constitutes the true economics of education.' (*Harijan* May 1937)

Gandhi had himself often admitted that he had hardly any knowledge of educational theory. He was primarily guided by his common sense, experience and intuition. Yet, his central thesis on viewing productive work as a pedagogic medium is widely acknowledged as a sound pedagogy for harmonious development of 'head, heart and hand' or 'body, mind and spirit' even today.[6]

B. Productive Manual Labour as Pedagogic Medium

The proposal to place productive manual labour at the centre of the school (or even college/university) curriculum, to view it as a moral and transformative force and to use it as a pedagogic medium was truly a revolutionary concept. It provided a materialist and scientific basis for constructing knowledge, evolving values and building multiple skills. Its civilizational, philosophical, and moral implications for reconstructing the very idea of education for social change could not be just wished away. The pedagogic potential of productive work was articulated by Gandhi so powerfully that it made the educational establishment of the British *Raj* as well as the elite sections of society, embedded as they were in Brahminical[7]-cum-colonial paradigm, visibly uncomfortable. Gandhi faced sharp criticism and protest, amounting to even ridicule. Attempts were made to reduce Gandhian 'basic education' to mere vocational education or to restrict its scope to rural population or the poor strata (see Section 7.0). The most potent cynical attack was in terms of divesting the entire proposal of its transformative potential by de-linking it from its civilizational, philosophic, and moral foundations.

C. Essentiality of the Mother Tongue

The use of the mother tongue in education and the development of Indian languages was one issue on which there was a fairly broad consensus in the nationalist movement (*Naik* 1979: p. 4). Gandhi contended that 'We have to make them [that is, Indian languages] true representatives of our culture, our civilization, of the true genius of our nation.' He warned that education through English medium has resulted in 'a permanent bar between the highly educated few and the uneducated many' and 'made our children practically foreigners in their own land' (*Young India*, 01 September 1921). In Gandhi's perception, 'the foreign medium has caused brain fag, put an undue strain upon the nerves of our children, made them crammers and imitators, unfitted them for original work and thought, and disabled them for filtrating their learning to the family or the masses... prevented the growth of our vernaculars...' (*Young India*, 01 September 1921).[8]

D. *The Principle of Self-Support*

What probably became the most controversial element in *Nai Taleem* was the principle of self-supporting education[9] advanced by Gandhi as being inalienable from his educational vision. This principle became intertwined with the issue of prohibition or foregoing liquor revenue. In Gandhi's words:

> The cruelest irony of the new Reforms lies in the fact that we are left with nothing but the liquor revenue to fall back upon in order to give our children education. That is the *educational puzzle*... It must be shameful and humiliating to think that unless we got the drink revenue, our children would be starved of their education. [emphasis mine]   (*Harijan* 21 August 1937)

He, therefore, attempted to resolve the 'educational puzzle' by advocating a national system of education that would be made self-supporting through sale of the products made by the students, provided 'the State takes over the manufactures of these schools' (*Harijan*, 31 July 1937)

The motive of the Gandhian proposal of using handicraft as a means of education came under suspicion precisely because it appeared to be a strategy to solve the financial question faced by the provincial Congress Ministries who were bound by their promise of total prohibition. Others contended, and rightly so, that it is the State's obligation to finance education. Still others attacked the idea by claiming that this would amount to legitimizing child labour. In September 1937, however, Gandhi warned against the assumption that the idea of self-supporting education sprang from the necessity of achieving total prohibition. 'Both are independent necessities,' he said as he responded to an educationist's queries. Gandhi continued, 'Let us now ... concentrate on educating the child properly through manual work, *not as a side activity, but as the prime means of intellectual training.*' [emphasis mine] The educationist was not convinced as to why this should be linked to supporting of school's finances. Gandhi responded that *'That will be the test of its value* [emphasis mine]. (*Harijan* 18 September 1937)'.

There are two ways of looking at the above response. First, Gandhi was primarily advocating a programme of vocational education that would promote rural employment. Second, the principle of self-support was indeed a part of his pedagogy of holistically integrating the education of 'head, heart and hand'. Here are some helpful clues that tilt the balance in favour of the latter interpretation. At the Wardha Conference (October 1937), Gandhi would emphasize that 'What I am going to place before you today is *not about a vocation* that is going to be imparted alongside education.' What followed was how the simple spinning device (*takli*) could act as a pedagogic medium for learning mathematics, physics and history. There is yet another argument. His clarification that it 'will be the test of its [that is, productive manual work's] value' has indeed deep pedagogic implications. Without applying 'the test of its value', the pedagogic power of productive work would steadily wither away. Any productive engagement implies *pre-planned, disciplined, assiduous and scientific work with tools and materials* until the intended product of social utility is ready. A lack of rigor in this practice is bound to lead to failure in 'the test of its [pedagogic] value', while also failing in the market!

An observation by Gandhi during the Wardha Address gives us further insight into his mind. While advocating that the value of the product from the handicraft should be adequate for meeting the cost of the teacher, he said: 'It is neither possible for us to keep waiting until the [British] government gives us adequate funds out of its treasury *nor until the Viceroy reduces the military expenditure* or some other similar way out is found.' [emphasis mine] (Mahatma Gandhi's address at the Wardha Education Conference, 22 October 1937)[10]

Clearly, Gandhi's insistence on self-supporting principle cannot be delinked from its historical context of the colonial government which was not expected to change its economic priorities in favour of the people's interest. It sounds reasonable

Countering Neoliberal Conception of Knowledge...

for him, therefore, to speak of self-supporting education, so that education can be spread among the masses. Hence the crucial question: *Would Gandhi, therefore, have given up his insistence on making education self-supportive if the issue of financing education is considered in the context of the State in independent India?* Gandhi himself provides a clue: 'The State must pay for it wherever it has *definite use* for it'[11] [emphasis mine] (*Harijan* 09 July 1938). He thus attempts to 'resolve' the 'education puzzle' (that is, prohibition vs. education) on the basis of certain premises which, however, do not appear to be grounded in the political economy that was emerging in the late 1930s. As we shall see in Section 7.0, the economic policies being adopted by the Indian National Congress at the time would not support his premises with respect to either the nature of the State or its vision of economic development in post-independence India. Gandhi's 'education puzzle' had thus assumed a new form—namely, the 'post-Independence Indian State vs. the people'—that was far less amenable to resolution than the 'prohibition vs. education' conflict!

6.0 Social Character of Productive Work and Knowledge: Radical Implications

We will now dwell upon how the Gandhian pedagogy constitutes a radical departure from the Brahminical-cum-colonial paradigm insofar it challenges the dichotomy between work and knowledge by placing productive manual work at the centre of school curriculum itself. This in itself delinks productive manual work from its roots of discrimination and injustice. Table 1 provides a list (not exhaustive) of Gandhi's choice of occupations to be brought at the centre of the curriculum:

What is striking about the above list is the social character of the occupations. Without exception, all the listed occupations involve productive manual work and are undertaken primarily by the lower classes/castes viz. *Dalits*, tribals, OBCs, and Muslim artisans, with the women in each of these social categories playing a significant role. In the Indian socioeconomic structure, these hereditary occupations have carried the stigma of being

Table 1

Occupations Selected for the Gandhian Programme of Basic Education

(Period: from 1938 onwards)

Spinning	Leather Curing (Tanning)
Weaving	Shoemaking
Dying cloth	Tailoring
Farming	Ironsmithy & Metal Work
Animal Husbandry & Dairying	Carpentry
Manual Agro-processing	Tool-making
Forestry	Printing
Horticulture	Construction
Building & Cleaning Latrines	Alternative Energy (e.g. Gobar Gas Plant)
Pottery	Gathering & Using Minor Forest Produce

inferior to the essentially non-productive and non-manual occupations of the upper classes/castes for centuries.

The political message is inescapable: *Accord these occupations and the communities engaged in them a place of dignity that was never their destiny in Indian history.* Gandhi had invariably recognized, as did Dewey (1907), the great American sociologist of education, almost three decades before him, that all such productive tasks had a strong knowledge-cum-skill content, including scientific, along with their context of socio-cultural history. This provided a rich pedagogical base for acquiring knowledge, value formation, and building skills. In a recent study of similar traditional occupations, Kancha Ilaiah (2007) provides rich documentation that substantiates Gandhi's rationale for selecting the above productive tasks of the lower social order for educational purpose.

This radical feature of the Gandhian proposal could not have been drawn at all from the Brahminical roots in ancient Indian traditions. Krishna Kumar (2005) writes that Gandhian pedagogy,

...implied a violation of India's old concepts of learning. The epistemology of 'basic education' was thoroughly radical, and there is no way we can place it in the context of ancient Indian traditions ...[it] involved direct conflict with the indigenous tradition because it introduced into the school curriculum a form of knowledge on which low caste groups had monopoly... In a school following this curriculum, a low-caste child would feel far more at home than an upper-caste child. Both in terms of worldview and functional skills, the curriculum of a 'basic school' favoured the child belonging to the lowest stratum of society. From this point of view, Gandhi's proposal intended to make the education system stand on its head...

(Kumar, 2005: pp. 179–80)

However, the above expectation will be sustained only if the present multi-layered school system rooted in discrimination is transformed into a fully public-funded Common School System based on Neighbourhood Schools aimed at guaranteeing free education of equitable quality to all citizens of India (NCERT 2007: pp. 54–62, 64–5).

7.0 Indian State and Gandhian Pedagogy: From Negation to Trivialisation

The 1937 Wardha Conference (Section 3.0) concluded in a set of resolutions which indicated some discomfort, perhaps unspoken ideological tension too among the participants, with Gandhi's Basic Education Scheme. This is evident in the four resolutions which reveal both a sense of hesitation and a lack of appreciation of its transformative potential (Fagg 2002: pp. 54–6). The Zakir Husain Committee, constituted by the Conference itself, basically followed the above resolutions in its Report (December 1937) but, at the same time, made some significant detours and departures as well (*ibid.:* pp. 57–60).

Even as Gandhi was developing and articulating his educational vision in 1937-8, the Indian National Congress was formulating an economic policy that was designed to take independent India in precisely the opposite direction. The Haripura Congress Resolution (1938) advanced two entirely contradictory policy objectives simultaneously, namely,

(i) Gandhi's educational vision that aimed at building a self-reliant decentralized vibrant rural economy, free of poverty, exploitation, discrimination and cultural obscurantism as well as undoing the parasitic relationship of the cities with villages; and

(ii) an economic policy aimed at rapid industrialization along with urbanization by promoting a Public Sector such that it would provide the much needed succour to the Indian capitalist class, that is, 'national bourgeoisie', thereby building an economic order aimed at centralization of wealth and means of production in the hands of few.

The above conflicting ideologies, representing two mutually exclusive models of national development, obviously could not be pursued at the same time. It is clear that the Indian State then taking shape had no intention whatsoever of instituting the Gandhian programme of educational and social reconstruction after Independence. This can be surmised in view of the negotiations that had already been essentially completed by 1938 between the Indian capitalist class and the political leadership of the Indian National Congress, requiring the latter to strategically 'promote' (read 'subserve') the vested interests of the former (Mukherjee 2002). If any evidence was needed, it came in the form of the well-known Bombay Plan or the Tata-Birla Plan (1944–5), prepared by the leading members of the 'national bourgeoisie', that was to guide the economic planning of post-independence India to protect and promote their self-interests.

While the State in independent India vigorously pursued its economic policy along the lines of the Bombay Plan through successive five-year plans, the political space for the Gandhian vision of moving towards a self-reliant decentralized vibrant rural economy was steadily, if not rapidly, obliterated. Nor would there be a scope for the evolution of the 'village republics' that Gandhi talked about. Since 1991, the Indian State has pushed neoliberal economic policies whose basic purpose is to subserve the needs of the global capital and market, even if these are contrary to the interest of the people or the nation. As in most other aspects of national life, the education policy, too, has been altered to serve the same purpose (Sadgopal 2010).

In line with the State's economic policy, the education policymakers, too, managed to find ways of successively diluting, distorting and ultimately trivializing the radical Gandhian pedagogy. This successive reductionalism is reflected in the policy recommendations or resolves for 'activity-based learning' (1944), 'work experience' (1966), 'Socially Useful Productive Work or SUPW (1977, 1978) or vocational education for 'entry into workforce' (1986, 1992)[12]. Significantly, Gandhi's educational vision of building Gramscian 'organic intellectuals' for social transformation stands ruthlessly replaced by the neoliberal conception of the Indian State using education to prepare highly skilled but inexpensive and subservient 'foot soldiers' for the global market!

8.0 Gandhi-Ambedkar Debate and the Context of Caste in Education

Dr B.R. Ambedkar, taking cue from Phule's scientific history of the caste system, entered into a historic debate with Gandhi in 1932. He questioned the very premise of the Gandhian logic of *Nai Taleem* and rural development. Citing from his in-depth studies of the history and sociology of *Varnashram*, Ambedkar argued that the village founded on the caste structure was the fortress of caste oppression. Any attempt to strengthen or rejuvenate village-based economy is bound to increase the stranglehold of the upper caste hegemony, thereby maintaining the same oppressive structure that had exploited Dalits, tribals, and other backward sections of society for centuries. While unwilling to accept Ambedkar's critique of the caste structure inherent in the Hindu society, that is, *Varnashram*, Gandhi advocated and assiduously worked for a programme for eliminating untouchability and transforming villages into 'Republics' founded on equality, justice, and enlightenment. There is, however, emerging evidence that Gandhi's own rigidity with respect to caste and *Varnashram* and its role in Indian society underwent radical change by late 1930s, presumably under the impact of Ambedkar's scholarly and powerful critique. How else would one explain Gandhi's radical proposal in 1937 of placing the productive tasks, performed by the lower classes/castes, at the centre-stage in the school curriculum of the education system of post-Independence India, thereby according the children of these downtrodden sections of society the role of providing leadership in the classrooms (see Section 6.0; NCERT 2007: Executive Summary)?

Throughout this period, from the early nineteenth century onwards, movements emerged against the caste structure and hegemony of upper classes and upper castes in different parts of the country. It was through

> radical questioning and rational social vision of early thinkers and leaders like Kandukuri Veeresalingam (Andhra Pradesh), Narayan Guru (Kerala), Iyothee Thassar (Tamil Nadu), Gurajada Apparao (Andhra Pradesh), Singaravelar and Periyar (Tamil Nadu) that public consciousness could be mobilized to challenge social stratification, oppose irrational traditions and practices and advocate education as a means of modernization of society.[13]

Ambedkar did not stop at merely disagreeing with the Gandhian development model but proposed an alternative economic model that is akin to State Socialism. In a memorandum submitted to the Constituent Assembly in 1946, he advocates nationalization of all key and basic industries and acquisition of all agricultural land by the State with collectivised method of farming[14]. He writes: 'land shall be let out to villagers without distinction of caste or creed and in such manner that there will be no landlord, no tenant and no landless labourer'. The outstanding feature of the plan was to include this model of State Socialism into the Constitution itself, without leaving any possibility for the Legislature or the Executive to 'suspend, amend or abrogate it'. He argues that, if this plan is not prescribed by the Constitution, the powerful capitalist class shall not allow this plan to take shape or may allow only a highly diluted form. Of course, as is well known, the Constituent Assembly did not accept Ambedkar's proposal. However, this did not prevent his following clarion call regarding education from reaching out to the subaltern classes and castes, most of whom are peasants and landless labourers of rural India:

Countering Neoliberal Conception of Knowledge... 257

My final words of advice to you are *educate, agitate and organize;* have faith in yourself. With justice on our side I do not see how we can lose our battle. The battle to me is a matter of joy. The battle is in the fullest sense spiritual. There is nothing material or social in it. *For ours is a battle not for wealth or for power. It is battle for freedom. It is the battle of reclamation of human personality.* [Emphasis mine]

(Speech delivered at the All India Depressed Classes Conference Nagpur, July 1942)

Addressing the socialists, Ambedkar asserted that they 'must recognize that the problem of social reform is fundamental' and contended that the socialist will be 'compelled to take account of caste after revolution if he does not take account of it before revolution.'[15] He urged them to appreciate that the 'caste system is not merely a division of labour. *It is also a division of labourers* ... it is a hierarchy in which the divisions of labourers are graded one above the other.' Hence his warning to the socialists, 'caste is the monster that crosses your path. You cannot have political reform, you cannot have economic reform, unless you kill this monster.' In his *undelivered* speech prepared for the Annual Conference of the Jat-Pat Todal Mandal of Lahore (May 1936), Ambedkar dares us to face the reality,

Yours is more difficult than the other national cause, namely Swaraj. In the fight for Swaraj you fight with whole nation on your side. In this, you have to fight against the whole nation and that too, your own... . More important than the question of defending Swaraj is the question of defending the Hindus under the Swaraj... only when the Hindu Society becomes a casteless society that it can hope to have strength enough to defend itself. Without such internal strength, Swaraj for Hindus may turn out to be only a step towards slavery.'

(B.R. Ambedkar
Annihilation of Caste, May 1936, Lahore)[16]

9.0 Capitalist Development Model vs. Socialist Transformation

This historical overview of the educational discourse will be incomplete, if not even skewed, if an appropriate reference is not made to the ideological challenge posed by the youthful revolutionary members of the Hindustan Socialist Republican Association (HSRA), a political party formed in 1928, before the leadership of the Congress Party. Led by Shaheed Chandrashekhar Azad and Shaheed Bhagat Singh, HSRA basically questioned the Congress Party's perception of the character and role of the 'national bourgeoisie' in the anti-colonial struggle and the confusing signals that the Congress Party was giving about its stand vis-à-vis *Poorna Swaraj* (complete independence) from the British *Raj*. This challenge continued until the martyrdom of Bhagat Singh, Sukhdev, and Rajguru on 23 March 1931. Clearly inspired by the scientific Marxist philosophy, HSRA gave the twin inter-linked call for not only liberating India from British imperialism but also for radical socialist reconstruction of Indian political economy and socio-cultural structures, through class struggle.[17] Class struggle, to be waged primarily under the leadership of the working class in alliance with the peasantry and the youth, will be aimed at establishing the control of the working class over the means of production, which were until then in the control of the Indian capitalist class and the feudal landlords. While defining socialism, Bhagat Singh contended that it must mean abolition of capitalism, transfer of means of production and domination of the working class. In 1928, Shaheed Bhagat Singh relates untouchability with the question of land alienation and rising competitive communal politics of the times and urges upon the 'untouchables' to mobilize and struggle for socialist revolution (*see* Chaman Lal 2004, Footnote 10(i): pp. 156–60). While questioning the role of Indian capitalist class in the national movement, HSRA ridiculed the Congress Party's alliance with the 'national bourgeoisie' and termed it as being against the interest of the masses. The Congress Party's leadership was hard-pressed to deal with HSRA's contention that freedom struggle without a programme of socialist reconstruction would amount to merely transfer of power from 'white sahibs' to their 'brown' counterparts, rather than liberation from British imperialism and colonial rule and emancipation of the exploited and oppressed masses. For education, it would mean that Macaulay's policies will continue to operate even after India's Independence!

Conclusion

The historical overview of the educational discourse and the related ideological debates during the anti-colonial struggle undertaken here is far from being either complete or comprehensive. By focusing upon Savitribai and Jotirao Phule, Gandhi, Ambedkar, and Chandrashekhar Azad-Bhagat Singh, it fails to do justice to the significant contributions made to this discourse by a host of outstanding social, cultural and political leaders. These would include Kandukuri Veeresalingam, Narayan Guru, Iyothee Thassar, Gurajada Apparao, Dadabhai Naoroji, Shahuji Maharaj, Gopal Krishna Gokhale, Singaravelar and Periyar, Subhash Chandra Bose, Ram Manohar Lohia, Jayaprakash Narayan, Zakir Husain, and Gijubhai Badheka, just to name a few of them. This comprehensive overview would have to be postponed to another space and time.

What we can record here from this limited study is the following principal lesson: The aspiration of the freedom struggle to build a fully public-funded Common Education System from 'KG to PG', capable of guaranteeing free, equitable, just, secular, scientific, and democratic education, will always remain a mirage as long as the national policies are aimed at promoting capitalist mode of development. There is no miracle which can move the education system in a direction that is contrary to the direction of the overarching architecture of socio-economic order, except for miniscule though innovative experiments. The question of socialist reconstruction of Indian society and its economic order can be ignored or postponed only at the risk of denying education to the majority of our children and youth, as has been the case with at least three generations since independence.

Yet, there is reason for hope.

There is hope because there is a clear path for moving forward. On the one hand, we must learn how to mobilize people for fighting and winning battles for their immediate and intermediate demands that either reverse or block neoliberal policy measures to commercialize education and lead to the strengthening of the public funded education system. On the other hand, we must also learn to pursue the scientific path of transformation from the capitalist mode of production to the socialist mode of production. *This path calls for unlearning our typically ahistorical, unscientific,* and fragmented *mode of thinking.* There is hope if we decide to learn from the twentieth-century history of socialist experiments in different parts of the world, especially from the present day Latin America. When we do this, we will ensure that we learn about the great potential of these experiments. At the same time, we will not ignore the inevitable historical errors and misjudgements that led to the fragmentation of the great socialist vision and weakening of the socialist movement during 1990s and beyond, as globalization advanced.

Indeed, historically speaking, there is no space whatsoever for frustration or despondency. Rather, it is time that we prepare ourselves for a protracted struggle with a view to decisively intervene in the State's prevailing socio-political and institutional structures and processes, which have now assumed dangerous neoliberal forms, in order to bring about pro-people changes therein. But this cannot happen without simultaneously mobilizing the masses to build resistance to the capitalist model of development and to explore and create an alternative socialist model. It must also be underlined that it is not enough to oppose the various agencies of the global capital – World Bank, IMF, WTO, and other international funding agencies, as several NGOs pretend or claim to be doing. That of course has to be done for the time being. Our real battle, however, is for demolishing capitalism and replacing it with socialism aimed at creating a new human being for a humane society.

Here, Shaheed Shankar Guha Niyogi's political philosophy of *'Sangharsh aur Nirman'* that is, 'Struggle and Reconstruction', developed during the historic struggle of iron ore mine workers in Chhattisgarh from 1977 to 1991, shows us a new radical path.[18] By treading on this radical path, we can hope to transform India as per the aspirations of the anti-imperialist freedom struggle and its outcome in the form of the Constitution, the latter's weaknesses notwithstanding. This calls for combining the essence of Gandhi's transformative civilizational vision of education with that of Phule-Ambedkar's historical critique of the oppressive and exploitative structures of caste and class and both with Shaheed Bhagat Singh's call for socialist reconstruction of the Indian society.

NOTES

1. An abridged version of this essay, in a different perspective, is included in Sethia, Tara (ed.) *Rediscovering Gandhian Wisdom*, Penguin, Under Publication
2. A similar concern was expressed by Phule regarding higher education under British Raj in his Memorandum to the Hunter Commission, 1882 (Deshpande, 2002)
3. The mythical cow that has the divine powers to fulfill all of one's desires
4. Source: *Hindustani Talimi Sangh*, 1957, pp. vii–viii. Translated from Hindi by the author
5. Adapted from Fagg (2002), pp. 8–9
6. Gandhi's conception of harmonious development of 'head, heart and hand' or 'body, mind and soul' is akin to the contemporary view of the taxonomy of education in terms of three major domains of learning viz. cognitive, affective and psycho-motor skills
7. The term 'Brahminical' is used in this paper strictly to refer to the historically embedded ideology of socio-cultural hegemony in India that has been systematically challenged by various social reform movements of 19th and 20th centuries, led by Phule, Periyar, Ambedkar, and Gandhi. This struggle greatly influenced the manner in which the principles of equality and social justice were enshrined in the Constitution, primarily under Ambedkar's visionary leadership. The term 'Brahminical', therefore, should in no way be seen as a reference to individual members of either the Brahman or other upper caste communities. On the contrary, one expects such upper caste/class citizens to join the traditionally exploited castes and other sections of societies in their continuing struggle against the ideology of Brahminism and for fulfillment of the goals of Indian Constitution.
8. The recent development of the concept of viewing 'mother tongue' in its multilingual context transforms the Gandhian insistence on 'mother tongue' as medium of education into a far more powerful site of resistance against the epistemic attack of neoliberalism than would have been the case with the earlier

perception of 'mother tongue' arguably as a static, rigid and even an exclusionary construct
9. This is not to be confused with the neoliberal conception of 'self-financing courses' being promoted in the higher education system in India as a public policy for the past two decades
10. Source: *Hindustani Talimi Sangh*, 1957, p. x. Translated from Hindi by the author
11. A statement made by Gandhi in the context of higher education in response to an educationist's query. Gandhi then provided a rather elabourate statement as to what, according to him, constituted 'definite use' for the post-independence State
12. The Gandhian pedagogy was misrepresented and reduced to 'activity-based learning' (Government of India, 1944, CABE Report), 'work experience' (Government of India, 1971, Report of the Education Commission, 1964–66), 'Socially Useful Productive Work – SUPW (Government of India, 1977, Ishwarbhai Patel Committee Report; Government of India, 1978, Adiseshiah Committee Report) and vocational education for 'entry into workforce' (Government of India, 1986, 1992, National Policy on Education – 1986, As modified in 1992). A detailed discussion of such reductionalism and trivialization in policy discourse can be found in NCERT (2007) and Sadgopal (2004, 2008)
13. All India Forum for Right to Education, Chennai Declaration, 2012
14. Memorandum on the Safeguards for the Scheduled Castes submitted to the Constituent Assembly in 1946 on behalf of the All India Scheduled Castes Federation and published in 1947 under the title, *States and Minorities: What are Their Rights and How to Secure them in the Constitution of Free India*. Source: http://www.ambedkar.org/ambcd/10B1.%20Statesand%20Minorities%20Appendix.htm accessed on 15 June 2013
15. Ambedkar, B.R. (May, 1936) *Annihilation of Caste*, Critical Quest: New Delhi, 2007, p. 14
16. Ibid., p. 50.
17. See (i) Chaman Lal (ed.), *Bhagat Singh Ke Sampoorna Dastavej*, Adhar Prakashan: Panchakoola, Haryana, 2004 and (ii) Bipin Chandra et al., *India's Struggle for Independence 1857-1947*, Penguin Books: New Delhi, 1988, pp. 247–59
18. Sadgopal, Anil and Shyam Bahadur Namra (eds.) *Sangharsh aur Nirmaan*, Rajkamal Prakashan: New Delhi, 1993

REFERENCES

Bagade, Umesh, 'Ambedkar's Historical Method: A Non-Brahmanic Critique of Positivist History', Unpublished Paper

Bhattacharyya, Sabyasachi (1997) *The Mahatma and the Poet*, National Book Trust: New Delhi

Deshpande, G.P. (ed.) (2002) *Selected Writings of Jotirao Phule*, LeftWord Books: New Delhi

Dewey, John (1907) *The School and Society*, Aakar Books (Indian Edition): Delhi, 2008

Fagg, Henry (2002) *Back to the Sources: A Study of Gandhi's Basic Education*, National Book Trust: New Delhi

Gandhi, M.K. (1909) *Hind Swaraj or Indian Home Rule*, Navajivan Publishing House: Ahmedabad, 1939

Gandhi, M.K. (1953) *Towards New Education*, Navajivan Publishing House: Ahmedabad

Giroux, Henry (2004) Public Pedagogy and the Politics of Neoliberalism: Making the Political More Pedagogical, *Policy Futures in Education*, Vol. 2, Nos. 3 & 4

Government of India (1944) *Post-War Educational Development in India: Report by the Central Advisory Board of Education*, Bureau of Education, India, January 1944

Government of India (1971) *Education and National Development: Report of the Education Commission 1964–66*, NCERT: New Delhi

Government of India (1977) *Report of the Review Committee on 'The Curriculum for the Ten-Year School'* (Ishwarbhai Patel Committee), Ministry of Education and Social Welfare: New Delhi

Government of India (1978) *Report of the National Review Committee on Higher Secondary Education with Special Reference to Vocationalisation* (Adiseshiah Committee), Ministry of Education and Social Welfare: New Delhi

Government of India (1986) *National Policy on Education-1986* and *Programme of Action-1986*, Ministry of Human Resource Development: New Delhi

Government of India (1992) *National Policy on Education-1986 (As modified in 1992)*, Ministry of Human Resource Development: New Delhi

Hindustani Talimi Sangh (1957) *Aath Salon ka Sampoorna Shikshakram*, Sewagram: Wardha, Maharashtra

Ilaiah, Kancha (2007) *Turning the Pot, Tilling the Land: Dignity of Labour in Our Times*, Navayana Publishing: New Delhi

Kumar, Krishna (2005) *Political Agenda of Education*, Sage Publications: New Delhi.

Mukherjee, Aditya (2002) *Imperialism, Nationalism and the Making of the Indian Capitalist Class, 1920–47*, Sage Publications: New Delhi

Naik, J.P. (1979) *The Education Commission and After*, A.P.H. Publishing Corporation: New Delhi, 1997

National Council of Educational Research and Training (1998), *Gandhi on Education*, NCERT: New Delhi

National Council of Educational Research and Training (2007) *National Focus Group Position Paper on 'Work and Education'*, NCERT: New Delhi

Parel, Anthony J. (1997) *Gandhi: Hind Swaraj and Other Writings*, Cambridge University Press: U.K.

Phule, Jotirao Govindrao (1882) Memorial Addressed to the Education Commission, 19 October 1882, in *Selected Writings of Jotirao Phule*, G.P. Deshpande (ed.) (2002) LeftWord Books: New Delhi, pp. 101–12

Sadgopal, Anil (2004) 'A Discussion Paper' presented at the first meeting of NCERT's National Focus Group on 'Work and Education', 27-30 December 2004, New Delhi (Annexure I of the National Focus Group Position Paper on 'Work and Education', in NCERT, 2007, pp. 74–89)

Sadgopal, Anil (2008) 'Deciphering Policy Discourse on the Place of Work in Curriculum', in *Perspectives on Education and Development—Revisting Education Commission and After*, Ved Prakash and K. Biswal (eds.), NUEPA and Shipra Publications: Delhi, 2008, pp. 323–42

Sadgopal, Anil (2010) 'The Neoliberal Assault on India's Education System', in *The World Bank in India—Undermining Sovereignty, Distorting Development*, Kelley, Michele and D'Souza, Deepika (eds.), Orient BlackSwan Pvt. Ltd.: New Delhi, pp. 296–313

Singh, Balwant (1956) *Bapuni Chhayaman*, Navajivan Publishing House: Ahmedabad

11

A Dialogue for a Mass Movement for a Democratic Education System

D. Ramesh Patnaik

To come straight to the point, there cannot be a democratic, secular and egalitarian education system in the country without abolishing commercialization of education at all levels. At a time when private initiative, in neoliberal atmosphere, is reduced to one of profiteering, the only way to spread education free of cost is State funding. So, one should make a clear resolution for a State funded public education system from KG to PG, and of course, leave a scope for non-commercial private initiative as well. For development of a harmonious society, education requires being free and equal at all levels and this is not possible without State funding. State funding, in a democratic polity, need not lead to State control over the education system. All educational institutions from school to university can be managed in decentralized and participative mode to advance the cause of democracy, which invariably includes plurality.

Obtaining Situation

During the last four years, the UPA Government stepped up the pace of neoliberal policy measures in the field of education, of course, as a part of an all-out systemic change on the basis of neoliberal approach. To a great extent, this became possible due to the combined effect of the cooperation of all political parties, media, and a high profile academia, who all believe in the axiom that the market can take care of development and distribution, quality and equality and freedom of the individual, sovereignty of nation, and peace of the world. Their integrity cannot be questioned, but one does not find an answer as to why these parties, institutions, and persons do not take note of all adverse effects of the pursued neoliberal policies for the last two decades.

Ill Effects of Commercialization of Education

With commercialization of education, the content of education is reduced to one of skill training, or at the best, professional training. Social Sciences, Natural Sciences, Humanities, Art and Literature, and fundamental research are looked down upon and are increasingly being replaced by professional and skill training required by corporate houses. The purpose of education is completely distorted. The purpose of education as was thought of by the pioneers of the modern republic system was to produce citizens with democratic, secular, and egalitarian outlook and with all intellectual and skill-oriented potentialities to advance the spiritual and material development of the society. Education was expected to develop all round personality of the individual and distributive development of the society. Commercialization of education replaced social interest by corporate interest and all- 'all round development of individual' by ability to earn. The private sector in education is running behind the trivialized concept of merit in marks and ranks, and the public sector is only destined to follow suit to stand in competition or else to perish. The result is a distortion of the very process of education. All pedagogical methods are replaced by memorizing and reproducing of a given material. There is no place now in India to really pursue innovative paths in pedagogy. The historical 'Hoshangabad Science Teaching Programme' is no longer possible. Today, no serious worker finds it interesting to pursue research in pedagogical theories. The mother tongue of the child is being increasingly replaced by English, killing the originality and creativity of the child on one hand, and alienating him/her from her own people and community on the otherhand. The commercialization of education, has reduced the student to becoming a customer, the teacher to a paid labourer, and the institution to a service provider. The Government of India has made 'offers' in 'education service', to the General Agreement on Trade in Services under the WTO regime. The 'offers' transform into 'commitments' automatically as and when the Doha Round of Trade Negotiations conclude, unless if the offers are withdrawn in time. This globalization of trade in education, requires universal quality parameters and will prove a deathblow to all needs of diversified cultures of India, for their development and democratization. All parts of India have not developed equally and this paper does not have space to go into the reasons for this differential development. In any case, if education is understood as a lever of development, it requires to be designed in the interest of local development. A centralized education system, could never allow decentralized planning. Globalization of 'education service' requires centralization of education administration and ends all hopes for a decentralized and participative mode of management of educational institutions. Commercialization of education not only strikes at the root of equality, it leads to the complete elimination of diversity. To put it all in brief, commercialization of education replaces genuine merit and social justice by money. It sings the last song for mother tongues, diversified cultures, hope for decentralized and participative management and all innovative pedagogical theories. It denies education as such to the majority and those few who get it, would not get anything of value. Any pro-people and pro-civilizational development in education, cannot be viewed without abolition of commercialization of education in all its forms.

The Acts and Bills

As far as the present trends in public policy are concerned, the 'Right of the Child for Free and Compulsory Education Act, 2009 (RTE Act)' pertaining to elementary education is under implementation from 01 April 2010. Six Bills have been introduced in the parliament over the last three years, which intended to bring paradigm change in Higher Education. This paper does not provide enough space to make a thorough analysis of either the RTE Act or the six Bills. However, let me make a brief statement. Even a lay man knows it very clearly that 'RTE Act' did neither abolish commercialization of education nor introduced Common School System'. A good number of people who were interested in a pro-people education system expected that the Act would strengthen Government schools, and regulate private schools. The Act belied even their hopes.

The Act does not provide right to either pre-primary, or secondary education. It is confined only to elementary education from Classes 1 to 8. The complete childhood is not covered by this Act. The Act does not have any provisions for retention of the children, even in the limited age group of 6 to 14 years. Even those, who come to school on their own would not get quality education because, the Act makes only those inferior provisions made in DPEP, regarding infrastructure and teacher posts, in its schedule. Even when the schedule of this Act is implemented, 80 per cent of primary schools in India would only get two classrooms and two teachers and the failed 'multi-grade teaching', would continue. That the governments failed to implement even this schedule, is a different matter. The Act, neither ensures retention of the children nor does it ensures quality education to all those who come to school on their own. As far as private schools are concerned, the Act does not provide for regulation of fees in private unaided schools. It is entirely left to the private managements. What is required of them is to make a public notice of fee structure in their respective schools before admissions every year. It is only a transparency clause. Above this, the Act provides for reimbursement of fee for 25 per cent of seats in private schools. This provision only siphons public funds to private agencies and is a well-known market enhancement programme of the State, guided by the World Bank. The Act does not regulate private schools; rather, it encourages corporate sector to establish a chain of low cost private schools to exploit the reimbursement provision. Further, as elaborated by the then Human Resources Minister, Shri Kapil Sibal, this Act empowers private agencies to increase fees to be collected from the students, and reduces the salaries of the teachers working there. This Act neither develops Government schools nor regulates private schools. Rather, its policy of fee reimbursement encourages children to join private schools there by resulting in closure of Government schools and enlarging the market in the private sector. The RTE Act is an act of fraud on the Constitution, as it is drafted against the Right to Equality, the basic principle of the Constitution. It only legitimizes the present multi-layered, inferior quality school education system where discrimination shall continue to prevail. Again, if we turn to the higher education sector, there looms a great danger. In the last three years, many Bills have been introduced in the Parliament. However, certain six Bills, as elabourated below, have got the potential for a paradigm change leading to thorough commercialization of higher education including professional education and bringing it under the direct rule of global capital: 1) 'The Foreign Educational Institutions Bill-2010', if enacted, opens the floodgates to Foreign Direct Investment in higher education and reduces education to a tradable commodity; 2) 'The Educational Tribunals Bill 2010' tribunalizes justice in the field of education which is already reduced to a trade; 3) 'The National Accreditation Bill 2010' provides for establishment of private accreditation agencies and the agencies, in turn, give accreditation to public and private colleges and universities and parameters of such accreditation cannot but be market oriented; 4) 'The Prohibition of Unfair Practices Bill 2010' reduces concept of fairness in management of educational institutions to one of transparency which only means that the managements *can* loot the people as long as they do same transparently; 5) 'The National Council for Higher Education and Research Bill 2011' establishes an 'Independent Regulatory Authority' in Higher Education (IRA in HE) in line with WTO guidelines, of course, with a different name 'NCHER'. This National Council for Higher Education and Research (NCHER) will be independent from democratic pressures of the people and will 'regulate' the 'trade in education service' in the interest of foreign and domestic corporate houses. The Government of India, as has been stated said earlier, has already made 'offers' to the World Trade Organization in Higher

Education Sector, which eventually will become 'commitments' if not withdrawn in course of the Doha round. All the reforms in the field of education the Government intended to bring about, will only establish a legal and institutional set up for operationalization of the agreement with the WTO immediately after completion of the Doha Round. 'The Universities for Research and Innovation Bill, 2012', introduced in the Parliament on 22 May, 2012, only adds another dimension to (all the above mentioned) market oriented reforms in education.

The End of Education

All the serious academics and activists in the country, who are all working on different aspects related to education, are increasingly coming to the understanding that, the cause they are pursing cannot be advanced, without freeing education from the clutches of the profit motive. Those who are working for quality education in Government schools, keeping the interest of the children from poor families in mind, understand gradually that, as long as the children of rich and middle classes go to the private schools, the ruling strata will not be interested in developing the Government schools. Neither the minister nor the Government regular teacher sends his/her child to Government schools. Government schools will develop only when the rich and middle classes send their children there. This requires the establishment of a Common School System. The academics and activists who are working in the field of pedagogy are increasingly realizing that creative pedagogical experiments cannot be taken up in school's running for profit and even in Government schools, which are only tailing private schools for their survival. So is the case with those who are working for a democratic language policy. Those who are working for the dignity of different cultural entities face the same experience. The people working for the disadvantaged, disabled, and the marginalized are increasingly realizing the real villain in commercialization of education. The debate of State List versus the Union List is losing all its relevance as, in any case, only trade is going to flourish. Those who value social sciences, natural sciences, humanities and art, and literature are noting with pain how their beloved subjects of study are being marginalized by market recommended courses. All social values are at stake as education and health are commercialized. Every finger is raised against commercialization of education. Of course, abolishing commercialization of education, in the given neoliberal atmosphere, is not an easy task, but it is inevitable if we are to sustain ourselves as a civilized society. Only the masses can reverse the wheel.

The Logic of Discourse and the Logic of Mass Movement

From the logic of discourse, one can make a conclusion that the abolition of commercialization of education and the establishment of a Common School System through neighborhood schools is the only solution to all the problems faced by school education in India and so is the case with higher education. In the course of the argument, we proceed from one stage to another stage within a few minutes. But, it may take years and decades to proceed from one phase to another phase in really building history. Every stage of discourse requires to be translated into a special phase of mass action. To make a brief elabouration of the idea, let us take Right to Education as an example. Parents, who are sending their children to Government schools, in the first instance, alone come forward to organize pressure on the Government to implement useful, and of course partial, aspects of existing legislations, rules, and regulations. Only at a later stage, do they come forward to demand that the government bring changes in the rules, regulations, and legislations to strengthen Government schools. Still later, they realize that Government schools cannot be developed in isolation without abolishing the commercialization of education and establishing a Common Schools System. Again, we know that people's struggle for democratization of education (*jnan*) does not proceed in isolation. Such a struggle goes hand in hand with other struggles for *jal, junggle, jameen,* and *jeevika*. An organization which realizes the solution through logic of discourse has to also understand the logic of mass action and stand with the people at every stage.

Activist Groups and Mass Movement

Do the Activist groups follow the logic of mass movement? Different students', teachers' organizations and groups working for educational rights of the people, generally, become active to resist new policy measures in course of commercialization or saffronization of education. Otherwise, they confine themselves to institutional issues. They sometimes take up the campaign for long-term goals but we do not find them engaging in consistent campaigns for short-term, positive, substantial demands. Let us say that if in a particular state, the Government makes a move either to close down some Government schools in rural areas or privatize some Government schools in urban areas, this will have become a common phenomenon in many states after the 'Right To Education Act' came into being. We find activist groups coming forward to oppose the move. But, we seldom find them taking up a consistent campaign, either before or after such a move, demanding development of Government schools to ensure quality education therein. To put it briefly, the activist groups only fight against new and immediate attacks on educational rights of the people. They sometimes take up campaigns for long-term goals like the Common School System or the Public Education System from KG to PG and the like. But, they do not campaign for short-term, positive, substantial elements of long-term goals. Let us enumerate some such substantial demands here for consideration. They may be: namely, i) abolishing child labour and establishing measures for universal enrolment and retention, ii) strengthening of all Government schools to the minimum level of central schools, iii) closing down all erring private schools and colleges not conforming to the minimum basis of the existing laws, iv) spreading the public education system at all levels, v) ensuring provision of student support measures like education material, health services and hostel facilities, according to the needs of the individual students to enable them to pursue their education at all levels, and vi) implementing 'social justice' in all institutes of higher education, including the so called centres of excellence, and legislating laws sensitive to gender inequality and the disabled and for other demands like these. If an organization is not fighting for these demands, they are not fighting for any greater goal. However, campaigning for such substantial policy changes can also be misguiding if, each of them is not framed against commercialization of education.

Conformist or Transformatory

Many organizations are working in the field of education. Some organizations take up partial and sectional demands, as enumerated above. However, they become only handy to the neoliberal policymakers if they do not, simultaneously, put up strongly their opposition to commercialization of education. They, in effect, only help in confining the people's opposition within the neoliberal paradigm and this trend can be called reformism. These forces support the policies of 'inclusion'. Anil Sadgopal, a renowned educationalist and social activist, concluded that the ruling forces are replacing the constitutional principle of equality by 'inclusion'. What is this 'inclusion'? Let us take the 'Right to Education Act' as an example. It is essentially drafted along neoliberal lines. It continues to promote and encourage the existing unequal school system, low standard Government schools for the poor, and incomparably provided schools for the rich. Now it proposes to 'include' a section of the poor into corporate schools. If the provision of 25 per cent reimbursement of seats is implemented, as calculated in Andhra Pradesh, six per cent of the poor, naturally the creamy layer amongst the poor, would get admission into corporate schools. That they will be further improverished in another matter. Six per cent will be 'included' and 94 per cent, will continue in the same poorly maintained schools. These schools would be further neglected. The campaign for quality education for the poor, if not associated with the struggle against commercialization of education, only leads to replacement of equality by 'inclusion' and leads to further intensification of stratification. That is why, a struggle for some sectional demand requires being associated with, struggle against commercialization of education to ensure that it serves the transformative goals, and not neoliberal policies.

Scope of Mass Movement

The democratic forces shall not think about the limited scope provided by the State as the conformists do, but, they shall operate on the basis of the scope for mobilization of the people at their present stage of experience and organization. People wage struggles for achieving different levels of demands, on the basis of the situation. People's struggles include struggles for protection of existing rights, expansion of rights, and even for transformation of system of education. However, the activists should be able to precisely estimate scope of democratic mass movement, in formulating their plan of agitation. The point that requires to be noted is that, people respond sharply when there is an attack on existing rights. The activists in the field of education have to take up the struggle for preservation of existing rights when attacked, mobilize the people in good numbers and also, in the course of development, motivate them and inspire them for struggles for extension of their rights to lead them to fight, for substantial elements of transformative goals and ultimately for complete transformative goals.

Historical Unity

There is a historical need for wider unity among educational rights groups. However, the basis for such a unity cannot but be, opposition to commercialization and saffronization of education and unity would be meaningful only if, each organization fights for all, or a minimum of one of the substantial demands, as listed earlier. The most important thing in the present context is that, sincere persons and organizations working with different democratic ideologies, should come together and work united to stall the onslaught of commercialization of education because, it is opposed to all great ideologies. All Gandhites, Lohiaites, Ambedkarites, socialists, communists and people committed to different ideologies, provided they are opposed to commercialization and saffronization of education, and stand for equality and diversity should stand united to resist the twin dangers.

Conclusion

An education system is expected to exclude all disparities, and include all diversities. Education should develop innate potentialities of every individual, and strengthen collective endeavour. Education should empower the people for protecting the sovereignty of the nation, and liberty of the citizens. Education should enable the people to analyse public policies, define the very concept of development to advance the civilization. The establishment of fully State funded public education system at all levels, can pave a path for building an education system that can suit the democratic aspirations of the people for building a democratic, socialist, egalitarian, secular, just, and humane society. It is time for activists and academics alike to go to the masses to integrate their subjective theories with the objective experience of the people, in order to advance the campaign for a democratic education system.

12

Afterword:
Narratives of Resistance: The Case of the Struggle for a Common School System in Tamil Nadu

Prince Gajendra Babu

> Even more important is the role of the education in achieving social and national integration. Indian society is hierarchical, stratified and deficient in vertical mobility. The social distance between the different classes, particularly between the rich and poor, the educated and the uneducated, is large and is tending to widen. Our people profess a number of different religions; and the picture becomes even more complicated because of caste, an undemocratic institution... The situation, complex as it was, has been made critical by recent developments which threaten both national unity and social progress [Section 1.07].
>
> The Kothari Commission (1964–6)

Education is one of the most important tools for social transformation and economic development. It generates hope and dares one to dream for a world free of inequality and exploitation. According to Albert Einstein and Dr B.R. Ambedkar, the aim of education should be to liberate the consciousness. Though the Right to Education was not included in the list of fundamental rights in the Constitution of India, Article 45 in the Directive Principles of the State Policy states, 'The State shall endeavour to provide, within a period of ten years from the commencement of this Constitution, for free and compulsory education for all children until the age of fourteen years'. It thus became more a duty of the state, to work in the area of public education, since equal access to type and quality of education was needed to level the playing field and help lift the deprived and the poor out of servitude, ignorance, and poverty.

After more than 60 years of Independence, the social transformation could not take place. Instead, many reports and facts claim that the gap between rich and poor, between the haves and have-nots has actually increased. The practice of untouchability and atrocities against women and the depressed sections of society are still prevalent. The Kothari Commission (1964–6) also found: 'Good education, instead of being available to all children, or at least to all the able children from every stratum of society, is available to only to a small minority which is usually selected not on the basis of talent but on the basis of its capacity to pay fees' [Section 1.37 The Kothari Commission (1964–6)].

The modern day slogan of 'Equality, Liberty, and Fraternity' has become a distant dream, as education is now a 'commodity' to be purchased in the market. And to legitimize the existing 'status quo' of the ruling class, there is an important ideological State apparatus, which is used as a means to mould the minds, to create assent in favour of the ruling ideas, to maintain the hegemony of one ruling class over the other, or to dominate any particular groups or castes over others in India.

The continuous withdrawal of public funded education has led to an increased mushrooming of the private educational institutes, which work with the motive of profit rather than any social or common good. This gave birth to multi-layered school system existing today, where one could purchase the amenities according to the strength of their pocket. Surprisingly, during colonial times, many states ruled by the native rulers saw to it that their population was provided with the free and compulsory elementary education. Thus, this fact forces us to seek an answer to the question as to whether the modern-day State, has taken a stride forward with everyone benefitting from education from it or are just a few? In order to understand this, let us take the case of Tamil Nadu.

In the then Madras Presidency, which consisted of the present State of Tamil Nadu, parts of Andhra Pradesh, Karnataka, and Kerala, the Provincial Legislature passed a Bill-TN Act 8 of 1920, that is, the Tamil Nadu Elementary Education Act, 1920 and Rules 1924. Even before this, 'The Tamil Nadu Educational Rules' popularly known as 'MER' (Madras Educational Rules) were in force from January 1892. This act was a progressive legislature of that period. It provided for Free and Compulsory Education from Classes I to VIII in selected *panchayats* with the mother tongue as the medium of instruction (education) and English as an optional language subject only, from Class VI onwards. Even modern-day infrastructure was included in the Act, with measurements for desk and benches, with backrests given along with drawings.

Around the same period, due to the efforts of M. Singaravelar, popularly known as the First Communist of the South India, who was in the Council of Corporation of Madras (Chennai) then, 'Nutritious Noon Meal' was provided for the children studying in the schools run by the Municipal Corporation. Later, in the 1950's, when K. Kamaraj was the Chief Minister, 'Mid-day meal' was provided to the children studying in all the public schools (schools run by the state, local bodies and the Board) throughout the State of Tamil Nadu.

The first state in the post-Independence era to bring in the legislation to provide 'Free and Compulsory Education' was the State of Kerala. The efforts by E.M.S. Namboodiripad, Joseph Mudachari, and Justice V.R. Krishna Iyer, even at the cost of their Ministry, stood firm in enacting the legislature which was taken as a model when the Right to Education Bills were drafted in later years.

The Acts passed by the Tamil Nadu Legislature in the post-Independence period did not move forward from the Act of 1920. In fact, it only pulled down the state by bringing in acts like the Tamil Nadu Compulsory Elementary Education Act, 1994 (TN ACT 33 of 1955) and Rules 1998. This Act repealed the TN ACT 8 of 1920 except for certain sections. The Rules framed under the Act define the school age as 6 to 14 and elementary education as 'up to 14 years' and that 'the Child will be in School up to class V'.

Thus, it could be clearly understood that the Government of Tamil Nadu, on the one hand provided nutritious noon meals, free uniform, free books, free education up to Class XII in public funded schools, and on the other hand, made sure that public institutes slowly phased out, hence creating space for self-financed Matriculation Schools to bloom. Slowly, all the Private Schools that came into existence from 1980 were granted affiliation either by the Board of Matriculation or by the Nursery and Primary School Board. It meant that there was no aided school and if it was to be found, it would have been of substandard quality.

There are five Boards of School Education in the state, and the curriculum is prepared by the state itself, which has to be followed by each of these boards. More than 80 per cent of the students appear for the SSLC Board Exams. These students are from Government and Government Aided schools, they are made to believe that their syllabus is 'Sub-Standard/Inferior' to that of the Matriculation or Anglo-Indian Board. A study conducted, has revealed that the content of the syllabus was same in all these four Boards, though they have different names. Dr S. Muthukumaran Committee, later appointed by the Government to recommend implementing a uniform system of school education, also concluded that contents of all the four Boards were same. Thus, it is clear that this was tactically done to promote private capital by highlighting its superior credibility and to create an idea of the private institutions where one's employability chances increases. This certainly attracted the bourgeoning middle class and they became the fierce propagators of it.

The struggle for the Common School System or for the equalizing process in the society was waged by various organizations together. The State Platform for Common School System (SPCSS) spearheaded the struggles for a uniform syllabus and Common School System. It was able to involve people from all walks of life in this struggle. The government clearly played into the hands of private capital by just appointing a Committee to look into the case, though it never recommended its proposals that were in favour of the uniform curriculum in the schools across the state or supported the Common School System. Instead, it instituted a common board, which has representation from the four boards. The TNUSSE Act, 2009 introduced a Common Syllabus, book, and one board exam at the end of Class X, instead of the earlier four exams. The introduction of the Common Syllabus can be seen as a step forward towards the struggle for the Common School System.

There has been an immense attack on the on-going struggle for a Common School System from the private capital. With the weakened organized Left force in the country post-2009 general elections, the market forces trued to influence the State government to replace the Common Syllabus with the same old Multi- Syllabus structure. The scathing attack on these alternative models can also be seen in regard to the global financial crisis. The crisis of capital accumulation—the declining rate of profit—has given an additional urgency to the neoliberal project for education globally. But the SPCSS has stood like a rock in fighting these forces adopting various modes from protesting to petitioning, using social networking to forming an alliance with the teachers, students, parents, and *karamacharis*. The interconnected solidarity between these different groups proves to be the main force behind their continued struggle.

For SPCSS, the issues do not cease at identifying problems, and recognizing the attack on education. In fact, it must build a movement to resist the onslaught of the market. The website launched by SPCSS in 2009, helped in exposing the Government's false statements and bias towards Private Schools. State Government, Private School Managements and the Confederation of Minority Schools together abolished the Common Syllabus. Meanwhile, the Tamil Nadu Government brought in an Act to regulate the fee collected by the private schools. Although, the Act was very vague and had provisions just to approve the fee structure submitted by the schools to the committee formed under the Act, still, it empowered and enlightened the parents.

The Private Schools approached the courts and the courts upheld the Act. But a single bench of the Madras High Court stayed the operation of the order of the Fee Determination Committee. The Government failed to appeal against the order. SPCSS, which was seeking to implead but was not allowed to do so by the single judge, sought special permission from the bench headed by the Chief Justice of the Madras High Court. Permission was granted, the appeal was heard, and the single judge order was struck down and the Fee Committee's order was allowed to be implemented. The legal battle that was solely fought by SPCSS in the interest of the parents—enlightened the parents of Private Schools—brought them close to SPCSS. The SPCSS seized the opportunity to involve the Private School parents in the struggle for a Common School System. Due to the sustained efforts put by the SPCSS, parents understood the politics behind the denial of equitable access to all children and pledged to carry forward the struggle for establishment of a Common School System. The parents of the Private Schools formed themselves into an association and linked the associations into a federation, namely Tamil Nadu Private School Students' Parents' Welfare Association.

SPCSS has gained popularity and support among the masses of the Tamil Nadu by their continued struggle. This was witnessed during the All India Conference for Abolishing Commercialisation of Education and Building a Common School System, held at Chennai by SPCSS in association with AIF-RTE. About 300 members of the Tamil Nadu Private School Students' Parents' Welfare Association served as volunteers. The entire of the expense incurred on this conference was collected from the general masses. This conference had delegates from all the parts of world as well as from India. After a nationwide debate, the Conference adopted and incorporated as campaign material suggestions put forward by various organizations and individuals.

To be sure, there are powerful forces trying to divert public attention from the Common School System agenda through clever devices. These include private schools running 'afternoon centres' for the poor, sections lobbying for 25 per cent reservation provision in the private schools for the poor children of the neighbourhood and proposers of school vouchers and public-private partnership model for backdoor funding of private schools out of public funds. These are the ways of justifying and legitimizing the present exclusionary system. The neoliberal policy followed by both the Union and the State Governments has started affecting every household. The private schools that enjoy complete freedom under the RTE 2009, are creating the future labour power without any critical insight that would make them realize their real predicament. The children grow in a demonized atmosphere. They are made to feel insecure and rely wholly on the parents even to do the projects under the continuous and comprehensive evaluation process.

Thus unless and until commercialization of education is abolished, establishment of Common School System is not possible. Without establishing CSS, Right to Education will only be a dream. To secure Right to Education for all children, the new liberal policy of the State has to be opposed. In this struggle, the entire community has to be integrated. The class struggle in Marxist sense foregrounded in the labour-capital dialectic, surplus value extraction or the structure of property ownership must be discussed and debated and taken to the masses. The form of the political education of the masses through different modes of struggle becomes utmost important and hence every movement must be seen in through the prisms of the class struggle.

Notes on Contributors

EDITOR

Ravi Kumar teaches at the Department of Sociology, South Asian University. His works include *Social Movements: Transformative Shifts and Turning Points* (Forthcoming, Routledge: Delhi); *Education and the Reproduction of Capital: Neoliberal Knowledge and Counterstrategies* (2012, Palgrave Macmillan: New York) *The Heart of the Matter: Development, Identity and Violence: Reconfiguring the Debate* (2010, Aakar Books: Delhi); *Global Neoliberalism and Education and its Consequences* (2009, Routledge: New York & London); *The Crisis of Elementary Education in India* (2006, Sage Publications: New Delhi). He is co-editor of a book series on *Social Movements, Dissent and Transformative Action* (Routledge: Delhi). His area of research includes political economy of identity politics, social movements, neoliberal impact on education and processes of knowledge production. He is Editor (South Asia) of *Journal of Critical Education Policy Studies (www.jceps.com)*.

CONTRIBUTORS

Anil Sadgopal is Member, Presidium, All India Forum for Right to Education. He has been consistently providing insights into the how state funded education has been destroyed by the interests aligning with private capital. His engagement in the field of education goes a long way. After obtaining his PhD in Biochemistry and Molecular Biology (1968) from the California Institute of Technology, USA, Anil Sadgopal joined TIFR as a

Fellow from where he resigned his appointment to organize a rural education and development programme through Kishore Bharati in Hoshangabad district, Madhya Pradesh and initiated the Hoshangabad Science Teaching Programme in 1972 with the Friends Rural Centre, Rasulia. He also conceived and led the Lokshala Programme for demonstrating an alternative vision of universalisation of elementary education through social intervention in the government school system. He has also served as member of various commissions on education of central government and state government and was member of Central Advisory Board on Education. He was Professor of Education and Dean, Faculty of Education at the University of Delhi and a Senior Fellow at the Nehru Memorial Museum and Library. He is a recipient of numerous awards and honours including the Jamnalal Bajaj Award (1980) and Rathindra Puraskar from Visva Bharati University, Shantiniketan (1984) for application of science and technology to rural areas, Vikram Sarabhai Memorial Lecture (1981), and UGC National Lecturer (1988). He has written extensively on education in journals and English and Hindi dailies. His publications in Hindi include *Sangharsh aur Nirman* (1993, Rajkamal: Delhi) and *Shiksha Mein Badlav ka Sawal* (2000, Granth Shilpi: Delhi).

G. Haragopal, a distinguished political scientist, is currently ICSSR National Fellow with the Tata Institute of Social Sciences, Hyderabad. He was with the University of Hyderabad as a professor in the Department of Political Science and later in the Center for Human Rights. He was also a Visiting Professor at Centre for the Study of Social Exclusion and Inclusive Policy (CSSEIP), National Law School of India University (NLSIU), Bangalore. He is a well known human rights activist. He has been with the Andhra Pradesh Civil Liberties Committee (APCLC) for several years and plays an important role in conflict resolution between the state and the Naxal groups. He has published extensively in *Economic and Political Weekly* and several other journals, apart from the Telugu and English press on human rights and politico-economic issues. His earlier works include *Administrative Leadership and Rural Development in India* (1980) and *Political Economy of Human Rights: Emerging Dimensions* (1997).

Notes on Contributors 285

Harjinder Singh 'Laltu' is scientist, poet, fiction writer, and commentator. He is currently a Professor at the Azim Premji University, Bangalore. He has worked at IIT-Hyderabad and Panjab University, Chandigarh prior to this. He has done extensive research in theoretical chemical physics and has been active in Hindi literature. His works of poetry include *Ek Jheel Thee Barph Ki* and *Dairy mein Teywees October* and his fiction is titled *Ghooghney*. He received the Young Chemist Award of Chemical Research Society of India (CRSI), Bangalore and has visited several institutions for brief stints including Princeton University, USA, IISc, Bangalore, RWTH, Aachen, and University of Bristol, UK. He also worked with EKLAVYA, MP, as a UGC teacher fellow.

Madhu Prasad taught philosophy at Zakir Hussain College, University of Delhi and is with the All India Forum for Right to Education. She has published extensively in journals such as *Social Scientist*.

Prince Gajendra Babu is General Secretary of the Tamil Nadu State Platform for a Common School System. He has been at forefront in struggles to provide better education in government schools in Tamil Nadu.

Radhika Menon teaches at Department of Elementary Education, Mata Sundri College, University of Delhi.

Rajesh Bhattacharya is with Public Policy and Management Group at Indian Institute of Management, Calcutta. He has a PhD in Economics from University of Massachusetts, Amherst, USA. His research interests are political economy of development, Indian economic history, and economic theory. He has published works on informality, exclusion and governance. He has published extensively in journals such as *Economic and Political Weekly*.

Ramesh Patnaik is with the Andhra Pradesh Save Education Committee (APSEC).

Samir Karmakar is a linguist by training. At present, he is working at Jadavpur University, Kolkata. Prior to this engagement, he worked at Azim Premji University and National

Institute of Advanced Studies. He has a PhD in Linguistics from Indian Institute of Technology, Kanpur. His area of interest is language and cognition. He is also interested in the sociopolitical construction of linguistic cognition with a special reference to India. He has written several articles on language and cognition in journals like *Science and Culture, Current Science, Poznan Studies in Contemporary Linguistics, Canadian Journal of Linguistics, Indian Linguistics*, etc. In addition to this, he has authored several papers for National and International conferences.

Srinivas Burra is with the Faculty of Legal Studies, South Asian University, New Delhi. Earlier worked with many international organizations. He obtained M.Phil and PhD in international law from Jawaharlal Nehru University, New Delhi. His areas of research and publications include human rights law, armed conflicts and international humanitarian law, international criminal law, refugee law, international law and legal theory. He has published extensively in journals such as *Economic and Political Weekly*.

Vikas Gupta teaches at the Department of History, University of Delhi. Prior to that, he taught Social Science in government schools in Delhi. His area of research includes themes in the history of colonial education, social aspects of knowledge 'production' and 'reproduction', and neoliberalism and its impact on the creation of inequalities in contemporary education. He has published numerous articles in leading journals such as *Economic & Political Weekly, Seminar, Mainstream* and in the *Proceedings of the Indian History Congress*. He has also delivered lectures at various nationally and internationally renowned academic centers. He is the Associate Editor of *Reconstructing Education*—quarterly publication of the All-India Forum for Right to Education (AIFRTE). Presently, he is working on a monograph on school education, where he is exploring the transition from colonialism to neoliberalism and how the mainstream education system could be reconstructed to nurture and promote pluralism and equality. He is actively associated with All-India Forum for Right to Education (AIFRTE), Dilli Shiksha Adhikar Manch (DSAM), and Sambhavana, which are striving for the universalisation of education of an equitable quality.

Index

ABP News 46
academic autonomy 99
accreditation systems 103
Activist Groups 272
Acumen Fund 132
Adivasis 227
All India Council for Technical Education (AICTE) 106
All India Educational Conference 245
Ambedkar, B.R. 15, 23, 255-7, 259, 276
Ambedkarites 274
American law school 222
  model in India 219
  system 220
American professors 227
Andhra Pradesh 67, 278
Anglo-American academic tradition 187
Anglo-American tradition 200
  in theory and methods 201
Anglo-American world 202
anti-colonial freedom struggle 23, 237
anti-reservation strand 229
anti-systemic political formations 13
Apparao, Gurajada 259

Arabic language 147
artificial consumption 80
Asiatic wider classes 88
Attlee, Clement 4
Aurobindo, Sri 25
avatars 8
Azad, Chandrashekhar 258-9

Badheka, Gijubhai 259
Bangla language 164-5
Bangladesh 141
Bankruptcy 134
Baptist Missionary of Shrirampore 164
Bar Council of India (BCI) 214-7
barbarism 76-7, 79
basic education scheme 245
Begums of Bhopal 90
Bengali 164
Bhakti literature 147
Bhargava, P.M. 61
Bhojpuri 169
Bhopal Judicial Academy 74
BHU 220
Bills 68, 74, 269
bleaker 22
BMC school 131
Bombay Plan 254
Bose, Subhash Chandra 259

bourgeois society 81
Brabeck, Peter 3
brahmanical order 153
Brahmanical system, traditional 86
Brahmins 90, 226
British capital 239
British Empire 237
British Raj 248
British trade and commerce 238
Brown 164
bureaucracies 7
bureaucratic governance 192
bureaucrats 5
business 170

Canagarajah 163
capital accumulation 2
capital markets 107
capital-labour accord 190
capitalism 8, 14, 99, 150, 191-2, 199, 208
    and democracy 189
    force and brutality in the 77
capitalist agricultural farms 193
capitalist class 199
    interests 37
capitalist ventures 44
Carry, William 164
castes 3, 251
    and class 261
        prejudices 93
caste system 87
caste/class, traditional hierarchies of 86
categories and regional distribution 39
Central Board of Secondary Education (CBSE) 51
Central Government 72-3
Central Schools 46
Chattisgarhi 169

Chicago School movement 80
child-centred pedagogies 23
childhood care 41
children of elites 32
children of the rich 90
China 199
    and environment, teaching 29
class 3
    contradictions 190
    formation 21
    inequality 24
    question 14
    struggle 258
    in Marxist sense 282
classical oriental learning 88
classical political economy 200
classroom culture 35
classroom learning process 27
classroom transactions 35
college education 139
colonial education policy 90
colonial framework 239
colonial India 203
colonial legacy 23
colonial masters 153
colonial power 149
colonial rule 87
colonial rulers 241
colonial system 24
colonialism and imperialism 150
commercialization of education 49, 267, 270-71
commercialization of higher education 269
committees and commissions 11
commoditization 67
Common School System (CSS) 11-2, 41-2, 85, 268, 270-2, 279-82
common syllabus 280
communal ideology 50

Index

communication 31
communism 77
competition 207
Congress Party 258
consumerist and free market world 5
copyrights 206
corporal punishments 122
corporate 22
corporate social responsibility (CSR) 48, 51
critical race theory 228
cultural and civilizational values 67
cultural and linguistic diversity 140
cultural and political leaders 259
cultural differences 151
cultural genocide 156
cultural heritage 34
   of India 30
cultural influence of the Mughal court 87
cultural socialization 162
cultural tradition 32
cultural worldviews 147
culture 149, 151
   and language 151
   battles 149
curricular framework 31, 35
curriculum 27-8, 51, 88, 124, 188, 217

D.S. Kothari Commission 92
Dalits 86-7, 149, 227, 239, 251
   intellectuals 141
   writing in India 146
Davis 196
decision-making 3
Delhi 116, 120
   and Agra colleges 87
   State schools 125, 130

Delhi Child Rights Commission 128
Delhi University 11, 220
   curriculum 61
democracy 194
   and capitalism 208
   and decision-making 3
   and working class mobilization 191
democratic dialogue 204
democratic education system 15, 275
democratization of education 271
Dewey 36, 252
disability law instruments 49
discrepancy 28
discrimination 34, 86, 125
   and disparities 29
discriminatory attitudes towards children 124
discriminatory order 21
discriminatory system 41
disparities 20
dissemination and citation 149
diversity 150
domestic trade 190
dominance and subordination 150
dropout of education 153
dropout rates 139
dual politics 194
dualism 193

East Asian developmental States 192
East India Company 87
ecological destruction 77
economic development 108
economic liberalization 221
economic neoliberalism 6
economic policies and globalization 224

economic problems in India 187
economic processes 189
economic system 105
economically disadvantaged groups 73
economy 13
education 8, 11, 14, 23, 105, 110, 151
   and health 2
   and knowledge 37
   and schooling 144
   colonial policy for 87
   commercialization of 266
   in India 10
   national system of 25
   of the masses 37
   political economy of 21-22
   socially inclusionist 227
   socially-oriented role of 24
   substandard levels of 49
   system 10-11, 13, 83, 90
      in India 10
Education Commission 60, 92
   elementary 3
Education Guarantee Centres 95
Education Guarantee Scheme (EGS) 37
educational crisis 14
educational demand 114
educational discourse 26, 52, 237, 259
educational inequalities 32, 41
educational institutions 27, 267
   militarization of the 10
educational management 42
educational planning 24
educational policy 82, 95
   and practice 36
educational sweatshop 124
educational system 59
   inequitous 41

educational theory 27
egalitarian vision 74
Eighth Schedule 170
elementary education 33, 38, 40, 43, 277
employment 88, 204
Engels 77
England 199
English 141, 155-6
   education 239
   language 149
      education 155
   medium schools 163
entertainment class 2
equal opportunity 105, 229
equalitarian 21
equality 19, 27, 41
   and justice 232
   principle of 38
   quality conundrum 33
equity and quality 39
European colonial masters 147
European languages 140
European modernity 140
exclusion 20
   and inequalities 23
exclusivist institutions 48
expansionism 23, 32
exploitation 239

Farahmandpur 5, 12
farmer suicides 9, 188
fascist forces 66
Federation of Indian Publishers 171
fees structure 217
feminist consciousness 62
feudal elite 88
feudal landlords 258
Food Security Bill 192
Ford Foundation 219-21, 227

Index 291

foreign capital 107
Foreign Education Provider (FEP) 106
Foreign Educational Institutions (FEI) 106
foreign universities 204
Forest Rights Act 192
formal education 49
free international 190
free markets 154
free trade 13
free-market capitalisms 189, 192, 195
freedom struggle 24-5, 100, 140
Freidman, Milton 80
fundamental right 19, 22-3, 38, 40, 132
  towards a duality 125

Gajendragadkar Committee 98
Gandhi, Mahatma 15, 25, 36, 91, 155, 242, 247-8, 250-51, 254, 259
Gandhi-Ambedkar Debate 255
Gandhian Civilizational Debate 241
Gandhian development model 256
Gandhian pedagogy 251-2, 255
Gandhian secular outlook 62
Gandhian thought 62
Gandhian vision of moving 254
Gandhians 199
Gandhi's conception of Nai Taleem 247
Gandhi's educational vision 255
Gandhi's transformative civilizational vision 260
Gandhites 274
gendered inequalities 3
General Agreement on Trade 267
General Agreement on Trade and Tariff 63-4
General Agreement on Trade in Services (GATS) 64, 101
Germany 199
Giovanni, Nikki 145
girls' schools, condition of 122
global capital 37, 68
global capitalism 22
global economy 205
global research frontier 203
global standards 204
globalization 223, 267
globalizing market 228
Gokhale, Gopal Krishna 91, 259
Governance of universities and colleges 98
Governance through competition 205
Government regular teacher 270
Government School 119, 123, 269-70
  system 94
Government teachers 130
Guru, Narayan 259

Haripura Congress Resolution 253
health 8
hegemonic nationalism 26
hegemonic normativity 21
hegemony in India 239
Henry 79
hierarchization 50
higher education 70-1, 95, 99, 107, 110, 187, 202
  and research bill 69
  funding 204
  in India 58
  institutions 188
  privatization and commercialization 108
  reforms 207

sole beneficiary of 67
value of 109
higher pedagogic levels 124
Hindi 169-70
    and Urdu languages 143
    journalism 154
    magazines 154
    poets 143
Hindu 143
    cultural world 27
    rashtra 34
    society 255
    upper caste 27
Hindustan Socialist Republican Association (HSRA) 258
Hirschman, Albert O. 198
Historical Unity 274
Hosen, Mir Mosarraf 165
Hughes, Langston 145
human capital 206
human civilization 161
human dignity 19
human life 142
human rights 180
human sense 151
human sociality 76
human values 77
humane society 260
humanitarian education 21, 37
hunger deaths 9
Hunter Commission 89
Husain, Zakir 259
hypocrisy 77

imperialism 77
included and excluded 20
inclusion ideology 20, 34
inclusionism 22, 34
inclusive education 22, 33
inclusivism 32
income inequality 99
Independent Regulatory Commission 69
India 2, 139-40, 161, 166, 191, 200
    economic performance of 186
    society 227
    tradition of economic thought in 200
Indian Advocates Act of 1961 217
Indian capitalism 190, 192
Indian capitalist class 193, 258
Indian economists 202
Indian education 40-41
Indian Education Commission 27
Indian education system 29
Indian educational policies 39
Indian higher education sector 204
Indian Institutes of Management 46
Indian Institutes of Technology 46
Indian judiciary 224, 227
Indian languages 140, 144, 147, 149, 152, 155, 157, 182
Indian Law Institute 220
Indian legal education 218
    system in Indian universities 219
Indian National Congress (INC) 91
Indian NGO 130
Indian Parliament 3
Indian population 191
Indian ruling class 39
Indian ruling elite 65
Indian social reality 226
Indian society 50
    plurality and diversity of 35
Indian State 68
Indian Supreme Court 226
Indian territory 168
Indian universities 202

and colleges 201
India's children 94
India's leading industrialists 101
industrial and agricultural India 179
industrial capitalism 196
industrial revolution 196
industrialization 190, 193
inegalitarian social order 41
inequalities 11, 26, 31
  and exploitation 12
iniquitous class relations 25
innovation capital 206
integrationalism 23, 28, 34
  and pluralism 27
integrationism 21
intellectual challenge 222
intellectual construct 147
intellectual power 59
intellectual properties 206
inter-religious dialogue 34
intercultural 34
Internet 156
intrinsic value and learning 82
Ivy League American Universities 132

Japan 199
Jawahar Navodaya Vidyalayas 125
job insecurity 13
Joshi, Murli Manohar 99
judicial intervention 40
justice, redistributive 20
Justice V.R. Krishna Iyer 278

Kalecki, Michal 196
Kayastha 87
Kendriya and Navodaya Vidyalayas 95
Keneysian and neoliberal policies 198

Keynes, John Maynard 4
Keynesian full-employment policies 200
Keynesian policy 196
Keynesianism 196
Khatri 87
knowledge capital dominates 205
knowledge production 14
knowledge products 207
knowledge system 229
Kolkata 165
Kothari Commission 28, 42, 60, 96, 276-7
Kothari, D.S. 27
Kumar, Krishna 252

labour 77, 81
  force 13
  market 13
Laitin 166
Land Acquisition Bill 192
language 162
language and culture battles 144
language curriculum 182
language of communication 163
languages and cultures 150
large-scale privatization 157
LatCrit Theory 228
Latour, Bruno 195
law schools 228
learning methods and curriculum 223
learning processes 82, 139
  of school 23
  of students 30
Left force in the country 280
Left politics 14
legal academia 212
legal community 212
legal education 212-3, 218, 221, 226
  in India 213, 219

in the traditional university system 232
reforms in 216
regulation of 214
socially inclusionist and egalitar 225
system 219
legal reforms, second generation 217
legal scholarship in India 227
legitimize inequalities 51
Lenin 78
Lewis, Arthur 200
liberalization 7
life and learning 82
lifelong training and upgradation of skills 103
linguistic determinism 147
linguistic right 180
linguistics contributes 167
LLB 230
programme 228
Lohia, Ram Manohar 155, 259
Lohiaites 274
loot 239
lower classes 203, 251
Lucas, Robert 197
lumpen class 67

Macaulay 179, 237-8
Macaulayian framework 241
Macaulayian policy in the Bombay Presidency 240
Madras Presidency 278
Maharaj, Shahuji 259
Maharaja of Baroda 90
mainstream 20-21
system 49
Maithili 169-70
majoritarian culture 27
marginalized groups 149
market 9, 114

creation 81
driven jobs 229
exchange 109
freedoms 9
friendly 229
interests of 10
rationality 6
marketability 204
marketplace 11
Marx, Karl 77, 196
Marxist philosophy 258
mass movement 271-72, 274
Maths and Science 118
McChesney 114
McKinsey and Company 130
McLaren 5, 12
medium of education 50
Mehran, Arthur von 227
Menon, N.R. Madhava 221-2
mental slavery 153
middle class male urban child 27
minorities 203, 227
minority institutions 49
model schools 46
modern education 24
modern industrialized Bangla 165
modernity 80
modernization 21, 23, 34
Morrison, Toni 146
Mother Tongue 151, 248
in elementary education 182
Mudachari, Joseph 278
Mukherjee, Alok 149
Muktibodh 146
multi-causal phenomenon 20
multi-layered 20
multilingual education policy 161
multilingualism 179
municipal and government schools 123
Muslim 251

in India 25
  elite 87

Nagpur Session (1920) 91
Nai Taleem 245, 247, 255
Namboodiripad, E.M.S. 278
Naoroji, Dadabhai 89, 91, 259
Narayan, Jayaprakash 259
Nation State 74
National Commission for Higher Education 70
National Curriculum Framework (NCF) 28-30, 33-4
National Democratic Alliance (NDA) 101
national education 24
  Tribunal 74
National Focus Group on Teaching of English 183
National Institute of Educational Planning and Administration 102
National Knowledge Commission (NKC) 103, 183, 229
National Law Schools 220-22, 225
  Bangalore 213, 219, 223
  model 212
  of India 222
National Law University 70
National Policy of Education (NPE) 28, 31, 93-4
national stature 155
national tradition 172
nationalism 156
nationalist discourse 155
nationalist struggle 140, 155
NATO countries 141
natural resources 3
Navodaya Vidyalayas 32, 46
Nehru, Jawaharlal 25
neo-conservative forces 38
neo-conservative groups 50

Neo-educational strategies 39
neoliberal capitalism 14, 82
neoliberal discourse and practice 36
neoliberal forces 58
neoliberal global capitalism 33
neoliberal ideology 22, 36, 39, 42
neoliberal mantra 7
neoliberal paradigm 8
neoliberal policy measures 125
neoliberal political economy 38, 51
neoliberal pressure 47
neoliberalism 4-5, 8, 10, 39, 44, 47-8, 114, 196, 237
  bankrupt public funds 236
  for education 15
new economic 4
New Economic Policy (NEP) 100
new economy 2
next generation reforms 217
NGO interventions 125
Niyogi, Shankar Guha 260
non-educational activities 48
non-egalitarian and hierarchized social structures 227
non-governmental organizations (NGOs) 70
norms 69
North East Delhi school 122
North India 152, 154-5
NREGA 192

OECD report 206
open competition 37
oppressed classes 38
other backward castes 106
other backward classes (OBCs) 226-7, 251
other backwards sections 239

Paash 145

Pakistan 141
Pandey, Gorakh 145
parents' interviews 124
Parliament 9
patents 206
patriotism 90
pedagogic interaction 35, 36
  transformative 37
pedagogical methods 82
Periyar 259
Persian literature 87
Phule, Jyotiba 15, 90, 239-40, 242, 259
Phule, Savitribai 90, 239, 259
  scientific history of the caste system 255
Pitroda, Sam 60-61
Planning Commission 199
pluralism 21, 23, 26, 28, 32, 34
  of thought 204
  philosophy of 33
policies and politics 11
political and economic hierarchies 76
political rationality 6, 14
politicians 5
Popper, Karl 145
post-Independence era 100
post-Independence India 27
post-Independence Indian Nation-State 23
post-Independence Nation-State 24-25
postgraduate programmes 230
Postman, Neil 141
poverty 8, 25, 61
  and class-inequalities 24
power relations 21
PratibhaVikasVidyalayas 46
Prince Gajendra Babu 15
private capitalist enterprises 190
private law school 217

Private Public Partnerships (PPP) 37, 42-3, 45, 51, 102
private schools 50, 123
privatization 7, 13, 107
  commercialization 67
professional education 269
public administration 6
Public Education System 272
public funded schools 50
public schooling in Delhi 134
public schools 115, 125
public system of education 45

quality and quantity 27, 41
quality education 273

Rabindra sangeet 143
Radhakrishna Commission 68
radical changes 82, 255
radical extension 81
radical measures 23
Rai, Lala Lajpat 25
Rajasthani language 147
Rajkiya Pratibha Vikas Vidyalaya (RPVV) 116, 125
  in Delhi 126
Rao, V.K.R.V. 200
rationalization and classification 170
redistribution 20-1
redistributive justice 27
  social 32
regional and global integration 7
regulation and rationalization of fees 105
religious agenda of Right wing Hinduism 33
religious education 33
religious houses 22, 48
religious organizations 37
reservation policy 73, 203
right and equality 52

Right to Education Act 38, 41-3, 49, 120, 272-3
Right to Equality 19, 27, 43-4, 51
Right to Free and Compulsory Education Act 95
right wing agenda 33
rights to justice 229
Roosevelt, Franklin D. 4, 181, 183
Rudolph 188
Ruling ideology 81

Saink Schools 95
Sargent, John 92
Sarva Shiksha Abhiyan 37, 120
Satyamev Jayate 46
Scheduled Castes 106, 226, 228
Scheduled Tribes 106, 226
    reservation 228
Schiffman 178
school and community 36
school and school learning 130
school choice 51
    campaign in India 93
school community interaction 30
school community interface 29
school community relationship 28
school curriculum 27
school education 42
    commercialization of 41
school enrolments 122
schooling 134
Schultz, T.W. 201
scientism against society 194
script 170
secular phenomenon 20
security systems 8
self-realization and self-growth 79
Sen, Amartya 58
Sheen Kaf Nizam 143
Sibal, Kapil 268

silent social revolution 246
Singaravelar, M. 259, 278
Singh, Bhagat 258-9, 261
Singh, Dr. Manmohan 58
Skutnabb-Kangas 150, 163
social 259
    accountability 111
    and cultural life 114
    and economic hierarchies 227
    background 225
    cohesion 33
    commitment 28, 38
    concerns 1
    context of language 147
    development 30
    equations and relationships 150
    good 67
    inclusionist judiciary 226
    institutions 81
    justice 1, 9, 19, 25, 105
        and equality 26
        equitable redistributive 23
    networks 124
    order 13
    reconstruction 254
    responsibility 19, 229
    revolution 203
    services 7
    transformation 23
socialism 260
socialist tradition 76
socialist view 22
socially disadvantaged sections of India 225
socially exclusionist policy 228
socially representative judiciary 226
sociocultural fabric 140
socioeconomic and cultural barriers 28

socioeconomic goals 236
South Delhi 116, 119
South India 12, 278
South Korea 199
spiritual and cultural heritage 34
Star Plus channel 46
student selection 124
subaltern legal theory 228
subaltern social groups 227

Tagore, Rabindranath 143, 155
Tamil Nadu 278
  Compulsory Elementary Education Act 278
Tarkalankar, Madanmohan 165
teacher training 131
teachers and teacher education 130
teachers' social background 229
teachers' training programmes 27
techno-bureaucratic efficiency 195
technological developments 32
territoriality 170
textbooks from NCERT 51
TFI training 131
Thassar, Iyothee 259
Third World countries 189
Trade Related Intellectual Property Rights (TRIPS) 64
trademarks 206
traditional responsibilities 22
transformation of system of education 274
transformative agenda 67
transformative education 32
transformative pedagogic programme 31
transitional bilingualism 183
Travancore-Cochin, rulers of 90
tribal groups 203
tribals 251

Tsunami 66

uncivil neo-rich 2
UNESCO World Conference 99
Unionism 81
United Kingdom (UK) 206
  advisory panel on Judicial Diversity 226
United Progressive Alliance (UPA) 102
  Government 265
United States 141, 199, 206
  Universities 219
unity and diversity 26
Universal Declaration of Human Rights 181
universal education 38
universal rights of citizens 82
Universities for Research and Innovation Bill 72
University Education 69
University Grants Commission (UGC) 9, 68-71, 97, 106-07, 214-5
university system 13
Unni Krishnan Judgment 38
unorthodox areas of research 204
upper castes 62
upper classes 62
Urdu 141

values 34, 131
  and goals 109
  and structures 69
  of assets 197
  plural 37
Varnashram 255
Veeresalingam, Kandukuri 259
venture schools 37
Vikal, Kumar 145
village schools 48
violence 22

culture of 140
vocational education 250
voucher scheme and PPP models 51
Vygotsky, Lev 85

weak children 48
weaker sections of society 51
welfare programmes 7
welfarist avatar 12
Western capitalist countries 198
Western capitalist economies 195
Western civilisation 243
Western economic discourse 200
Western economists 198, 201
Western liberal 191
Whorfianism 146
women 203

Woods, Despatch 88-9
working class 258
 politics 14
World Bank (WB) 67, 74, 93, 99
 report 104
world economy 100
World Trade Organization (WTO) 71, 74, 101-2, 267
 negotiations 196
World War 190
 Second 195
world-class universities 187

Yashpal 69
 Committee Report 103

Zakir Husain Committee Report 91

Rosa Luxemburg Stiftung

The Rosa Luxemburg Stiftung (RLS) is a Germany-based foundation working in South Asia as in other parts of the world on the subjects of critical social analysis and civic education. It promotes a sovereign, socialist, secular and democratic social order, and aims to present alternative approaches to society and decision-makers. Research organisations, groups for self-emancipation and social activists are supported in their initiatives to develop models which have the potential to deliver greater social and economic justice.

Rosa Luxemburg Stiftung—South Asia

Centre for International Co-Operation
C-15, 2nd Floor, Safdarjung Development Area (Market)
New Delhi 110 016, INDIA

Tel.:+ 91(0) 11 49 20 46 00 I 49 20 46 40 (D) I Fax : +91 (0) 11 49 20 46 66